Two Years on Two Wheels

or

The Travelblogs of an Accidental Klingon

A True Story of an American Kiwi's adventures across two hemispheres in search of Freedom, Happiness and a good cup of Coffee!

By

Rod Slater

Published by RSAAA

First published in New Zealand in April 2022

Second printing (revised) May 2022

This is a true story. Names of places and events, when noted, are real. Some names have been revised to provide a basic level of privacy to those people. The timeframes noted and travel routes are also true. However, there are periods where the imagination of the author, while being accurate to his mental state at the time, may have blurred the lines between reality and imagination. These should be relatively obvious to the reader and have been retained from the original log book and held in the spirit of the adventure.

Cover design, artwork and photographs by Rod Slater.

ISBN Softcover-978-0-473-62509-2

ISBN Softcover POD-978-0-473-62510-8

eISBN Kindle 978-0-473-62511-5

www.rodslateraaa.com

To the memory of my mother and father

who taught me all things are possible,

to follow my dreams and

never give up.

"Life is either a daring adventure or nothing."

Helen Keller

Contents

Prologue

MD 143.12.23.14.27[1]
December 22, 2016

Riding at 100 kilometers per hour can get chilly after several hours in the saddle, but the Southern Hemisphere's spring was in full effect and making way for summer. Overhead, the sun was shining, the sky was blue, there wasn't a puff of wind, and my leather gloves, chaps and jacket were keeping me warm.

All my objectives were falling into place, and with my Harley Super Glide rumbling away beneath me, I felt the full exhilaration of a glorious ride in grand weather. A contented man, alone in his element. What a day!

Just outside of Te Kuiti, in the Waikato region of New Zealand's North Island, lies the Mangaokewa Scenic Reserve. In high spirits, I turned off the highway and down the short drive to the free camping area. I was unsure what to expect, but nothing could have prepared me for the thrill of seeing what appeared to be a winter wonderland, spread out before me. With temperatures of 75 deg F (24 C), I knew it couldn't really be snow, and yet …

Turns out, the cottonwood trees were in full bloom. White drifts lined the road with cotton blown aside by vehicles entering and departing the campground. Their dual tire tracks through the whiteness reminded me of a snow-covered road. The green grass beneath perpetuated the illusion of a light dusting of snow in late autumn. The beautiful deception extended up onto the roof of the toilet block. Fluffy cotton seeds floated lazily towards the ground. In this part of the world, it was about as close as you could ever come to a white Christmas.

Laughing with enjoyment, I went about the task of setting up my tent, followed by an exploratory walk around the campground and along the river.

---

1. MD = Motorcycle Date. The date derived from the inception of the Harley-Davidson Motor Company in 1903 and paying tribute to the adventurous life, as we know it, eventuating from that point in time. Ie MD 143.12.23.14:27 translates to (1903+144) = 2016 December 23rd at 2:27pm.

The longest day of the year had just passed, and it was still light as I crawled into my sleeping bag for the night.

The next morning, with the illusion of snow still covering the ground, and with December the 25th just around the corner, I couldn't help but sing Christmas carols as I headed south in a jubilant mood. Let it snow, let it snow... (even if it's only cotton)... let it snow.

The turns and hills of the Mangaokewa Gorge required complete concentration and provided a challenging ride. I passed numerous empty logging trucks coming the other way and assumed the loaded ones were coming from behind or up ahead; but so far, I hadn't seen any. They were probably booking along at the same speed I was.

On the other side of the road, facing in the opposite direction, I caught a glimpse of a *Welcome to the Waikato Region* sign out of the corner of my eye. I was leaving the province, but the sign was just what I needed for a photograph. The only problem was, I'd need to turn around. *No worries*, I thought shifting down to first gear, and laid the bike over for a sharp U-turn. In my haste I neglected to feather the clutch during the slow maneuver. Then the engine's high piston compression caused the motor to stall and the bike's forward momentum to suddenly disappear.

Buggers!

The bike itself weighed 650 lbs (300 kg). Add to that all my gear and a tank of gas and we are talking a bit of weight. With the loss of momentum and the steep heel, I couldn't hold her from tipping over. Down we went.

And there I lay, under the bike, in the middle of a narrow road, on a downhill slope, on a curve, my left leg pinned under the motor. A truck coming downhill around the bend wouldn't be able to stop in time, or swerve to either side to miss me.

"Oh my goodness! This is not good," I said. Or words to that effect.

They say that when death is near your whole life flashes before you. Well, it was something like that for me. This wasn't my first adventure, or my first scrape, and I couldn't help thinking about what had led to the reason for this ride, or the need for a photo of that stupid sign.

Perhaps knowing the shenanigans we might get up to, or what moral evils may await us in some secluded spot, my parents barred us kids from owning a car until after we graduated high school. The only problem was, we needed to get around and, by some strange contradiction, it was deemed OK to own a motorcycle. These days, most parents worry more about their kids succumbing to death or crippling crash injuries than a bit of touchy-feely in the backseat. But there you go. Times have changed.

Our hometown was Miles City, Eastern Montana was our stomping ground, and the year was 1967. While The Beatles' "Sgt Pepper's Lonely Hearts Club Band" boomed out of car stereos around the world, Johnny Cash and June Carter's "Jackson" was our sound of choice. The TV Star Trek series was in its second season. Pickups, with rifles hung across their rear windows in gun racks, dominated the road. Seat belts were optional, and many cars didn't have them. Helmets were not required for motorcyclists, and – best of all – in daylight hours there was no speed limit, right across the state.

At fifteen I received my license, and a few weeks later, became the proud new owner of a second-hand black Honda 90 cc street bike.

At the impressionable age of seventeen, my attention was grabbed by an exciting new TV series called *Then Came Bronson*. Bronson, a young idealist of indeterminate age, played by Michael Parks, cruised the West Coast on a Harley-Davidson Sportster. Wearing pilot's sunglasses and a black stocking watch hat, he rode from adventure to adventure with his sleeping mat rolled up and tied off to the handlebars above the headlight. By the end of each episode, Bronson had exhibited an impressive range of skills, endeared himself to those around him, and solved some sort of mystery or overcome a problem – all within the confines of a one-hour time-slot.

It was the life for me. And so inspired, in the summer of 1969, between my junior and senior year of high school, having upgraded to a black Honda Dream 250 cc, I tied my sleeping bag onto the handlebars, attached a small suitcase to the rear seat, put on my black knit stocking hat and German-made pilot's sunglasses, mounted my beautiful bike and headed out.

I was only forty miles down the road when reality burst my idealistic bubble. The sleeping bag sagged down onto the front fender, applying pressure to the tire and causing a horrible screeching noise and billows of smoke. Then the front wheel abruptly stopped, scaring the daylights out of me as I scrambled for balance and control. Once safely at a standstill, shifting the sleeping bag to the rear of the bike resolved the issue, and although I no longer looked quite as cool as Bronson, I was still on the road to adventure.

৵৽৻

The journey assailed my senses. The unimpeded wind blew over my handlebars as I traveled around eastern Montana, Northern Wyoming, Yellowstone Park, then back into central Montana. Bugs plastered my clothes, leaving behind off-green and yellow splatters.

Without the confines of a closed-in vehicle, my visibility was three quarters of a sphere. Odors were strong and immediate as I rounded each corner onto each new stretch of the road – alfalfa, wheat, road kill, lilac and exhaust. The texture of the asphalt, a mere six inches under my feet, changed as my speed increased. I was right there, in the midst of the air and the weather, keenly aware and in awe of my surroundings, and each fluctuation of temperature had an impact on my sensations and comfort.

Rain pummeled me like nails until I found shelter under an overpass or tree. After stopping, the hair on my arms, now devoid of wind, would continue to vibrate and tingle as if covered in ants. With no tent to block my view of the stars, it was bliss to sleep on the ground on fine summer nights.

Traveling in a car is like watching the world pass by on a screen. But on a bike, choosing your own destination, path and speed, you become the star of the movie. It was a sense of freedom unlike anything I'd experienced before.

After a month or so of following my bliss, I ran into my cousin Don in Harlowton, Montana. Don had a black Honda Dream just like mine but with a bigger 305 cc engine. After hearing my stories of life on the road, he excitedly insisted on riding along. "No problem," I said. "So long as you wear a different style of sunglasses and no stocking hat." I didn't want competition for who looked coolest. A few days later, the two of us set off to discover America. By some coincidence, the film *Easy Rider* was released around this time, but Don and I were living it for real.

As we traveled along through the Little Belt Mountains, we played a game called "swivel hips." This entailed increasing speed while zigzagging between the dotted center lines without touching them. As a bonus, there were red survey tags stuck in the asphalt at intervals. While swerving over to kick at these, I happened to notice a cab-over-refer semi-truck coming up from the rear at pace. In the presence of the encroaching big-rig, I straightened up to ride more sensibly. Realizing Don hadn't seen the truck, I decided to have some fun. Riding alongside him, I waited until the huge semi was right behind us before I gave my horn a couple of beeps. Don looked over and I nonchalantly indicated over my shoulder with my thumb. He glanced back and nearly fell off his bike when he saw the driver looming ten feet away and high above us.

Starting up a long stretch of up-hill road, the truckie was determined to gather as much momentum as he could, maximizing the truck's speed until gravity took over and slowed his progress.

While building this highway, the engineers had removed a significant volume of mountain and hill-tops, and used the cut material to fill gorges and valleys, creating an even, albeit steep, grade. We were just approaching one of these valleys where the highway was set atop 150 feet of fill. The embankment fell sharply off each side, and the make-up of the downward slope consisted of loose gravel and boulders ranging in size from basketballs to Volkswagen Beetles. I noticed them about the same time the semi pulled into the other lane and began to pass.

The truck's engine changed timbre as its momentum declined and the big diesel began to carry the full weight of its payload. Occupying the entire width of the highway, the three of us proceeded upwards toward the mountain cut. With engine roaring and smoke billowing out its stacks, the semi's speed slowly diminished until it was nearly equal to ours. Then, with the truck about halfway past, another semi crested the hill, coming in our direction.

It immediately became obvious to everyone involved that our truck didn't have enough speed to get by. It was too late for the truckie to break and pull back. In his wing mirror, I could see the concern in his eyes. He shifted his gaze to the other semi... then us... then the other semi. His face contorted with trepidation over the implications of the impending decision. And then, his mind was made up. His eyes hardened... Bye-bye bikers! The huge vehicle pulled back into our lane, and there was no place for Don and me but over the edge.

I slammed on the rear brake as I bounced onto the shoulder and flew over the lip. The downward slope was so steep I slid forward onto the gas tank until the handlebars hit my crotch and stopped me from going over the headlight. The bike's rear end fishtailed back and forth as I revved the engine while downshifting through the gears, fighting to keep control. I navigated between the boulders as best I could and was soon caught up in a minor avalanche of rock and debris.

With a flash of hope that I might just live as I neared the bottom, I overcompensated on the handlebars and collided with the edge of a boulder about the size of a La-Z-Boy recliner. By now I was only going about five miles an hour, but the bike went onto its side and I flew over. The engine began to rev and, still in gear, the rear-wheel spun madly. Gas began seeping out of the tank across the engine to the ground. Fearing it would catch fire or explode, I bounded back up through the avalanche, grabbed the bike, stood it up, and killed the engine.

I was shaking so hard I could hardly stand upright, and my knees felt as if they were about to give. I didn't know if I was holding up the bike or it was holding up me. A foul stench filled the air. I looked down and noticed I'd soiled myself.

Looking back up the hill, I saw Don still descending in my direction, looking much the same as I must have looked a few moments before. He was revving up as he downshifted through the gears, the handlebars in his crotch, his right foot pressed down on the rear brake, fishtailing back and forth, trying desperately to get his bike under control. For one long, horrifying moment I thought he was going to run me down, but he managed to miss the boulder that had put me out of action, pass me by and continue on until he reached the bottom of the incline. He finally skidded to a stop, slid back down off the gas tank, and turned off his engine.

A few stones continued to slide down the hill, rattling and grating as they fell.

Then,

silence.

Don got off his bike,

put the kickstand down,

leaned back onto the seat, and

crossed his legs.

He reached into his shirt pocket,

took out a packet of cigarettes,

10

removed one and tapped it on the back of his hand.

He placed it between his lips,

took out a book of matches,

removed a match,

struck it on the matchbook, and

lit the cigarette.

He slowly inhaled, and

shook the match out,

returned the cigarettes and book of matches to his pocket, and

removed the cigarette with is right hand.

Exhaling the smoke, he looked at me.

And with a great calmness and certainty, said,

"The main thing is… never get excited."

A pearl of wisdom I still carry with me today. But one thing's for sure, by the end of that trip, the taste for adventure was well and truly cemented in my being.

Book 1

New Zealand

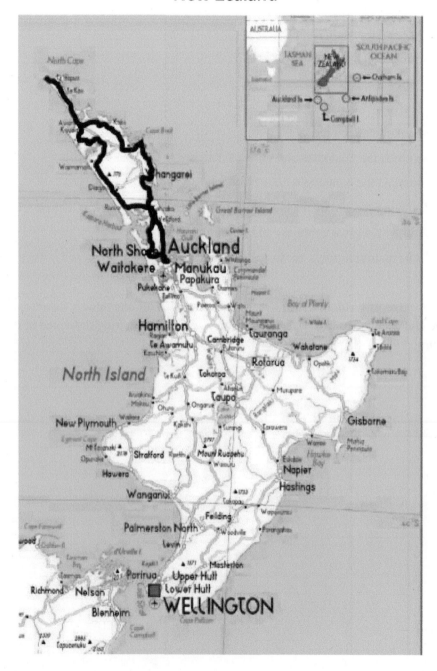

A Spark Ignites

MD 136.9.12.14:30
September 12, 2016

Time, as it does, passed by. After my first summer on the road with cousin Don, God continued to bless me with an adventure-filled life. I graduated high school in 1970, found work on the Milwaukee Railroad as a conductor/brakeman, achieved a degree in Art and Architecture from Montana State University, moved to Seattle, got married, purchased a 30-foot Baba cutter rig double-ender yacht named *Bontekoe* and set off to sail around the world. As you do.

My wife and I arrived in New Zealand, way down in the South Pacific, a few years later, and low on funds, I practiced my architectural profession and replenished the coffers to fuel my sailing passion while awaiting the birth of our perfect daughter, Tristin. Then, out of blue, I found myself not only single again, but also fulfilling the role of solo parent. That's when the adventures really began! And they continued as Tristin journeyed through the stages of life, emerging as a talented and beautiful young woman. But throughout it all, buried deep in my subconscious, remained a spark of desire to ride again.

One day the burdens of life and family responsibilities started weighing so heavily on me that something gave way inside. The shift fanned the spark. The spark smoldered and became a glowing coal. The coal erupted into flame. And soon, the flame was all-encompassing. I had to have another motorcycle! A big cruising bike so I could escape the mounting pressures of my daily life.

When I took up residency in New Zealand, I failed to transfer my United States motorcycle license, so a test was required to regain my riding privileges. No problem – off I went to fulfill the requirements.

Turns out, you can't just walk in, take the test and leave again. In the New Zealand regulations, everything is broken down into a time-delayed step-by-step process.

Step One: Complete a basic handling course. Take the written test. *Fair enough.*

Step Two: Wait thirty days. Take a vision test to ensure your eyes are OK. *Why not at the same time as Step One?*

Step Three: Wait another thirty days. Take a Learner's riding competency test that allows you to operate a 250 cc bike by yourself during daylight, in town, with no passengers, and displaying a yellow "L" for "Learner" sign on the back. *Expected. But again, why the wait?*

Step Four: Wait six months. Take a restricted riding test that allows you to operate a 250 cc bike on the motorway between 5:00 am and 10:00 pm. No passengers, and with the yellow L sign still on the back. *OK, I suppose. Time to gain experience for new riders. But I was already experienced...*

Step Five: Wait twelve months. Take the final riding test. This allows you to ride any size bike you want with passengers. *Really? A whole year?*

All this added up to nearly two years until I could buy a cruising bike! That couldn't be right. I've heard of delayed gratification, but this was ridiculous. The painful process seemed to be geared towards a total novice who had never had a vehicle license of any kind.

It just wouldn't do. Upon completion of Step One and full of self-importance, I marched into the licensing office where I was waited on by an officious woman with the intellectual agility of a small, oval soap dish.

I tried to explain. "I've ridden motorcycles for twenty-some years, starting from the age of fifteen. Can I just take the written and final test?"

"No. You must pass each of the allotted steps in the specified order, after the required timeframe."

"Surely I could skip all that preliminary stuff, sit with a tester to verbally verify my skills, then take a practical test to demonstrate my competence?"

"You must pass each of the allotted steps in the specified order, after the required timeframe."

"Why can't I take the eye test and the written exam on the same day?"

"No. You must pass each of the allotted steps in the specified order, after the required timeframe," responded the looped recording.

Thus stonewalled, I had no other option but to abide by the rules. I borrowed a 250 cc motorcycle from a friend, took the learner's competency test, returned the bike, waited the appropriate time period, then diligently stepped my way through the process until I passed the final riding test.

The very next day, I went shopping for a big, heavy bike for long distance riding. Adventure was nearly with my grasp. Remembering the dreams of youth, my mind was fixed on a used Harley-Davidson Sportster like Bronson's... until that new 2009 Super Glide glimmered in the showroom window. A member of the Dyna family, she had a 96 ci (1583 cc) engine on a semi-large frame – ideal for switching between city and highway travel. The black paint and seat made the aluminum wheels, chrome exhaust and trimmings pop. She ticked all the boxes before I even took a test ride.

I purchased her that afternoon and named her Black Beauty. She soon became my preferred mode of transportation, and as we got to know each other over the next several years, we canvassed a large percentage of the paved roads of New Zealand.

If you ask me, Kiwis are the nicest people in the world – until they get behind the wheel of a car. With hands tightly wrapped around the steering wheel, they immediately switch to the Dark Side of the Force. Previously polite and kindly folk suddenly pop blood vessels and begin shouting, "Get the hell out of my way!" Speed limits are typically 100 kph (62 mph) on the open road and 50 kph (30 mph) in town. But, inexplicably, people drive 70 kph in town, and only 80 kph on the highway. You take your life in your own hands by riding a bicycle. And motorcyclists are just about as vulnerable.

The most important aspects of motorcycling are never covered in any training or testing. There are a large number of non-taught rules, but there are three in particular of which every biker should be intimately aware.

Rule number one: You are invisible. This is the single most important thing to know about riding. Imagine walking into a convention center where a seminar has just let out for a lunch break. Hundreds of young people are walking towards you at speed with headphones or earbuds on full volume and their eyes glued to their cell phones. Oblivious to their surroundings, they are focused only on updating social media or sending a text. That's what it's like riding a motorcycle in traffic. It's up to you to keep out of everyone else's way.

Rule number two: Riding in the rain is like riding on an ice-skating rink. Two wheels simply don't have the same stability and traction as four. Oil, petrol and diesel residue continuously spill onto highways. Adding water brings those substances to the surface. If there has been a long dry spell and you go riding during or just after fresh rain, the odds of sliding and dropping a bike escalate exponentially.

Rule number three: Riding after dark is like riding with your eyes closed. Looking through a bug-splattered or scratched plastic faceshield or windshield reduces a dark road lit by a single headlight to foggy shades of gray – a situation that is only made worse in the glare of oncoming traffic.

Violate all three of these rules at once, and the chances of an accident are inversely proportional to winning the lottery. Imagine skating at speed across a crowded ice-skating rink where everyone, including yourself, is blindfolded. The odds of a successful outcome are not in your favor.

Once back on a motorcycle, remembering and obeying the rules came back quickly. Feeling comfortable riding on the opposite side of the road didn't take long either.

Astride Black Beauty, my morning commute was cut from an hour to just fifteen minutes. The return journey, however, often took several hours, as I frequently passed my exit and just kept going. Evenings, Saturdays and Sundays were spent on longer and longer rides. And with the addition of saddle bags, it wasn't long before I loaded up my bike with a tent and sleeping bag. These overnight trips morphed into week-long excursions, then two separate month-long rides to the South Island.

I became a member of the Harley Owners' Group (HOG), a community of likeminded people – which is to say, a community of people always up for a ride. The group held annual rallies, where a couple of thousand members from all over New Zealand gathered to celebrate the biking lifestyle with music, food and showing off their beloved rides.

Life was beautiful again.

North Island to the Top

MD 143.3.13.08:18

March 13, 2016

The Iron Run was the pinnacle of the HOG calendar. After the previous year's rally in Queenstown (at the bottom of the South Island), Paihia (in the north of the North Island) would host the 2016 event. Of course, I wanted to attend.

Life was cruising along OK. Tristin was away at university and I was living at Bayswater Marina on Auckland's North Shore aboard Bontekoe, the beloved 30-foot sailboat that I had purchased in Seattle and was still faithfully mine after many years and many miles traveled. But my thirst for adventure was never far away, and something new was stirring.

One of the big problems of living in a small country is distance, and how to make a ride last. It was an easy four-hour trip from North Shore to Paihia. That made it hard to use the whole week I had allowed to get there. So I joined up with several other HOG members who had planned a zigzag route that would take at least four days. Diesel was a Road Captain from the club and would lead the ride.

Bikers often acquire a pseudonym from their mates. This guy had stopped to put petrol in his bike one day and inadvertently put in diesel. From that day forward, the event was memorialized whenever he was addressed by the other riders. I never knew his real name.

Thunder of engines filled the air on the day our small contingent departed. The late summer atmosphere was warm and dry. Billowing cumulus clouds speckled the rich blue sky. We held to the western side of the North Island, primarily vacillating between State Highways 12 and 16. The long arms of Kaipara Harbour's many inlets kept us away from the coast, and eventually we rumbled into the small town of Ruawai on the banks of the mighty Northern Wairoa River. There we stopped at the local pub for a break and some lunch.

Framed photos on the walls of the pub showed sailing ships of yore that had plied the river and the harbor's vast expanses. One framed image was a chart showing the location of various wrecks. Beyond the harbor lies a notorious coastline, where the Tasman Sea washes up full-force on the beach from Australia. It has been the graveyard for many a ship over the last 200 years.

"Some of those shipwrecks are now re-emerging from the shifting sands," beamed the waitress as she shepherded us to our table, "and all sorts of artifacts are popping up!"

At the dangerous mouth of the Kaipara Harbour, the remote Pouto lighthouse sits atop sand dunes. I was fascinated.

Diesel made a suggestion. "We could carry on to Dargaville and cross over the river as planned, but then take the road most of the way out to the dunes, if you like. But it'd be a bit of detour."

"That's OK," I said, "I'll add it to my list of future rides."

"Great. Then we'll continue the route I've laid out and carry on heading north through the Waipoua Forest. I've reserved some rooms for us tonight in Kaitaia. And tomorrow we'll ride to Cape Reinga. Then it's back south to Paihia in the Bay of Islands on the east coast."

About an hour after lunch, we entered a strange kingdom of ancient subtropical growth, winding our way up into the hills. Morning mist still hung in the air in the narrower valleys. The road was so narrow the trees seemed to reach out to embrace us as we carved turn after turn through the dense forest. A biker's dream, really. Soon we would encounter the marvels Waipoua is most known for: its giant kauri trees. And one in particular: Tāne Mahuta, lord of the forest.

It was a humbling experience to stand at Tāne's base, with the canopy high above. He is estimated to be somewhere between 1250 and 2500 years old, with a girth of 13.77m (45.3 ft) – the oldest and largest kauri known to man.

These trees pretty much grow straight up with a bunch of branches at the top, delivering high yields of knot-free timber that was once considered ideal for harvesting. Māori had long used them for sculpting large canoes called waka. One such waka seats a hundred warriors and rests under cover in Paihia. In the 1800s, European sailors loved the long, straight, unblemished lengths for masts and spars for their tall ships, then settlers felled the trees en-mass for housing. So much so, the slow-growing species was nearly wiped out. A thriving, but ultimately finite, logging industry continued until the early part of the 20th century.

Between mouthfuls of burger during lunch, Diesel had already filled us in on some other details of local history. The kauri trees left behind huge gum deposits, often thousands of years old and buried in swamp lands. This gum, which turned hard with age, was found to have many useful properties, from jewelry, fire starting and tattoo ink to additives for varnish and even linoleum. Realizing the value of this resource, early pioneers set out to extract as much gum as possible.

After identifying old swamp areas where kauri had been previously grown, they drilled into the promising ground with hand-held augers, sometimes up to their knees in mud, until a gum-deposit was located. They became known as the "gum-diggers", and people came to New Zealand from as far away as Croatia to make a living.

"Sounds like a lot of hard work for not much pay," said Crash, one of the other riders.

"Yeah, but at one time there were up to 20,000 people in the gumfields," the well-informed Diesel concluded.

And a lot of people think bikers like Diesel are just a bunch of grubby dumb guys riding motorcycles.

The day was nearly shot as we pulled into the backpackers' in Kaitaia. The accommodation was modest, but they had a large secure garage where we could store our bikes for the night. After a great dinner of fish and chips, we gathered to discuss the next day's ride.

"Tomorrow, Ninety Mile Beach will be off to our left as we head north for Cape Reinga," said Diesel.

"Why is it called Ninety Mile Beach?" asked Sunshine.

"The story goes that someone rode a horse the full length and, judging by the time it took, declared the distance to be ninety miles. Only thing is, he forgot to allow for the slower pace of riding on sand. It's actually only fifty-five miles," the ever-informed Diesel explained, "which is still pretty long. From there it's on up to Cape Reinga and the end of the road north."

"Can we ride clear out to the lighthouse?" asked Crash.

"Not quite," said Diesel. "Māori legend teaches that the souls of the dead depart from the cape as they make their way back to their spiritual homeland

– making it tapu, or a sacred place. We'll leave our bikes in the carpark and walk the last bit. It's a spectacular spot and the forecast is for another sunny day."

Diesel was right.

We stood there at the tip of the North Island, looking out at the meeting place of the Tasman Sea and Pacific Ocean. Under the lighthouse we were further rewarded with an Iron Run patch for our vests.

Walking back up to the carpark, I do believe I heard the passing of several souls on their way home.

Although I was enjoying myself, riding with a group had been a different experience for me. On longer trips I mostly travel solo. People often say they want to come along, but when push comes to shove, they usually drop out.

Case in point was my good friend Paula. We'd successfully been on several afternoon rides together, with Paula riding pillion, and enjoyed each other's company. A few years ago, we were talking about life in general and our plans for the summer when I casually said, "I'm planning on taking a trip to the South Island."

"That sounds like fun. Can I come along?" she asked, surprising me.

"Sure," I said offhandedly. Actually, I was quite enthusiastic about sharing the wonders and excitement of traveling by motorcycle.

I explained that there would be limited space on the bike. The tent would remain at home and we would stay at backpacker accommodation for economic reasons. We would have one saddle bag each, and I emphasized the limitations of that space by indicating the dimensions with my hands – about 150 mm wide, 300 mm high and 450 mm long (6 in x 12 in x 18 in).

"But what should I bring?" she asked.

"Three tops, three changes of socks and underwear, and one pair of pants – in addition to what you're wearing."

A week before we were due to leave, she rang up and asked again, "What should I bring?"

"Three tops, three changes of socks and underwear, and one pair of pants," I reiterated.

On the day before, the phone rang again. She was still not sure what to bring. I repeated the same instructions and said, "Don't worry, just do your best. I'll help you sort it out when I get there."

When I arrived, she said, "I'm still struggling and really need your help." We went into the bedroom. On her bed was a huge pile. "These are all the things I have to have," she said.

Dumbfounded, I began going through the items. "What do you need two hot water bottles for?"

"In case I get cold!"

"But it's summer and we're sleeping indoors. What are the slippers and bathrobe for?"

"In case I have to get up in the night and walk down to the toilet."

"What's this?" I asked, holding up a large cotton sheet.

"A sleeping bag liner."

I stared back.

"Surely you don't expect me to sleep in the same bag for the whole trip?" she continued.

"There's not enough room! You can wash the sleeping bag just as easily as the liner." (Although I have to confess, I only wash my sleeping bag once every five or six months. But there you go.)

I whittled down the items, discarding one after another, as she became increasingly sullen. The final straw came when I said the small suitcase full of makeup and beauty products would have to remain behind.

"Well, if it can't go, then neither will I!"

"Look. I'm not a magician. Just look at the bike. Where would we put it? Can't you just take a compact?"

Turned out, it was a solo trip to the South Island after all.

Among the various activities offered by the head office of the HOGs in Australia is something called an ABC competition. The objective is to visit a city for each letter of the alphabet. Proof of attendance is accomplished by taking a photo of your bike in front of a government building displaying the name of the place, along with a copy of the latest HOG magazine. Points are also awarded for national parks, Harley-Davidson dealerships, countries, big things, US states, Australian states, New Zealand regions, official rallies and a few other things. Come December, the photos are packaged up along with an entry form and fired off to the HOG judges. And, like so many things in life, whoever has the most points, wins. The first three places included a cash prize.

Without really reading all the fine print, I decided to give it a go. A thought had been rattling around in my brain about riding Route 66 in the USA. That opened up the chance to earn way more points than if I was only riding in New Zealand. But collecting that first point by attending the Iron Run Rally was high on my priority list as our small contingent departed Cape Reinga and headed south towards the Bay of Islands.

The Bay of Islands had been my first port of call in New Zealand. Sailing into that sailors' paradise had cast a spell over me in 1993, and my anchor's been stuck in this beautiful country ever since. Because I'd explored most of the islands and inlets in the area, I felt quite at ease just relaxing in the quiet, laid-back environs of its main town, Paihia. Well, the normally quiet town. Now it was overtaken by the rumble of hundreds of Harleys.

I wandered around town trying to take in all the events. A "Show and Shine" was underway. Here, members displayed their pride and joy, cleaned to showroom perfection. Exotic modifications and paint jobs made each bike unique and fun to compare. People voted for a winner by putting one or two-dollar coins in a bucket near each entrant, and the collected money went to charity.

I signed up for a demonstration ride on a Road King later in the afternoon and checked out a number of the merchandising tents selling t-shirts, hats and upgrade parts. Another tent had a motorcycle mounted on a fixed stand that allowed riders to accelerate through the gears and feel the motor vibrating between their legs.

Oftentimes a rally would have various riding competitions. But not usually for speed. Five parallel two-meter-wide lanes, running fifty meters long, were painted in the grass. The winner was the last one to cross the finish line without his or her feet touching down. Another competition involved a pillion passenger placing tennis balls on top of orange road cones as the rider weaved between the cones without stopping. These contests required first-rate handling skills.

A celebration dinner, followed by live music, was held on the Waitangi Treaty Grounds at the edge of town. This was the historical location where British and Māori had gathered to sign the Treaty of Waitangi, bringing the two peoples into partnership, under the protection of the crown, and thus creating Aotearoa New Zealand, on 6 February 1840. The treaty still plays a key role in our country today.

"First time I've ever been here," said Crash. "I mean, in school we covered the history and all. But it's pretty impressive to stand in the place."

"Did you see the 100-man waka yet?"

"No."

"Follow me." I led him down to the beach and the large canoe. The long waka rests under a roof on rail tracks, which allow it to be easily launched. During construction, several trees had been hollowed out and attached together to form one boat. Intricate carvings adorn the huge tail section, and run along the top rail to the bow, finishing with a fierce figurehead to lead the way.

"I've been here on Waitangi Day and seen the celebrations with singing and dancing. This and other waka are launched to paddle around the bay amongst the modern naval ships and sometimes old tall ships."

"Did you see the haka here too?"

"Of course," I said. "That's the best part."

The haka is a traditional challenge performed in unison with body movements and a chant calling on the strength of past warriors for support. The most famous haka is performed by the New Zealand All Blacks rugby team at the beginning of all of their matches. Kiwis take great national pride in the haka, performing it with gusto. And rightly so.

We studied the construction and intricate carvings of the waka a bit longer, then wandered back to the live music and continued socializing with copious amounts of beer until late. But not too late, as I intended to take part in the Thunder Run the following morning.

A Thunder Run occurs whenever a large number of bikes ride together. In this case, roughly 1,300 rally bikes headed north to Keri Keri, and the resultant thunder from the engines reverberated through the countryside. Highly organized, runners were sent out ahead to block off intersections and

23

direct riders on the correct route. All along the streets and highways people lined up to watch us pass by. It was like being in a parade. There were so many bikes involved that the leading bikers arrived back in Paihia just as the last ones left, 45 minutes later! It always feels good to be part of something bigger than yourself.

After the rally ended, I spent another night catching up with an old friend, while most people, including those I rode up with, headed home. Fully refreshed, I set out solo the following morning down the east coast back towards Auckland. As usual in Northland, I had to dodge plenty of possum road-kill, but nothing could steal my bliss. The narrow road continuously rose up and down steep hills. Sometimes plunging into the bush, with visibility reduced to the next curve in front of me, and only three feet between me and the edge of the road. Then suddenly, I would come around a corner and break out into a broad vista of rugged coastline and uninterrupted deep-blue ocean.

The Poor Knights Islands could be seen offshore, appearing rough and inhospitable as they erupt from the ocean surface – a divers' paradise that I had visited in the past.

Several times the road descended right down to the shoreline. Sandy beaches were sporadically placed between jagged rocks and colorful outcrops, inviting me to stop frequently, dig in my toes and gaze out to sea. I passed numerous people basking in the sun along the shore.

"Hi you baskers!" I shouted as I rode by.

Little towns and destination campgrounds appeared along the way. I stopped at the marina in Tutukākā for fish and chips.

As I sat soaking in the sun at the outdoor table, a shadow appeared over my food. It was a lanky elderly man leaning on a single crutch. "Mind if I join you? I need to rest a while."

"Sure, plenty of space," I said, moving over.

"That your bike?" He pointed his crutch at Black Beauty.

"Sure is."

"How's your ride going?"

"Great. Lot of possum road-kill though." These furry nocturnal marsupials had been introduced to New Zealand in the 1850s to establish a fur-trade. The little Aussie critters took to the place with great enthusiasm and flourished to the point where they are now a constant threat to the native ecology. With no natural predators, they devour trees like there's no tomorrow.

"A damn nuisance if you ask me," said the old man. "You can't hardly drive at night without hitting five or six by the end of the trip."

"Yeah, it seemed like I passed a dead one on the road every five or six minutes."

"Do you know how many possums it takes to make love?" he asked abruptly. "Three," he said before I could respond. "Two to do the act and one to watch for cars."

Back on my bike, I carried on along the water's edge until I was eventually forced to turn inland in order to clear Whangārei Harbour, but I pushed back to the coast again as soon as I could. At Ruakākā I stopped for a long walk along the beach, viewing the dynamic Whangārei Heads across the bay.

It's funny to think that the outlying islands like the Poor Knights, Hen and Chickens, and Sail Rock are really the peaks of mountains that begin under water. Tips of an iceberg. But, looking at the Whangārei Heads, I began to comprehend the continuity of the countryside and imagine what lay beneath the sea. So much of life is spent looking at the tips and imagining how everything else supports them – looking at the appearance of things and wondering what lies beneath.

It was late afternoon and the offshore sea breeze turned cool. As I dug my toes down into the warm sand, I became philosophical. Perhaps it's time to actually dig down below the surface and see how much of what I've always imagined is actually true.

On the final stretch home, the evening skyline of Auckland appeared and all the colorful experiences of this short holiday began their fade into black and white memories. Black Beauty had exceeded all expectations. After eight hours of riding, I pulled into the marina and unloaded my gear. Once it was off and stowed, I sat back down on the bike to think a bit. And I thought, Y'know, I might just go for a quick ride around town.

So I did.

Auckland – East Cape

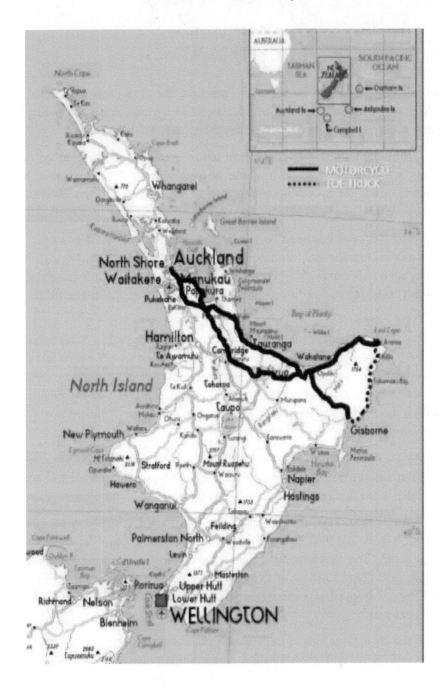

March 27, 2016

So, there I was, sitting in *Bontekoe*, watching the days growing shorter and colder and, more often than not, accompanied by rain. A certain pining for warm waters and longer days filled my thoughts.

Tristin would be at university until winter break, when she planned to go skiing with her friends, leaving me no real reason to stick around New Zealand during the upcoming winter months. But for now, it was essential to take some time and think about my options.

Easter weekend I decided on one final autumn ride down the coast to Castle Point Lighthouse. I find it relaxing to take those long journeys, camp out in my tent, sleep on the ground and see the countryside for a few days. It doesn't take long to clear my mind and gain clarity of purpose when I'm riding.

I washed and waxed Black Beauty to make her presentable, loaded the saddle bags with the required minimal necessities, and set off with a full tank of gas and a smile on my face. Unfortunately, I dawdled a bit before starting and wound up leaving in rush hour traffic. With a top speed of 30 kph (18 mph) it took forever to get out of Auckland and find an exit from State Highway 1 South so I could head for the hills.

My plan was to cut across the Coromandel Peninsula then take the coast road through the Bay of Plenty and around East Cape, one of a handful of unridden roads demanding exploration, to Gisborne.

Towards the end of the first day, the bike started acting strange, cutting out every now and then. It was an alarming, "total electrical failure" type of cutting out. The problem continued to get worse as evening approached. Rather than going all the way to Whakatāne, the last major center in the Bay of Plenty, I stopped at a campground for the night, about 20 km (12 miles) short of town.

In the dwindling light, I undertook a once over of everything on the bike to do with wires and spark plugs. Finding nothing obviously wrong, I didn't bother removing the battery cover as there would be nothing more than a couple of terminals to look at.

The electrical issue had shaken me up. To relax, I set off for an evening walk along the beach, listening to the rolling surf as it rushed up to greet my bare feet then reluctantly receded. Over and over again. I had a strong premonition that I should be "receding" back to Auckland, but for now I pushed away the thought.

The next morning, within ten minutes of leaving for Whakatāne, the bike began cutting out again. And the closer to town I got, the worse it became. To complicate things, it was Good Friday, and everything was closed. I decided that if I could get things running properly, I would head back home. Finally, I surrendered and called the local AA emergency call-out service.

"Hi. I've got some electrical problems on my motorcycle."

"Where are you?"

"At the northern edge of Whakatāne on the crossroad just across from the mall."

"Well, I'm only 200 meters from the intersection. If you can get it to my shop, it'll save the towing fee."

What luck! Black Beauty sputtered and coughed towards the garage and then I finally pushed her the last 50 steps to the front door.

"I've checked all the electrical connections and looked for loose wires," I informed the mechanic with a confident air. "I'm pretty sure it's something to do with the electronic ignition."

"Well, I always start at the beginning to rule out the easy stuff," he responded removing the battery cover. I watched in disbelief as the battery's two terminal bolts dropped to the ground.

"Looks like that's the problem," I said with my face glowing fire-truck red. I thanked him profusely, paid for his time, and headed back on my merry way into town.

After backing the bike into a spot in Whakatāne's city center carpark, I settled down for my morning coffee and to contemplate the wisdom of carrying on with the trip. Once fortified with caffeine, things looked more optimistic. I decided, since all was well, to proceed with my original plan.

Once back on the road, the reason for any hesitation was soon forgotten as the sparsely populated landscape became mesmerizingly beautiful. The comforting vibration and sound of Black Beauty's big Evolution 1583 cc (96 ci) engine rumbling under me would make the next 350 kilometers (220 miles) fly by.

Of course, the East Cape lived up to its reputation of wild countryside and thrilling roads.

And, of course, when I reached Hicks Bay, roughly half way around, and started looking for a campground, the bike started acting very skittish and wobbly.

Now what?

The rear wheel bearing had given out. I couldn't believe my luck – or lack thereof.

An interesting point of geography: Hicks Bay is the furthest point you can get from a certified motorcycle repair shop anywhere in New Zealand.

Once again, I called the AA roadside service. A tow truck arrived about dark thirty and we loaded the bike on the trailer then headed further south towards Gisborne. It was equidistant to go backwards or forwards and I was determined not to retreat. In the hustle-bustle of loading, I set my helmet on the picnic table next to where the tow truck collected me, and where, I realized about an hour and a half later, it still remained. Bugger! Things just kept getting worse.

I didn't make it to Castle Point, but at least I'd completed the trip around East Cape – although not all of it on the bike or during daylight. I spent a lovely Easter Sunday and Monday camping by the beach waiting for Gisborne's repair shops to open. Fortunately, one of the motorcycle shops had a helmet on sale that fit. Things began to look up again. While there was no Harley-Davidson dealership in town, the Honda dealer employed a mechanic versed in Harley-speak, and by Wednesday afternoon I opened up the throttle on the road back home.

With new bearings, tight electrical fittings and the soothing rumble of the motor sending vibrations through my entire body, the trip home breezed by. The lighthouse at Castle Point would have to wait till next spring or summer.

The downtime reclining in Gisborne had given me copious space to make the decision to follow through with my plans for the upcoming New Zealand winter. Rather than procrastinating (as I usually do) about that Route 66 trip in the States, I'd grabbed the bull by the horns and, taking advantage of an early bird promotion, made plane reservations from inside my tent. The loose arrangement was to go to the States on the first of June and buy a Harley. I'd ride Route 66 and perhaps some of the eastern states, then head back to South Dakota by the third week in August for the Sturgis HOG Rally. After that it'd be on to my hometown in Montana for the All 70s High School Class Reunion in the first week of September, stopping at the houses of my siblings along the way to remove all the belongings they had so patiently and kindly stored for me over the years. I would ship these personal effects back to New Zealand, along with the new bike (if I couldn't sell it before I left) – thus killing several birds with one stone.

The plan was made. The goals were set. The tickets purchased.

All was under control.

The day after I arrived back in Auckland, I ran into my friend Cindy, who was home on leave from her teaching job in Taiwan. We'd met about a year and a half earlier when she'd previously been back in New Zealand. As well as being a teacher, Cindy was an artist, and a singer in a couple of bands. There seemed to be a strong connection between us – strong enough, in fact, to invite further investigation. Prior commitments prevented her from traveling Route 66 with me, but instead she suggested I come and explore Taiwan.

Suffice it to say, all was no longer "under control."

After a lot of discussion and some investigation, followed by a few days of deliberation, I delayed the date of my departure for the US. Thus forfeiting all my early bird purchase savings, I bought tickets to Taiwan for a three-week stay. There should still be sufficient time to ride Route 66 after that. A level of "control" was returning again.

In the midst of preparations, I was offered some architectural work. Feeling the financial pinch of my recent motorcycle repairs, and relishing the design opportunity, I accepted the commission. I knew the timeframe would be tight, involving several intense days just before I left for Taiwan, but I wasn't too worried. Most of my architectural career had been spent working 12- to 15-hour days, seven days a week.

Life was under control, but now somewhat shaky.

Then, out of the blue, one week prior to departure and in the thick of the design commission, a young woman called to look at *Bontekoe*. Tristin was keen for me to buy a bigger boat, so a few months earlier I had half-heartedly listed the yacht for sale.

"I love her!" said the young woman. "I want to buy her. I just need to organize a loan."

"Fantastic," I said, "but I'm leaving in seven days and don't see how you can organize bank approval, a haul-out, survey and a sea trial in that timeframe." *Not to mention me having time to remove all my belongings.*

"I'm sure we can arrange it," she replied ever-optimistically. "We can finalize everything when you get back in three weeks."

My life was becoming a yo-yo.

There hadn't been much interest in the boat, but when it rains, it pours. Two days before I was due to leave, another potential purchaser entered the mix. And showing the boat was eating away my precious time.

The upshot of all this was that my life was definitely not under control. I boarded the plane to Taiwan with unfinished drawings, short on sleep and with two offers on the table for *Bontekoe*. Not to mention a huge wave of uncertainty as to why on earth I was going to Taiwan when my primary intention had been a motorcycle trip on Route 66.

I can't figure out if it's optimism, naivety, poor planning, the luck of the draw or plain stupidity that gets me into these circumstances. All I can say is it doesn't seem to happen as often to other people.

This new adventure had begun on a radically different tack than I had envisioned. But how can one really ever plan an adventure? There would always be a "what if?" hanging over my head if I hadn't decided to follow this road and see where it led. And anyway, it's the unplanned bits that add the surprise, excitement, variety and joy to the best stories in life.

Book 2

Taiwan 2016

June 2, 2016

"How was the flight?" asked Cindy, giving me a big hug at her front door. She had organized for a taxi to collect me from the Taipei airport and drop me off at the base of her six-story apartment block overlooking the city.

"Quite restful, actually," I responded. "The noise-canceling headphones I bought almost completely blocked out the kid next to me who wailed the entire trip."

"Told you that you would like them," she said with a satisfied smirk on her face. "Well, get some rest. We're going to dinner tonight at the place where I'm opening my painting exhibition," she said as I carried my suitcase up to the room where I would be staying. "School ends in three days, which should give you time to recover from jet lag before we go exploring."

And hopefully complete most of the work on my design project, I thought.

৵৽৹ৎ

It felt good to be on the island of Taiwan. The day was hot, the water warm, and music from the previous night's concert was still ringing in my ears as we walked hand in hand along the waterline at the local beach. We stopped for coffee. "This afternoon we'll catch the train to Hualien and then a shuttle to Silk Hotel in the Taroko Gorge. It's so beautiful there – I hope you like it," said Cindy.

What wasn't to like? "Taroko" means "magnificent and splendid" in the local language and it certainly lived up to its name. The spindly roadway diverged and split, following the Liwu River but frequently breaking off into tunnels. Buses, scooters, motorcycles and scrambling pedestrians all competed for space. The wild water flowing under bridges called for attention as it cascaded over boulders on its way down the gorge. All this entertained us as the bus climbed from Hualien towards the 9,700 ft (2,957 m) peaks.

"This road was just a trail until the mid-1950s," lectured a tour guide sitting behind us with her group. "Over the course of 1956 to 1960 the trail was made into a highway, and during that time 225 lives were lost. Mostly from avalanches and people falling off the trails. Cyclones often stopped progress. Once, a newly installed bridge was found six miles downstream, two days after a huge cyclone had passed."

I could see that work was ongoing, with the addition of extra roads and tunnels to accommodate the increasing volume of traffic. The abrasive water had cut a swath through granite, leaving smooth flowing shapes and colors. *Not unlike the Badlands of Arizona,* I thought, *but different colors.*

"Our bus driver is obviously in some kind of competition to beat the fastest time to the hotel," I observed. "He's had the gas pedal floored from the moment we left the parking lot."

As if to validate my comment, we rounded a corner on two wheels and squeezed into a tunnel with thirty mopeds approaching us head-on.

"Hang on!" laughed Cindy as she slid into me. "It's not for the faint-hearted, that's for sure."

"Wow, look at that!" I pointed. The gorge walls had given way to sheer drops on both sides. Half the road was cut into the cliff face while the other half was cantilevered over the river with no visible support. *What's holding us up?* I worried.

Somehow we arrived in one piece and, over the next few days, we set off from the hotel on several walking tours as we got to know each other better. Although still hot, the high altitude meant the temperatures were more tolerable and even though there was quite a bit of rain, it seemed to hold off whenever we were outdoors.

Signage on the various trails warned us to keep a sharp eye out for poisonous snakes and venomous giant hornets. We didn't spot any snakes, but we did see hornets the size of hummingbirds that sounded like Chinook helicopters when they passed overhead.

Along the gorge, little temples and monasteries perched picturesquely on jagged rock outcrops or on the tops of peaks. The design and detailing inside of some of them simply took our breath away.

We had just arrived at the Eternal Springs Shrine, where artesian water gushed from the side of the mountain, when disaster almost struck. "Look out!" I shouted, and quickly pulled Cindy to the roadside as a bus careened around the corner.

Now it was our turn to be the hapless pedestrians scampering out of the way of buses and mopeds.

"How does it feel?" I asked laughing.

"Not as much fun being the dodgee as the dodger," she responded.

Dense green vegetation clung to the steep walls and cliffs of the mountainsides. The white temple with its red clay roof tiles sat to one side of the waterfall, connected by a bridge to a pagoda supported by red columns on the other side.

The dramatic effect of the torrent, surrounded by the shrine where it spewed forth from the rockface and found its own way to the valley floor, left a powerful impression on me. *Man successfully working with nature*, I mused.

Being thrilled as passengers when riding on buses, frantically terrorized as roadside tourists, eluding hornets on hikes, guarding our lunches from wild monkeys and exploring peaceful shrines built in improbable settings – it all added to the excitement and local flavor of the gorge. Not to mention the happy memories for Cindy and me.

દ∞ઉ

Riding the slow train on the way to and from the gorge, which stopped about every seven minutes at some small town or another, I had an opportunity to hear and read the digital announcement boards for each stop in both Mandarin and English.

By the time we were back in Taipei, with the support of Cindy's language skills and the Chinese app on my phone, my command of the language had improved immensely. I can now read and say, "The next stop is Taipei" (or Tainan, or Anping etc.) and "Mind the gap when alighting to the platform" … Although I sometimes struggle to bring these phrases into everyday conversation.

MD 143.6.10.15:54
We had three days to discover and explore Taipei before heading to the south end of the island on the High Speed Rail (HSR) train.

The next morning, I made my first interesting discovery. In these parts, the garbage trucks play a little tune similar to the ice cream trucks of yore. When the sound is heard, everyone brings out their garbage. Meanwhile, there's me standing on the sidewalk with change, waiting for an ice cream.

"I figured, as an architect, you would want to see Taipei 101 – the tallest building in Taiwan," said Cindy as we rode the escalator up from the subway system on the third day of our explorations.

"I do believe you have me pegged," I said stepping into the daylight and leaning back to look up at the impressive edifice.

At 1,670 ft (509 m) Taipei 101 sports 101 floors and boasts the fastest lift in the world. We rose from the fifth floor boarding area to the observation deck (90 floors) in 38 seconds! My ears popped more than they do in an airliner. The swift acceleration may or may not have had something to do with activating the black beans consumed the night before, I'm not sure. But the good thing is we were only in that confined space for 38 seconds.

"Let's go to the observation deck first," said Cindy grabbing my hand, "and get some fresh air."

We were very fortunate to have a semi-clear day and could see quite a long way across the city. After a comprehensive stint on the exterior deck, I took the lead.

"OK, my turn. Let's drop down a couple of floors and take a look at the anti-sway ball."

"The what?" said Cindy.

"Anti-sway ball – a six-ton ball suspended by cables and shock-absorbers," I informed her. "Skyscrapers use mass to counteract the shock from earthquakes and high winds."

The shape of the ball was formed by a series of thick disks. Painted gold and hanging within a black backdrop, it more resembled a piece of art than an engineered dampening devise.

MD 143.6.14.10:15
"There's really no need to own a car here," said Cindy as we set off the following morning on our newest adventure. "Public transport is so efficient. I just love it."

Yeah, but from what I had seen so far, it would be hard to justify owning a motorcycle bigger than a moped too. And everywhere was wall to wall people, giving me a hemmed-in feeling. I was sorely missing riding my bike.

We took the subway to the HSR terminal where trains arrived every 30 minutes to whisk you away. "I'm very impressed," I told her as we boarded the sleek southbound train for Tianan. I was relishing the opportunity to improve my Mandarin language skills. Soon we were comfortably in our seats.

"I really like living here because it's not only safe to walk around but theft is minimal," continued Cindy as she promoted the positives of Taiwanese life. "People leave their cell phones and purses laying on the table at restaurants to reserve their seats as they go to the buffet or toilet."

"I've noticed that. Even though people are compressed into small spaces, they all seem to get along," I agreed. "The worst thing I've seen was a bit of yelling in a parking lot when some idiot cut off a man heading into a parking space." Then I reasoned, "But who could begrudge a guy venting in a situation like that?"

Able to travel up to 180 mph (290 kph), riding on the HSR was smooth and quick. The scenery was beautiful and we were making incredible time. But looking out the window as country roads weaved in and out of small villages and fields, I became somewhat despondent. I got that feeling I was watching someone else's film. I longed to be riding those roads through the rice paddies on my motorcycle and once again be the hero of my own movie. I tried to shake off the feeling for now.

"The next stop is Anping," I informed Cindy in plausible Mandarin. "Mind your step when alighting to the platform," I added as we disembarked.

"Just get the luggage," she said in a rather exasperated tone.

MD 143.6.16.12:05

We spent the next couple of days in Anping as tourists. During the day, we visited the "Treehouse" at Tait & Co Merchant House (so called because a banyan tree has taken over the old ruins), the street markets and Fort Zeelandia, which was built by the Dutch in the 1600s (derivatives of "Zealand" seem to keep popping up in my life). Then, in the cool of the night, we wandered the streets, visiting intricately designed shrines and stores that stayed open till late.

The place has a fascinating history. Formosa (an earlier name for Taiwan) had been controlled by the Dutch in the early 17th century, then the Chinese, then the Dutch again, then the English, then the Japanese, then the Chinese again, and pretty much everyone else over the years. And yet, despite everything, the local population have retained their own identity.

☙❧

"OK. Tell me again why you wanted to come to Tainan?" requested Cindy staring forlornly at the industrial end of the city.

"When you asked what I wanted to do while I was in Taiwan, the only thing I knew about the country was that my boat was built here in the Ta Shing Boatyard," I answered trying to explain the tenuous link.

Cindy humored me and we flagged down a cab. The excursion may have seemed logical when I first suggested it, but less so now as we continued deep into the city's industrial boondocks. When we arrived, the yard was silent... hardly surprising seeing as it was lunchtime on a Saturday. I could see people napping in shaded areas. But I strutted right up to the gate like I was in charge and knew what I was doing.

"Hi. My name is Rod," I informed the drowsy guard in English. "My Baba 30 was built in this yard in 1978 and I would like to visit your site." And then, observing his blank look, I switched to Mandarin. "Ne Hou. The train has arrived in Tainan." Followed by, "Mind your step when alighting to the platform."

That got his attention! He shouted into the phone and two security guards arrived almost immediately. One was carrying a white jacket. I can only assume these guys hadn't ridden the train very often.

Luckily, Cindy jumped in as I tried a second time to explain why we were there. Cindy's language skills were met with much more success, but still doubtful looks, as the guard got on the phone again.

He received instructions, then, "Office," he said escorting us to an administration building. There we met a hesitant gentleman named Andy Chung, Senior Vice President of the Ta Shing Yacht Building company.

"What you want? My English not good," he tried.

With a sketch pad in hand, Pictionary type drawings, frenzied hand waving, occasional words in Mandarin and English, along with photographs

39

of *Bontekoe* from my cell phone, we discovered Andy had been with the company for over 45 years and had worked his way up the ranks.

Then he announced, "I work on you boat. My job not builder but add part."

"Well, you did a fine job," I said, and with the aid of a globe sitting on his credenza traced my finger along *Bontekoe*'s route from Seattle to Alaska and then on through the Pacific Islands to New Zealand. "This is where she has sailed."

He was notably impressed and seemed pleased to see the fruition of his efforts so long ago.

After a short tour of the sleepy plant, he offered to take us back towards the city where we could find a cab. All things considered, I really enjoyed myself and I think Andy, although perhaps still a little dazed and confused by our unexpected arrival, was happy we had come.

MD 143.6.23.11:25
With the boatyard tour out of the way, Cindy and I boarded the HSR to Xin Zuoying and transferred to a bus bound for Kenting. The school holidays were in full swing and this tourist destination was in a festive spirit when we arrived. After we checked into the hotel we ventured out amid the "great unwashed."

Main Street was defined by a highway that sliced through the center of town. Throngs of people, food stalls, live music, food stalls, games, food stalls, pop-up bars and more food stalls, with their rich aromas, filled the air.

"I'm kind of hungry," said Cindy. "How about you?"

"Me too. Let's see what's available," I said as we pushed our way through the masses.

You could get wieners on a stick, some sort of green stuff (kelp maybe?) wrapped in Chinese pancakes on a stick, corn dogs on a stick, corn cobbs on a stick, fish on a stick, prawns on a stick, and my personal favorite...

"I'll take a squid on a stick," I said indicating the delicacy soaked in teriyaki sauce and hot peppers slow cooking over coals. Despite being analogous in consistency to chewing on a large rubber band, it was delicious.

The squid eventually breaks down but not before giving your jaw a strenuous workout.

"I'll stick with the corn dog," said Cindy giving a skeptical sideways look at the squid tentacles protruding from my mouth.

Phenomenal sunsets had illuminated the beach every evening, with blue skies every day since our arrival. Besides leisurely walks along the water's edge or just lying on deck chairs tanning, we took a short trip to Eluanbi Park and lighthouse. There, the heat and humidity took its toll on Cindy.

"I need a day of rest," she said. "And I'm not leaving the air-conditioned hotel."

"OK, get some rest," I said and set off alone towards Sheding Nature Park on foot... on foot, because I'd failed to made reservations for the tour bus a day in advance.

There were few clouds and almost no wind. By 10:00 am, my clothes were saturated and the salty sweat running down my legs had filled my shoes to the brim. The result was a squishing sound that scared off all the native deer and agitated the throngs of cicadas surrounding me. By noon, that air-conditioned room was beginning to sound pretty good.

My reserves and electrolytes had worn thin by the time I left the park; then I came upon a sign stating that it was still another four miles back to Kenting. No way was I going to walk. I stuck out my thumb, and amazingly enough, the first car stopped. The driver was a friendly man with his family sitting in the back seat. I felt kind of bad that I was sloshing around the front seat and dripping everywhere. When we arrived at a junction, the signs said Kenting to the left and Henchun to the right. He looked at me with an uncertain look.

"The train is now arriving at Kenting," I said and he pulled over since he was going to Henchun. I opened the door and rode the surf out, leaving his car seat looking like it had been occupied by a giant slug. I apologized profusely, tried to wipe down the upholstery and offered to compensate him for the ride. But he wouldn't accept any money.

"Thank you so much," I said and waving good bye added, "Mind your step when alighting to the platform." Which he seemed genuinely delighted to be told.

Back in Cindy's company the next day, a short bus ride took us to the southernmost tip of Taiwan and a quaint seaside bed and breakfast surfing resort called Summer Point. The heat continued to affect Cindy and was exacerbated by the broken air-conditioner in our unit.

"I'm sorry," she said falling onto her back on the bed, "I just need to sleep."

"No worries." I opened the doors and windows to try to get some cross ventilation. The thick white and colored plastered buildings, set against the dark green brush and azure-blue skies, looked like a cross between the Mediterranean and the Mexican Riviera. The setting was all very low key, but superb, as I looked out from our balcony at the surf breaking in the bay. It seemed like the perfect place to paint or author a book... once the air-conditioner was repaired, mind you.

"I'll just try to sort out some of the issues back home while you rest," I said opening my laptop.

Negotiations for the sale of my boat and questions from the city council about my house designs kept interrupting what I'd hoped would be stress-free days. I promised myself that after this, I would never, ever, ever again try to sell something or do work projects while on holiday. Ever!

After all the back-and-forth communications and negotiations, there were too many unknowns regarding the boat sale. I could no longer make further changes to my US flights without total ticket forfeiture. Life was suddenly getting incredibly complex and running full speed into a time barrier. So much for planning ahead.

Cindy, struggling with heat sickness, and me with my head buried in my problems, drifted off into our own separate worlds.

Pressure, of course, facilitates mistakes. Finally, I just pulled the plug and said, "Enough!" If someone wanted to buy my boat, they could wait until I returned from the States in September. I would resolve the outstanding design issues now, but not entertain any new ones. It may cost me financially, but emotionally and stress wise, it was the best decision.

With those burdens removed from my shoulders, I went outside for a walk and met a couple of Harley-Davidson bikers staying at the B&B next door. That lifted my spirits. They spoke no English but even with the language barrier, as bikers, we were able to communicate just fine. Smiling, pointing and nodding with some occasional thumbs-up gestures, proved adequate to ask how the bikes handled, if the aftermarket air filter increased the horse power and whether the spring tension was sufficient when banking at high speeds while carrying a pillion. Of course, that rejuvenated my desire to get back on a bike and travel.

MD 143.6.27.13:30

Cindy slept for the entire return trip to Taipei on the HSR. I amused myself by watching the scenery speed by, amazed at the countryside and how it supported so much agriculture. A large number of small farms occupied the landscape. As we passed through each of the many communities, I noticed that there was always a definite edge where built-up areas stopped and the country began. This was so unlike the urban sprawl and strip phenomenon happening in the United States and New Zealand.

When planners haven't thought ahead or provided proper direction, and expansion by developers is allowed unabated, the result is a continuous infill of buildings along highways and primary roads between towns. Without signage, you have no idea when you have left one town and entered another. The old Sunday drive in the country has been lost, along with the appreciation of the rural landscape.

I was once again mentally riding the narrow country roads when we passed several cemeteries that caught my eye and piqued my interest. Each culture treats their dead differently and cemeteries speak volumes about how the dead are honored. Instead of tombstones, the treeless burial lots of the Taiwanese countryside consisted of low, walled-in spaces. Some had building works, like thrones, at the head. Others featured miniature temple facades. Stone lanterns and brightly colored ceramic inlays were common. Several appeared to be larger shrines, which I assumed were mausoleums of sorts. I took photos as best I could.

MD 143.6.29.07:25

"I have band rehearsal today for our concert this weekend," said Cindy. "Are you going to be OK here at the flat?"

"Actually, I'm feeling confident about using the transport system. I think I'll take a day trip around Taipei by myself," I said.

The intent of my mission was to find a Harley-Davidson dealership. It sort of gave the day purpose. People were really friendly and helpful when I asked for directions. After a couple of rail transfers and a short walk through the humid streets, I was met with success. And surprised at the size of the place.

Turns out Harley-Davidson are doing a booming business in Taiwan. But with a society that is used to scooters by the hundreds of thousands, I suppose it's only natural to want bigger and better.

After getting my fix sitting on several newer motorcycles, I retired for a flat white in the HOG members' room. Eventually, armed with a new Taiwan Harley-Davidson T-shirt, I set out to inspect the Taipei Fine Arts Museum, the Grand Hotel and an outdoor water exhibition in a park, before heading back home

☙❧

My last day in Taiwan was spent sitting on the grass watching Cindy perform with her band for the Canada Day celebrations. The next morning, the time came for me to depart.

I thanked Cindy for her hospitality and the outstanding job she'd done organizing everything. I would never have visited the place on my own, let alone seen the best parts of the country. The intense time we had spent together was wonderful and enlightening. Although it had been special, we both realized that, even if we overcame the many obstacles in front of us, our paths lay in different directions. It was time to move on with my plans for the coming months and I was getting antsy.

Tristin's winter skiing plans had fallen through in New Zealand, so she had flown to the USA instead to stay with my sister, Judy, in Washington State and do some travel with her around the western part of the country. I was excited about seeing her there. Meanwhile, the date for my class reunion in Montana remained fixed. In the scant nine weeks left, I'd need to fly from New Zealand to the States, find and buy a bike, travel to Chicago, ride Route 66 to LA and return to Montana.

New Zealand – In Retrospect

MD 143.7.01.11:05
July 1, 2016

There are times when life can get ahead of you. It happens to all of us – things both within and out of our control. It doesn't really matter the event or the cause, so much as the feelings we encounter in the moment, the impact they have on us and the resultant choices we make.

The stresses and pressures I had faced because I went to Taiwan had indeed induced mistakes. These, combined with a series of unfortunate events, a harsh word or two, a couple of miscommunications, a stupid action and an inappropriate response, culminated in the floor of my world suddenly breaking apart. While trying to hold things together, I watched in helpless disbelief as my self-confidence fell, hit the floor, rolled around precariously for a while, then nearly disappeared altogether as it slipped through the cracks.

Without my self-confidence, I'm like a fish flopping around on the beach. Even though I may see the water and its offer of normality and safety, I have no way of propelling myself in the right direction. No matter how valiant the effort, the struggle is useless and ultimately appears quite pathetic to the casual observer. Without a helpful push, the odds of getting quickly back on track through this ungainly flopping about were minimal.

That push came as I was sitting in a fog of self-doubt at the Auckland International Airport terminal. The loudspeaker burst forth with several names of people who should urgently report to their respective departure gates. You can imagine my surprise when I heard, "Paging passenger Rodney Slater: please come to Gate 5. The aircraft is ready to depart. All of the passengers are on board and we are waiting for you!"

I bounded off the seat with bag in one hand, jacket and iPad in the other, and raced down the corridor. Seems I wasn't the only one flopping around on the beach. There was a school of several other paged passengers racing alongside me towards their destinations. We all had that terrified look in our eyes as if a barracuda was cutting a swath through our number and we knew at least one of us wasn't going to make it.

Proceeding through the gauntlet of jeers, boos and evil-eyed looks I settled into my seat aboard the aircraft. As we lifted off, I realized (once again) that whatever has happened, it can't be changed. The plane was going to continue on, with or without me on-board. As would life. And I had a choice to make.

Life is for the living and suddenly I felt ready to climb aboard and live again. Trying to be someone I'm not had just confused me and everyone else. And there was no way I could please everyone anyway. Having relived the situation over and over in my head, I knew I couldn't fix it anyway. My choice was to stop, breathe deeply and take a minute to remember who I was. Then focus my energies on where I was going. And trust in God that all would work out OK.

Which, of course, it does.

Book 3

USA 2016

HOG Heaven

MD 143.7.3.7:08

July 3, 2016

Thus, with realization of surroundings, clarity of purpose and self-confidence on the mend, I arrived in Spokane, Washington State, hired a car, drove to my sister Judy's house in Liberty Lake. She and Tristin were away road-tripping, so I had the place to myself. I made camp, bought a phone and began inquiries about purchasing a bike. By the end of the next day, I had found, bought, insured and licensed my new motorcycle. Phew! Amazing what you can do when you put your mind to it.

OK – so it wasn't brand new – but it was new to me. I had found her just over the state line in Idaho. She was a red and black 2005 Harley-Davidson Softail Heritage. The original owner had painted her with *Pirates of the Caribbean* images and named her the Black Pearl. The back fender was emblazoned with the phrase, "Dead Men Tell No Tales." Being a sailor myself, it seemed somehow appropriate. If there were any chrome extras available, factory or after-market, it had them – including matching clock and thermometer. I had to wear sunglasses just to look at the speedometer in bright sunlight.

The test ride provided a pleasing double surprise.

Firstly, helmets are not required in Idaho, so that left me with substantially improved hearing compared to removing my hearing aids and covering my ears with a helmet. Secondly, the Vance exhaust pipes pretty much let the sound from the engine run unchecked out the back. Starting her up for the first time, I was enveloped in an impressive rumble. I could tell I was going to enjoy this trip to the max!

The hardest thing was determining how much power this bike had compared to my Super Glide back home. When I opened the throttle, the deep rumble turned into a throaty, high decibel roar that scared the socks off me. Since the speedometer was in miles per hour, the needle moved more slowly when I accelerated, compared to the Super Glide's kilometers per hour. The overall impression was of making a lot of noise but without much get up and go… Until I passed the 35 mph speed sign and looked down to see I was doing 60 mph!

Yup, this would do fine.

Not all states in the US allow riders the freedom to determine whether or not they need a helmet, so I would be required to wear one while passing through regulated areas. Personally, I like to wear a helmet when it's cold or raining. Raindrops feel like nails being driven into your face when you're riding along at 75 mph (120 kph), which might take the shine off an otherwise nice ride. But, in the same breath, I detest anyone telling me that I *have to* wear one.

I found a place having a sale on helmets that suited my budget. A salesclerk appeared as I was trying one on.

"I'm glad to see you're interested in purchasing a helmet," he began confidently. "I'll be glad when they make it a law for all bikers to wear one in this state."

"Why's that?" I asked through the open visor.

"Well, statistically, if a motorcyclist is involved in an accident, they stand a higher chance of injury or death without a helmet," he said.

"Is that so?"

"If they aren't smart enough to wear one, we need to make a law to protect them," he said, unaware he was waving a red flag to a bull.

"Exactly how many actually die from head injuries?" I asked.

"Well, I'm not positive," he hesitated. "But even if it saves one life it's worth it."

"So, what about cars?" I asked.

"What about cars?" He looked puzzled.

"Well, don't some of the accidents involve head injuries? Like in convertibles or soft tops, for instance."

"Well, yeah, I suppose so," he responded tentatively.

"Then shouldn't they have helmet laws for drivers and passengers of cars?" I asked.

"Statistically, it would be a much smaller number than motorcycles. And everyone in a car wearing a helmet would be inconvenient and expensive."

"I'm sure that *statistically* helmets would save at least one life due to head trauma in a car crash. Therefore, how come it's not worth it to save *that* one person?"

"It's a very small risk. There are a lot more cars than motorcycles after all. Cars are much safer... and not wearing a helmet is a risk I'm willing to take," he added confidently.

"Do you ride?" I asked, selecting another helmet to try on.

"No."

"When it comes to yourself, you're willing to take the risk. But when it comes to something you know nothing about, you want to make laws that have a cost and affects others. To 'protect them.' Taking away their right to make a choice. Isn't that a bit hypocritical?" I said, while wearing an open-faced helmet.

"I don't ride because I had a friend who was seriously injured on a motorcycle."

"Do you know anyone who was injured or killed in a car crash or plane crash?" I asked.

"Well, yes," he said cautiously.

"And yet somehow you're still OK to ride in cars and fly in planes?" I said removing a helmet.

"I believe they're safer."

"A vast number of laws are passed by people trying to impose their beliefs by telling others how to live. Imagine my surprise to discover that those in favor, like you, are seldom affected by the new law – leaving an abundance of idiotic laws, while politicians claim they're doing something positive and businessmen ensure their product has a guaranteed sale. If you feel it's important to wear a helmet when riding a motorcycle or bicycle, by all means, put one on. It doesn't need to be a law."

"That sounds a bit fatalistic."

"Don't get me wrong – I have no desire to die in an exploding bike crash. However, I will not let that fear dictate my life and the freedom, happiness, satisfaction and contentment I experience when I'm riding my bike. All I ask is to be allowed to make my own decisions."

During the conversation I found a helmet I quite liked. The whole front hinged away so I could look down while zipping up my coat. In addition to the clear visor, there was a second pull-down tinted visor, eliminating the need for sunglasses. While the fit was quite tight, I reasoned it would loosen quickly... especially after I noticed the expensive price tags on some of the other options.

Then off I went, leaving behind a thoroughly bemused, and perhaps chastened, salesman but having ticked all the boxes for a legally compatible, safe and fully stocked journey.

As Bruce Cockburn sings in "Each one Lost," there are unlimited ways to die, ranging from battlefields to the safety of our own homes. But eventually, we're all headed in that direction. My choice is to live my life right up to the point that I give up the ghost. I know too many people who are walking around dead already – hiding in fear, safely in their lounge chairs, watching other people live through a TV screen.

Two days later, Judy and Tristin arrived back in Liberty Lake from their travels around the western US. They'd been in the confines of the same vehicle for the last 18 days, but they were still smiling! Always a good sign.

On the Fourth of July we went to the local parade and watched the golf cart floats. Some were quite creative, with red white and blue bunting galore. Judy had a large number of her friends over and we drank Rainier and Pabst beer, and ate hot dogs, hamburgers, potato salad, dill pickles, Jell-O, along with other traditional American holiday delicacies. Fireworks exploded continuously, sending Judy's miniature Schnauzer under the table. Later, we wandered down to the lake to watch the community night fireworks display. It lasted a full 20 minutes with launch sites at either end of the water. Fireworks in stereo!

The next day we drove to Lookout Pass, which borders Montana and Idaho. There we met my brother, Allen, and his wife, Becky, over from Kalispell, Montana, and the five of us hired bicycles to ride the Hiawatha Trail.

This trail is the former main line of the old Milwaukee Railroad (or, as it's most accurately known, the CMSTP&P – Chicago, Milwaukee, Saint Paul and Pacific Railroad). The route starts at the top of the pass by entering a 1.6-mile tunnel, then travels downhill on a two percent grade through four or five more tunnels and over several trestles as high as 100 ft (30 m), as it winds through the glorious Rockies.

This ride was special to me because of the eight years I had spent as a conductor/brakeman in Montana. Information placards along the way told familiar stories. Blue skies and perfect weather made for a nice afternoon reminiscing about the old days of riding the rails. But boy was I glad to be riding a motorcycle for my big trip, rather than a bicycle. Give me engine power over leg power (and a plush Harley seat) any day.

A few days later, we loaded Tristin on a plane for home. By then, I'd put a few hundred miles on the Black Pearl trying to get the feel of her, and re-calibrating my New Zealand brain for riding on the "wrong" side of the road. Quite frankly, the bike felt pretty good. Next, I took a longer day ride, right around Lake Coeur d'Alene – the first time I'd ever made that trip. Long rides in this comfortable saddle were certainly not going to be a problem.

Then, after spending several hours experimenting with luggage combinations, different tie-down options and determining what really wanted to be where, it time to head out at last.

Washington, Idaho and Montana

MD 143.7.11.16:49

July 11, 2016

Having double-checked my packing methodology and bungee cords one last time, I left Liberty Lake in the morning light and settled into rumbling down the two-lane highway at a nice easy stride. Pine trees lined the sides of the road as I made my way deeper into the Rockies.

I was wearing my new helmet, and it sure was snug. Unfortunately, as well as squeezing my forehead, it was pinching my cheeks together at the jaw intersection, making it hard to keep my mouth closed. Chewing gum or anything else was impossible, because I kept biting my cheeks. After a while, my mouth kind of assumed an "O" shape – like a permanent look of surprise. I didn't worry about any of this too much, until I stopped for dinner.

When I removed my helmet, I discovered I had a huge ridge running down the front of my forehead, making me look like a Klingon! As I stepped into the café, I noticed several other Klingons, who looked surprised to see me. Sensing comradery, I went over and joined them. It's kind of nice bumping into other bikers along the way and share an innate knowledge about riding without having to say a whole lot of anything.

Seems there had been a sale on those helmets across several states.

I was singing "Going to Montana" by Frank Zappa and laughing at the absurdity of dental floss bushes when I crossed the border from Idaho into my home state.

With absolutely stunning scenery the whole way, I decided to play tourist and stop at all the roadside attractions. It seemed forever since I had last seen them. The Kootenai Falls were simply exquisite – a series of turbulent waterfalls, each with their own unique personality, but difficult to photograph. Many had calm crystal-clear pools at the base just begging me to jump in for a swim and cool off. But I knew better. Even this late in the season, it was still snow-melt water. Cool me off indeed. Freezing would be more like it.

"This bike has always been stored in a garage at night," the previous owner had informed me. "She's never been dropped. And I never rode her off paved roads or in the rain."

Well, some of that was about to change.

The rain chased me for several hours but I had managed to elude it until just before Kalispell. Usually, I'd have been able to stay with Allen and Becky, but they were away, so I needed to find alternative accommodation. With twilight imminent, I chose a campground supposedly ten miles out the other side of town. No camping fee was the clincher, saving me $9 over the one closer to Kalispell. I was on a budget after all.

About 30 miles later, in diminishing light, heavy rain, on an unpaved slippery, muddy road, dodging several white tail deer, I arrived at Avery Lake campground. I pitched the tent and slept to the tune of raindrops dancing on the nylon fabric. Just so she wouldn't feel too neglected, I placed a bike cover over the Pearl. We each had our own tent, as it were. It was a beautiful spot. And even more so in the morning after the rain quit and the mist began to rise.

Breaking camp, I headed back to Kalispell on a nearly empty fuel tank. After spending an extra $2 on gas for the mileage out to Avery Lake, plus $12 removing mud at the car wash (best laid plans), I rationalized that sometimes saving money costs a little more – but it's usually worth it.

With rain forecast on my chosen route, it made sense to do some mechanical work and ride in the sun the following day. I proceeded to the Harley-Davidson dealership, and arrived five minutes after they opened.

"Good morning," I said moseying up to the workshop counter. "I'd like to schedule a 13,000-mile service check and a new front tire."

"Good morning, sir," he smiled. "You are number 14 in the queue."

"You're kidding!" I stammered.

"No, but I think we can probably still squeeze you in before end of day. You'll have plenty of time to explore around town."

"Great. I'll go for a wander and see you this afternoon."

The nearby Salvation Army Store had books on sale for half price, requiring a huge outlay of 78 cents total for two books. Thus began a pattern of treating op shops, and such, as libraries along the way, turning in read books and checking out new ones for a pittance.

"Good as new," said the Harley mechanic when I got back. "You do realize that your tires were the originals?"

"Yeah. I can't believe they only lasted 11 years," I kidded.

After collecting the bike, I made my way on up to Whitefish and pitched my tent in a lovely campground right on Whitefish Lake. I was getting spoiled pretty fast. But what a way to go! Due to my old age, I was able to purchase a National Park pass that allowed me free entry to all National Parks and half off all National (and some State) Campgrounds. Such a deal. I planned to frequently use my pass in the up-coming months.

By the time I departed for Glacier National Park the next morning, the weather had improved. Not quite one of those perfectly clear blue-sky days that you dream of, but magic nonetheless. Again, playing tourist, I stopped at every pullout along the way to read plaques and take photos.

You have to be there to fully appreciate the raw beauty of Glacier National Park. The scenery changes with every turn of the road as you climb up and up. Snow drifts appeared near the top and I couldn't resist the temptation to get off the bike and play a bit. Imagine throwing snow balls in the middle of July!

After clearing the 6,646 ft (2,025 m) pass on the aptly named Going-to-the-Sun Road, the clouds dissipated steadily until I arrived at the park's eastern gate under that clear blue-sky of those dreams I mentioned.

My face hurt from smiling the whole way.

There are many similarities between the Taroko Gorge road in Taiwan and the Going-to-the-Sun Road – stunning locations, significant engineering and weather challenges, tough decisions by those in charge to make the projects happen and four years to build. I can only thank the people who made these routes possible; both roads provide an exciting opportunity for those willing to travel them.

Over the course of my life, I've been blessed with many good friends. While each has their special place in my heart, there's something about the old friends from my youth that just cannot be beat. There's a long history and we accept each other for who we are. Warts and all.

I met up with several of these friends in Helena, and we reminisced and told stories (with hardly any exaggeration) until late. Many more lived around this neck of the woods, and whenever convenient, I planned to stop and see them along the way. Any I missed, I'd probably see later at the upcoming reunion.

With its daytime speed limit of 80 mph (130 kph), Central Montana went by quickly. There was a new and interesting sculpture outside of Miles City in the form of a herd of metal horses. From a distance they looked real, and their metal heads, fabric manes and tails moved in the wind. I had seen a similar herd further west and was puzzled when they didn't stir as my roaring bike hurtled past. Usually, the loud Vance pipes would send a peaceful herd of almost anything into a frenzied stampede. Now I understood. It's hard to run when you're a metal horse.

In Miles City, I made time for the short trip to the cemetery on shady hill just outside of town and had a good long visit with my mom and dad. I had missed them and their wise council terribly over the years. It was a difficult conversation, expressing my emotions and listening to their comments from the past, but I felt a great weight lift.

It had been some time since I'd been east of Terry, so when I was back on the road I slowed down to enjoy the scenery on the frontage roads. Big thunderheads billowed all around me in the vast sky. Rain squalls, concealed in the angry deep blue clouds, headed in my direction, but somehow I managed to dodge each one. This big sky country, with its nearly limitless views of landscape and skyscape grandeur, lifted my soul and simultaneously left me feeling insignificant.

How I love Montana!

Arriving in Glendive, close to the North Dakota state border, as I headed ever eastward, the streets were wet and trashed with leaves and branches. When I looked closer, I saw drifts of white all over – piles of hailstones about the size of marbles. Glad I missed that!

On the outskirts of Glendive, in Makoshika State Park, I set up the tent on a high spot between small drifts of hail. This park, and its surrounding area, are home to many fossil discoveries, and the next day I wanted to do some dinosaur hunting of my own.

I awoke to heavy fog – a rare event in this part of the country. Unperturbed, I motored up into the hills until I ran out of paved road. After parking the bike, I set out on foot up Radio Hill Road. I wasn't keen to ride the Harley on gravel roads, if I could avoid it. Rocks not only chip the paint but can get caught between the belt and pulley, causing the belt to break and leaving me trapped in the middle of nowhere. Not to mention the fact that, as I found out later, belt replacement is expensive.

When I finally reached the upper ridges, the fog had burned off and the scenery was dynamic! Taking the first side trail off the main road rewarded me with stunning vistas in every direction under the rich blue skies overhead.

Every school kid in Montana knows about the nature of the clay in the surrounding hills. Hard as stone when dry, it can cut you if you fall on it. But it turns to powdery dust when crushed by traffic and becomes a soft malleable gumbo after a rain. In this gumbo state, it sticks to everything but itself. If you step in it, it sticks to your shoes and they lose their traction. The same thing happens with car tires. Extreme caution is advised when wet!

I somehow neglected this local knowledge as I started down a narrow switchback towards a natural land bridge I was keen to see. About half way down, the track swung back into the shadow of the hills, were it remained wet from the previous day's rain and hail. I stopped and thought, *This looks like it could be slippery.* Followed by a cautionary, *Perhaps I shouldn't go down there.*

While standing still, contemplating the wisdom of proceeding, I noticed some sagebrush moving up the slope. It took a moment for the penny to drop – It was me who was moving downhill and quickly realized the decision had already been made. I had to get out of there.

Running uphill was like being on a treadmill. No matter how fast I moved, I couldn't make headway. My only accomplishment was gumbo build-up on my pant legs, then hands and sleeves when forced to drop to all fours. The more gumbo I accumulated, the heavier I became and the faster I slid in the wrong direction.

I could see the headlines: "FORMER LOCAL MAN IGNORES CHILDHOOD TEACHINGS. SUCCUMBS TO GUMBO." And the news at six coming live from Makoshika State Park "...where, earlier this afternoon, a six-foot ball of gumbo was discovered at the base of Johnson Trail by park rangers. While investigating the possibility of a new dinosaur dig, excited archaeologists discovered fresh human remains within the ball. After extensive investigation, it's believed Mr. Slater ventured out after heavy rains into wet gumbo with a plastic pail and shovel to search for fossils. In the course of events, it appears he must have lost his footing and rolled down the steep embankment. Kids, let this be a lesson!"

I probably should have just let myself slide to the bottom and gone to see the land bridge, since I was nearly there anyway. But fear of the headlines and a deep inner will kept me going. Eventually I managed to gain some traction by grabbing handfuls of grass and stones at the side of the track. It seemed to take forever, but I finally arrived back on solid ground. Taking a different trail (read, "dryer trail"), I managed to view the land bridge from a safe distance. I'm sure it looks just as good from further away as it would have up close.

Despite my gumbo experience, I vowed to return to Makoshika someday. I still had dinosaur fossils to find.

Someone I knew once said, "Any time spent outside of Montana is just wasted time."

I hit the starter button to bring the Black Pearl's big 84-cubic-inch engine to life, squeezed the clutch, toed the gear shifter down with a resounding *thunk* and set off to waste some time in North Dakota.

North Dakota

July 16, 2016

I stayed on the Interstate Highway for most of the ride through North Dakota – primarily because that's the only asphalt road there is if you want to go west to east, and I was interested in making time.

But eventually, the Teddy Roosevelt National Park called me off the Interstate and I killed the motor as I slowed to a stop next to an information booth.

"Mornin'," drawled the plump woman behind the counter.

"G'day," I replied. "I was thinking I'd just explore the old buildings here then jump back on the highway."

"You could," she said. "But the cost is the same and you would miss out on the real reason for the park."

"Yeah?"

"Yeah. You see, Teddy came out here as a sportsman to shoot buffalo. But once he arrived, he could see they were nearly wiped out already. He realized the need to protect wildlife from extinction if people wanted to hunt in the future, and became a conservationist instead."

"I thought he was a Rough Rider," I said.

"That too. Riding through this area he became enamored with the intrinsic and wild beauty of the land. Putting the two realizations – preserving animals and land – together, he became responsible for establishing most of the national parks in the US." She was beginning to sound like a brochure.

"Go Teddy!" I said.

"You should look at his cabin and then take the loop road to get a good view of the landscape and the animals." Noticing my reluctance she added, "It's paved."

"Worried about losing tourists to gumbo, eh?" I said under my breath.

"What?"

"I said, the big loop or the little loop road?"

"Oh," she responded, "the big loop road, definitely. You'll see wild horses at the first turn, buffalo along the creek and pronghorn antelope on the flats. No deer this time of day I'm afraid."

The landscape was similar to Makoshika State Park, but riding versus walking allowed much more exploration. As promised, all the animals were present and the raw beauty of the land was spectacular. I pulled off the road at a safe distance to watch a huge bull buffalo rolling in a dirt bath. Dust billowed all around when he stood and shook. Then he kicked up more dirt with his hooves and tossed it over his back. The fact that we can see these creatures today is all thanks to the foresight of a handful of people.

I was hardly underway, but during the trip I'd already managed to lose things. I'd lost my hat twice, and had luckily returned to find it both times – usually laying off to the side of the road. Then I lost my glasses. Then my Buff face mask. Then my glasses case... not so lucky finding that one intact.

I had a tendency to set things down on the saddle bags at the back of the bike when I stopped. Then forget and drive off. It seemed like I was doing things I couldn't remember doing and couldn't remember the things I knew I'd done! Maybe it was old age, or schizophrenia, or just my Alzheimer's kicking in again.[2] In any event, it was really annoying. And once again, I had to backtrack three miles to find my hat after watching the buffalo.

In parts of the USA, it seems to be a source of great pride for a person or place to have the *biggest* – it doesn't matter what, just so long as it is larger than anyone else's. New Salem, North Dakota, has "The World's Largest Holstein Cow" – Salem Sue – and you can see her from miles away. I'd been making pretty good progress with taking photos for my entry into the HOG ABC competition, so I pulled into the carpark next to a beat-up old pickup and got off to take a picture.

2   *He doesn't really have Alzheimer's.; I'm his alter ego and just messin' with him* – Worf

"We built her back in 1974," said the old geezer in the pickup's passenger seat. "She's 38 feet high and is a hefty 12,000 pounds. Made outta fibreglass on a steel frame."

"Impressive," I said looking at the giant beast atop the short hill.

"Yup. But not as heavy as Dakota Thunder." And noticing my blank look added, "That's the world's biggest buffalo. He's over in Jamestown. Built in 1959, he's 26 feet high, and weighs in at a massive 60 tons."

"Wow!" I said, taking note to stop there for another photo.

"A local custom for the graduating high school class," he continued, "is to sneak up and paint the buffalo's anatomically correct genitalia the school colors of blue and white."

I chuckled at that. "I notice there's a lot of big things in these parts. Like your mosquitoes. Where I live, in New Zealand, we call them mozzies, but they're a lot smaller and quieter."

"Oh yeah, the skeeters," he smiled. "Last year was a bad un. We had problems with them procreatin' with the chickens."

"The chickens?"

"Come huntin' season, we shot em with shotguns, hung em on the shed to dry," he continued. "Used em for milking stools."

"How about this year?" I asked laughing.

"I thought I saw two skeeters carry off a small dog the other night. You wouldn't want to venture out alone at twilight, that's for sure," he added with a knowing look.

Right! First liar doesn't stand a chance around here.

In any event, one or two would always sneak into my tent at night and were impossible to find until morning, when they lumbered about fully laden with my blood. I used that opportunity to retaliate and smash them against the tent. Over-sized or not, they were the bane of my camping life. The number of red blots along the nylon walls increased daily.

At Mandan (named for the Mandan tribe that had once lived there), I visited Fort Abraham Lincoln – the former home of General George Armstrong Custer's 7th Cavalry. They'd been posted there to protect the expansion of the Northern Pacific Railway, and it was their departure point when they set out in their fateful search for the Sioux in the late 1800s. The Battle of Little Bighorn was the result. Apart from the reconstructed buildings of the fort, there was also a replica Mandan village. It was interesting to compare the old lifestyles of the indigenous people and the white man.

The white man built timber buildings with green wood, raised up on stone foundations. As the wood dried, cracks appeared. The prairie winds, pushing sub-zero air through those cracks, would have been awfully cold in winter and they nearly froze to death. They didn't last there for long.

Meanwhile, the Mandan lived in large villages comprised of roomy timber huts covered with insulating earth. Their settlements had moats and walls surrounding them for protection – similar to early European fortifications. They lived this way for centuries. Quite peacefully, I might add.

The young squaw, Sacagawea, hailed from this area and became a guide for the Lewis and Clark Expedition in the early 1800s as they set out to find the source of the Missouri River. Without her knowledge and skill, their expedition would have surely been more difficult. In my opinion, Sacagawea's life and the exploits of the Lewis and Clark Expedition rank amongst the most exciting adventures ever undertaken.

Sunday morning in Jamestown, I attended an old country church in a historic replica of a western town. We sang songs popular from the 1850s that are still appropriate and just as meaningful today. Afterwards, I photographed Dakota Thunder, then toured the buffalo museum, where I was able to see a very rare white (albino) buffalo.

I bid farewell to Thunder and rumbled out of town. The plains rolled by at 75 miles an hour (120 kph) and the temperatures continued to rise into the mid-eighties (29 C) as I headed east and crossed into the land of 10,000 lakes.

Minnesota

MD 143.7.19.19:32

July 19, 2016

Fargo and Moorhead are pretty much one city, making it hard to tell the moment when you've left North Dakota and arrived in Minnesota. Luckily, I stumbled upon an information center shortly after crossing the state line.

What I discovered was a wealth of helpful material for motorcyclists. Maps for the best rides were available for the north, central and southern parts of the state, with color-coded routes showing scenic (green), hilly and curvy (yellow) and just nice pleasant rides (red). I immediately set about plotting my course.

It's due to lakes, rather than mountains and hills, that the yellow, curvy routes exist. The definition of a "hill" in this flat state is anything over 50 ft high. If you want to go downhill skiing, your best bet is Bull Run, and it only has a 395 ft (120 m) vertical drop.

Because of the low-lying nature of the landscape, there's nowhere for the water to drain, which results in the state's "10,000 lakes." Pretty much everyone has a lake in their back yard. No matter where you go on the road, you're bound to pass a lake or two every 15 minutes. It makes for superb riding with lots of bird life and little vistas around every other curve. It must have been a real challenge naming them all and keeping them separate. I kept my eyes peeled for Lake Wobegon but failed to find it.

All was well, but as I curved around yet another lake-edge, the Black Pearl started making a disconcerting noise that sounded like an intermittent metallic grinding. First thing Monday morning, I found a Harley dealer in Alexandria and took the bike in for inspection. Seems a nut in the primary crank case had worked loose, and I'd sought out mechanical help not a moment too soon. Another day or two and there could have been serious damage.

Besides the large number of lakes, the other thing I couldn't get over was the abundance of corn. It must have been a good year too as the stalks were already taller than me. Even though there wasn't a breath of air in the campground at night, you could hear the corn growing in the dark. Its eerie rustling and crackling made me all too aware of how stories like *Children of the Corn* were conceived.

I was really looking forward to reaching the city of Owatonna. Just for the name of it. When we were kids, we use to initiate newcomers into summer camp by having them learn the secret chant:

Owa

Tonna

Siam

They were told to repeat it faster and faster while we shouted encouragement and agreement until they realized what they were saying.

Riding around the central city square, the simple elegance of a particular building caught my attention. Suddenly my architectural schooling kicked in, my history professors lectures came flooding back and I shouted, "I know what that is! It's the famous Wells Fargo Bank building." I had forgotten it was in Owatonna. I quickly located a parking space out front and went inside.

The reception clerk must have been used to people wandering around and staring up at the vast and ornate space with their mouths open. She volunteered, "Designed in the early 1900s by Louis Sullivan."

"Yeah I know," I said with a touch of awe and reverence in my voice, "and still elegant after all these years. But what surprising use of color." The monolithic smooth brick exterior was adorned with ornate green terracotta tiles and a slender band of blue, green, brown and white mosaic tiles. A single large arch signified the entry and framed the windows at each elevation.

"The tiles and large murals have been left pretty much intact since completion," said the clerk. "As have the teller cages and meeting rooms."

"I love how the light floods in from the arches and the enormous central sky light," I said, still wonder-struck.

"If you enjoy architecture, there's also a house in town designed by Frank Lloyd Wright, who was an employee of Mr. Sullivan. It's not far from here."

"You're making my day," I said.

I made a side trip to see it and, since it's privately owned, I had to be content with viewing the exterior from the street boundary. But I wasn't disappointed. My passion for American architecture topped up, I headed out of town with fond thoughts of Owatonna.

It felt really good to travel the back roads. Very little traffic and the interaction with the country felt more personal as I followed the river through the Richard J. Dorer State Memorial Hardwood Forest. While I enjoyed the forest in its present garb with all its shades of green on green, I couldn't help but think how lovely a ride it would be in the fall, when all the leaves were changing color.

There were quite a number of historic marker boards along the way and I stopped to read most of them. Since the country was mostly settled from east to west, it felt like I was tracking back in time.

Eventually, I ran into the Mississippi River at La Crescent, which marked the defining edge of Minnesota.

And the beginning of Wisconsin.

Wisconsin

MD 143.7.22.15:11

July 22, 2016

Crossing the Mississippi River by bridge at La Crosse, I arrived in Wisconsin – the Dairy State, and the home of Harley-Davidson. I wanted to find another information center, which I figured would be on the main road. So, I crossed back to Minnesota, rode north for three miles and crossed the Mississippi again, this time on the Interstate Highway. It's a big river, even from way up there on a bridge, and seeing it three times was spectacular. But my imagined information center did not exist.

Having acquired a knack for the laid-back life while traveling the backroads, I saw no reason to change as I left the main road again and carried on across the state. The heat had been rising during the day and continued to do so. Daytime temperatures were well up into the low nineties (low thirties in Celsius) with humidity in the high eighties every day.

This leg of the trip began with field after field of corn but soon gave way to lovely treescapes and intermittent prairie views.

One of the neat things about riding along in these parts was the ever-present Milwaukee Railroad. In addition, many local parks displayed old train engines and cabooses. I recognized most of the town names from the old bills of lading we used to carry. The names always conjured up images of exotic places, both to the east and west of the Rocky Mountain Division where I worked. Of course, those fantasy images began to lose luster when I saw the places in real life. Well not completely, but the world did seem slightly smaller.

When sleeping in the campgrounds close to the tracks, I discovered that the trains ran almost constantly. It wasn't the noise that bothered me, so much as the nightmares that I was late for work because I'd missed my train.

I stopped in a campground called Yogi Bear's Jellystone Park, because all the other camping areas were full. As the name suggests, it's set up for kids, and it cost a fortune. But the worst part was when I discovered a hornets' nest in a hole over the outdoor sink. Several of the vicious creatures dive bombed me as I went to brush my teeth. One got me on the left ear lobe, then two others stung me right between the shoulder blades as I sprinted away swinging my towel and shouting salty profanities acquired from bars frequented by sailors and cowboys. These imaginative phrases made me less than popular with the parents in surrounding campsites.

In the heat, all three stings swelled terribly overnight. My suffering was compounded by the fact that somehow I'd left the tent screen open too long and a squadron of mosquitoes arrived. They attacked my face and honed in on the blood-gorged earlobe with a vengeance. After sunrise, I exacted my revenge by adding to the collection of red dots on my tent, lined up on the nylon like kill marks on the fuselage of a fighter plane.

Wisconsin Dells is an amusement town with a little bit of Las Vegas, Knot's Berry Farm, Rainbow's End, Disneyland and a few others thrown in for good measure. I could see how this would be a fun stop for a family, but I had planned to buzz right through – until I noticed there was a Star Trek conference going. I love Star Trek. I decided to stop and go in – just for the air conditioning, if nothing else.

The heat had forced the helmet ridge running down my forehead to become more prominent than usual. Adding insult to injury, a large number of the mosquito bites accentuated the vertical line. Combined with the golf-ball-sized ear lobe covered with red bumps and my "O" facial expression – not to mention the swelling between my shoulder blades, which was making me lean forward menacingly – I was indeed a strange and ominous sight as I lurched towards the entry in my black leathers.

The good news was, I not only gained free entry because I was considered to be "in costume" but won a merit award for the most authentic Klingon makeup. I suddenly found myself warmly embraced by a community of fanatical Trekkies and with honorary membership to a weird and alternate bunch of people.

Looking forward to visiting the Harley-Davidson Museum, I kept up the big push to get to Milwaukee. This attraction, housed in a 130,000 sq ft building, is a Mecca for Harley owners, and at least once in their lifetime, all such riders should make the pilgrimage to view the original 10 ft x 15 ft shed where it all began.

I had set aside the whole afternoon to leisurely stroll through the vast temple of engineering and speed. Long corridors displayed 400 to 500 pristine motorbikes, following the company's manufacturing history from No 1 through to the latest release.

Three quarters the way along the panhead display, two bikers walked up and introduced themselves.

"Hi. I'm Zinc and this here is Smudge," said the big guy. He glanced down at the patches on my jacket. "You're a long way from home. New Zealand, huh?"

"I am. Actually, I'm from Montana originally, but I've been in New Zealand for the last 25 years. Rod's my name," I volunteered, sticking out my hand.

"Nice to meet you, Rod," said Smudge, and Zinc nodded likewise.

"This is quite a place," I said, making conversation.

"Have you seen the exotic bike display yet?" asked Zinc. "The Captain America chopper replica from *Easy Rider* and the war time motorcycle ridden by Captain America in the Marvel movie are both there."

"My favorites. No, I haven't seen them yet," I said excitedly.

"Follow us."

Around the displays were video screens showing clips from various films, but I only had eyes for the *Easy Rider* chopper.

"Some of the motorcycles are pretty outrageous," said Zinc. "Like that one that looks like a stretch limo." He pointed to an extra-long bike that bragged two motors, two gas tanks, a fin on the rear fender and exhaust pipes to Africa.

We were like kids in a candy shop. Eventually, the staff asked us to leave so they could close up. We walked the short distance across the plaza to the biker bar for a bite to eat and to review what we'd seen over a brew.

"What's your plans for tomorrow?" inquired Smudge. "We're going to the engine plant just north of Milwaukee for the morning tour."

"I'm in," I said.

The following day, I arrived 20 minutes early, but Zinc and Smudge were already there. Their two spotless bikes – a gray Fat Boy and a midnight blue Road King – were parked near the entry. I was excited. This is where the engines on both my bikes had been made.

The three of us went inside, signed in, took the safety briefing, put on our eye and ear protection and followed the tour guide around.

The plant, sprawling over several acres, was interesting – but not what I had envisioned. Almost everything was automated. A series of huge boxes with vision panels allowed us to see fluids and metal filings flying as robots carved clutch shafts, crankcase housings and drive shafts out of larger pieces of metal. Employees moved large bins of finished parts from the lathes to the polishers and onwards to the inspection booths.

Afterwards we went for breakfast to discuss what we'd seen.

"I'm a bit disappointed," I lamented. "Probably naïve, but I had this vision of people laboring over a half-assembled motor. Lovingly inserting piston shafts into the engine block. Not robots."

"Me too," said Zinc. "At least all the humans I did see looked happy to be there."

Changing the subject, Smudged asked, "So, what kind of work do you do in New Zealand?"

"I'm an architect. But mostly retired now and concentrating more on my art."

"Ever design any police stations?" inquired Smudge.

"Several as a matter of fact."

"Oh yeah? Zinc and I are both retired police officers."

"How is it on the streets with all the shootings?" I asked.

"It can be tense. But contrary to what Hollywood tells you," explained Smudge, "the average US police officer has never drawn their gun while on duty. I know I certainly never did."

"New Zealand police don't even carry a gun as part of their standard kit," I informed them. "There are special cases where a designated officer or special unit will be armed though."

A heavy rain had been falling as a front passed through while we discussed the state of the union, their working conditions and the recent Las Vegas sniper killings that were in the news. But now the weather had run out of steam and the sky began to clear.

"We're going to catch a ferry across the lake to Michigan in a few minutes. Where are you headed from here?" asked Zinc as he looked down at his watch then reached for his gloves.

"I was hoping to ride up to Green Bay along Lake Michigan and then visit the Milwaukee Arts Building. There's an exhibition of the Chinese terracotta soldiers on right now." This reminded me that there were things other than motorcycles – like art and architecture – that I should be spending some time exploring. "But there's so much I want to do and I'm running out of time, and I think I'm going to have to give it a miss."

"Well, I'm sure everything will sort itself out the way it's supposed to," said Zinc.

"Ride safe, brother," they chorused, and with a shake of the hands they were off.

The most interesting people can be found riding bikes.

But my interest in riding Route 66 was still my main objective, so onwards, south to Illinois!

Illinois

MD 143.7.24.08:14

July 24, 2016

About 20 miles (45k) over the border from Wisconsin into Illinois sits Zion State Park. It's right on the shores of Lake Michigan and about 50 miles (80k) from the heart of Chicago. This was the only campground to date that I'd stayed at for more than one night. I figured it was cheaper to ride into town and back than pay $200 a night for a hotel room. Plus, I was able to see more of the surrounding area traveling back and forth.

Although there was a heat wave and the temperature and humidity continued to rise, Lake Michigan hadn't been informed. I could only stay in the water for ten minutes at a time. Luckily, that was more than sufficient to successfully drop the body temperature enough for a good night's sleep.

Having had my fill of viewing motorcycles for a while, I headed out at the break of dawn to look at some of Frank Lloyd Wright's works in Chicago's Oak Park. There are a number of houses and a church, as well as his own home and office, all located within a short distance of each other. Interestingly, these buildings were being designed around the same time the Harley-Davidson Motor Company was starting up in 1903, and seeing the adjacent homes, constructed in the standard style of the times, really showed the true genius of Mr. Wright's creations by comparison.

First off, though, I took in the stunning Robie House – another brilliant example located in a different part of town.

The Robie House sits on the fringes of the university campus, and directly across the street they have recently completed a new complex. It's a very modern building that takes most of its forms from the Robie House, which still looks cutting-edge some 100 years after Wright conceived his design.

Over the decades, the house had been used by various people and even as a dormitory at one time. A recently completed major restoration effort has brought the structure back to much of its original glory.

Wright's style of architecture became known as the "Prairie School" because it drew inspiration from the long horizontal lines of the surrounding landscape. These became evident in the low-pitched roofs, with their extensive overhangs, and long banks of leaded glass windows. Wright was a stickler for detail. To further accentuate the horizontal elements of the Robie House, he used red roman bricks, which were longer and thinner than regular bricks. But the real kicker was the use of red mortar for the vertical joins and white mortar for the horizontal joins. The overall effect makes the elevations read as a series of red and white horizontal lines. Masterful!

The 97 degree (37 C) temperature and 85 percent humidity of midday found me in Oak Park taking in the walking tour. Actually, it was more of a sloshing tour for me as sweat dripped from everything. But it was still worth it. All the books and photographs simply do not adequately prepare a lover of architecture for the experience itself.

Heading back to the campground in rush hour traffic didn't seem like a smart idea, so I went against the flow, into the heart of the city instead. A clever move, because the shade of the skyscrapers helped keep me cool.

After finding a parking garage and grabbing a bite to eat, I went to the top of the Willis Tower. At 1,450 ft, it is the second highest tower in the USA. The ride to the top was slightly slower than the ballistic elevator in Taipei 101, but impressive nonetheless, with fabulous views of Chicago and out over the lake as the sky turned a dull yellow pewter with the onset of dusk.

The observation level included glass boxes protruding about four feet outwards from the exterior wall. Now, when I say glass, I mean *only* glass. Top, sides and bottom. Looking out from a tall building over a city skyline is relaxing. Looking downwards over the edge can be a thrill. But looking straight down between your feet to the sidewalk below is definitely not for the faint-hearted.

It was great sport watching a robust middle-aged woman with a large handbag tentatively put her foot onto the glass then slowly add weight, like testing the ice of a frozen pond, whilst desperately trying to avoid looking down. Once she gained a level of comfort, I pointed to the lower corner of the booth and asked, "Is that a crack?"

It was still plenty hot on the ride back to the Zion State Park campground, so another quick dip in the lake was in order. Both to cool down before bed and hopefully help reduce the new swelling around my eye.

Taking stock of the previous 30 days, I realized that within the space of a month, I had swum in the China Sea and the less warm Lake Michigan, and been to the top of Taipei 101 and the Willis Tower. Both buildings claim to be taller than the other, depending on whether you count floors or antennas. Turns out, everyone wants to have the biggest. Just to make sure I'm covered, I've done both.

Within a week and a half of departing from my sister's house at Liberty Lake in Washington, adjustments to camping life were complete. I was sleeping better than I had in a long time. Waking up to a different view with each new locality, striking camp became a routine I could efficiently accomplish in ten to 15 minutes, and setting up camp took no longer.

With a few exceptions, my day started in the cool of the morning with stretches in the tent, before the sun made the heat unbearable. I performed leg lifts, dead bug, back arches and core body exercises designed to strengthen the lower back for long days of sitting in the saddle. These stretches and exercises were followed by the number of my age in push-ups.

Next, I'd head out for two miles of fast-paced walking. If there was a lake nearby, I'd take a short swim; but if not, a shower or, worst-case scenario, a spit bath from a spigot or the water jug. I'd prepare a cuppa while I packed the bike, and contemplate what might lie ahead of me as I sipped the hot, caffeinated brew.

Side attractions out of the way, it was now time to focus on the primary reason for this trip. I headed south again towards downtown Chicago, and after a brief search, on Adams Street I found a sign that clearly marked the beginning of Route 66 and the true purpose of my adventure.

Onto Route 66

MD 143.7.26.10:08

July 26 2016

Full of enthusiasm, I parked my Heritage underneath the Route 66 sign for the obligatory photo – a significant feather in my cap. The Pearl's 84 ci engine caught and roared into life the instant I hit the starter. She was as ready to go as I was. And we were on our way.

Then things hit a snag. Despite all that promise and my high expectations, the great American journey began with a bit of an anticlimax and a certain amount of anxiety. It took forever to get out of Chicago, with thousands of stop lights, stop signs, jogs and turns, and 25 mph speed limits. I confess, I wasn't feeling very comfortable. My primary concern was the one per week murder rate in the city at that time. Fearful of losing my way and venturing into the wrong neighborhood, I paid close attention to the route signage, and prayed I'd be safe.

Well, I needn't have worried. Eventually the freedom of the open road welcomed me, and my worries fell away.

Out in the Illinois countryside it was corn, corn and more corn. Somewhere in the midst of all that corn, I found accommodation in a public park campground, and there I ran into a young woman from England.

"Mind if I share the campground with you?" I asked, pulling into the empty spot next to her tent and bicycle.

"All good," she responded. "Nice bike."

"Thanks," I said, taking my tent and sleeping bag off the back. "From the looks of things, you're a biker too."

"Yes. But you probably cover greater distances than me. I only make about 70 to 100 miles a day."

"Wow! That's impressive actually. I usually only go 200 to 300 miles myself. Where did you start?"

"Boston," she answered. "I'm going to Seattle. I've been riding through corn for five days. I never thought there was this much bloody corn in the whole world," she said distractedly. "But I'm concerned because my map isn't very good. I can't carry much water and I try to find water stops every ten to 25 miles. But it doesn't show the villages between these cities," she explained opening the map and pointing out the route through North Dakota and Montana.

"That's because there aren't any," I informed her. "Your map is correct. That's all there is. I'm from eastern Montana and those 'cities' have a population of about 10,000 maximum. And the small towns are all at least 30 to 40 miles apart."

"Oh no! That can't be?"

"Trust me, it is. You'll need to carry more water because it's going to get hot," I said. "Also, this route you've marked here is the Beartooth Highway and runs through Yellowstone Park. It's about 11,000 feet high and pretty steep." Seeing the shocked look on her face, I added, "But very nice scenery."

"I didn't know there were mountains there. Are there many?" she asked forlornly.

"Uh. Well yes. The Rocky Mountains run from here to there," I said pointing at the map. "And the passes are here, here, here and here. Most are about 6,000 ft (1,830 m) high."

"I had no idea…"

"You've come a long way already," I pointed out, trying to cheer her up. "You'll do just fine." *I'm sure glad my bike has an engine,* I thought to myself as I continued to set up camp.

The truth is, if we actually understood all the obstacles facing us before we began a journey, we might never start. Sometimes, the unknown is the best thing for us.

The heat wave continued into the low 100s every day, with the humidity close behind. The dried red dots had now baked into the tent fabric and become a permanent feature.

Illinois is known as the land of Lincoln, and along the way, I stopped at the Lincoln Cemetery, where thousands of white military tombstones stand at attention over treeless fields of grass. The hardest part was seeing all the new ones. Occasionally I'd catch sight of the bereaved – such as one young woman I saw sitting on a blanket, with a small child, talking to the partner she'd lost. Politicians need to visit these places more often. Especially when there are threats of war. Not just on Memorial Day for two hours at dawn, when everything is fancied up by ceremony, flowers, speeches and cameras. But on a normal weekend or weekday like I did. Stay there and randomly read the names and dates of those buried. Consider each person and their short life. And see who comes to grieve. I was somber as I got back on the road.

The city of Pontiac features a town square where murals are painted on the backs of buildings to create the illusion of a 1950s street-frontage. There's also a life-size bronze sculpture of Ol' Abe Lincoln himself, leaning up against a split rail fence. When I stopped to take a selfie, I realized what a tall drink of water this guy was! I asked a passer-by to take a full-length photo of the two of us. Standing in the same pose, the top of my head only just reached Abe's eyes. And I've always thought of myself as a rather tall guy.

Springfield has restored Lincoln's house and the surrounding neighborhood, where large trees cast shadows on gravel streets. Abe often entertained large groups of people at his home and it wasn't really all that spacious inside. Seems too that he was not fond of the stick, as his children were well known for their pranks and rambunctiousness.

Presidential elections back then were substantially different to today's. For example, on the campaign trail, candidates would actually express their intentions for office rather than just pointing out their competitor's shortcomings. What a concept. In all fairness though, perhaps the main difference was that newspapers and journalists reported the news, instead of offering tabloid headlines skewed by one-sided opinions.

A short distance away from Lincoln's house, I saw a number of motorbikes lined up in front of a bar, so I pulled in to have a squiz. The place was decorated with an interesting collection of old furniture, flags and motorcycle bits. Unused during the current summer months, a large homemade barrel wood heater sat in the middle of the room with a horizontal chimney running below the ceiling to retain as much heat as possible. I wandered over to order a beer.

"This is a private club," said the bartender, his hands firmly planted on the counter. Everything had stopped, and the other patrons were staring.

The awkward silence was broken when a guy at the pool table pointed at my patches and said, "Are you really from New Zealand?"

"Sure am, mate," I replied, trying to use my best Kiwi accent.

"Aw, give him a beer anyways, Pat. Put it on my tab." Then, reaching out his hand, he said, "I'm Speed. You here for the Catfish Festival?"

"Cheers, mate," I said as a beer appeared before me. "When's the Catfish Festival?"

"It's fully underway right now. Whole town turns out for the celebration," continued Speed. "They close the main street off to traffic and everyone puts up stalls to sell pretty much anything a person might want."

"Sounds like it's pretty full on," I observed, still not sure what catfish had to do with it.

"You bet. There's an AC/DC rock and roll tribute band playing later tonight. Should be some tickets left."

"Tempting," I agreed. But it was still early afternoon and I decided to move on after checking out the festival stalls. "Thanks for the beer, Speed. Enjoy the concert."

"Ride safe, brother."

The riding surface of Route 66 offered plenty of variety. Parts of the road featured the original paving, with its brick base course. In other places, the route opened out into four lanes. Meanwhile, restored gas stations and diners dotted the roadside all along the way.

There were photo opportunities everywhere as people turned up in classic cars and parked in front of these old establishments. One such place was a Standard Service Station that had been restored to the 1950s era. I had pulled in, parked under the canopy and set myself down on a bench to admire the surroundings and rest a spell, when next thing I knew, I had company in the form of an old Indian Motorcycle, a 1962 Oldsmobile Starfire and a 1956

Pontiac Torpedo. They all looked brand new, right off the assembly line. With the exception of the uniformed attendants who used to wait hand and foot on motorists, the illusion of golden age America was more or less complete.

As I approached the Mississippi River, I could see the St. Lewis Arch in the distance. I took a slight detour to cross the original Route 66 bridge. On foot – though not by choice. These days, there's a park on either end and vehicles are prohibited. Known as the Chain of Rocks Bridge, a series of long riveted steel Warren Truss spans bounce from one concrete pylon to the next, with a distinctive 22-degree jag away to the right in the middle as the structure hops its way across the Mississippi. Did I mention this is a very big river?

Then it was back on the bike, and across the new bridge – as uninspiring and boring as it is technologically advanced – into Missouri.

Missouri

MD 143.7.27.13:34
July27, 2016

Missouri is known as the "Show Me" state, so naturally I wanted to see what it had to show me. The St. Louis Arch was a perfect start.

Eero Saarinen was another one of those architects who inspired me at university. In 1957, he was commissioned to design the St. Louis Gateway Arch to commemorate the 100-year anniversary of the Lewis and Clark Expedition and expansion into the west. He died in 1961, four years before his architectural masterpiece was completed.

The elegant three-sided silver arch – a real engineering achievement – is inspiring in its simplicity. The view from the top was spectacular with the city spread out below. Out one side, I watched a steamboat paddle up the river, while on the other, I searched the western horizon across the Missouri plains.

To get to the beginning of Route 66, I'd had tracked backwards through much of the territory Louis and Clark had explored, and now I had arrived at the starting point of their expedition. After the exploring was done, Sacagawea had settled in St. Louis, where she gave birth to a baby girl. Although I had read about all this in history class and followed many of Louis and Clark's expedition trails, everything was beginning to gel and make sense. It felt special to be standing there where it all began. And I began to feel like an explorer myself.

Soaking it all in, I suddenly remembered that I was now progressing westward – entering the flow of the natural migration of American settlers across the continent.

And the recession of its indigenous peoples.

All this excitement really drew up a thirst in me. I decided the best solution was to take a tour of the Anheuser Bush Brewery, which had been opened in 1852 by the German immigrant, Adolphus Bush. This National Monument opened up yet more intriguing stories from times past, including the creation and development of the plant and its products, its struggles during prohibition, and the rise to national and worldwide status as a fine beer. The brickwork-clad architecture was industrial in nature but pleasant to observe – much more so than the metal-clad warehouses of today.

The elegant interior housed giant copper vats viewed through full-height glass walls, ceramic tiled floors, wrought iron railings, chandeliers, and a huge mosaic mural on one of the walls. Not at all what I'd expected to see in a brewery.

But I confess, after the tasting was over, I sort of forgot most of the details. Except for being told to get off the brewery's Clydesdale. Evidently, these horses are only supposed to pull wagons. Somehow, I was still able to saddle up and more or less safely ride out of town on the bike and pitch my tent for the night. Good beer though.

Mark Twain is another famous character from this neck of the woods. He was born and raised in Missouri, and the National Forest named for him covers a significant area of the south-eastern part of the state. Signs kept popping up to let me know the beautiful trees I was riding through were all part of this vast area of natural growth.

The sheer extent of the forestation astonished me. For some reason, I had pictured Missouri as a Great Plains state, sort of flat and barren. Then, looking at the map, I noticed it's adjacent to Kentucky and Tennessee, and I realized I was riding in the Ozark Mountains.

As I approached the town of Stanton, I came upon the Merrimack Caves – a favorite hideout for the Jesse James Gang. The exploits of Jesse James were the stuff of western comic book legend, familiar to everyone I grew up with. But the story had special significance to me because, back in my university days, I'd played the role of Frank James in a musical called *Diamond Studs*. Now I found myself taking a trip down memory lane, and I sang the old show tunes as I motored along. The James Gang had led a colorful life and became folklore heroes; but in the end, they were nothing more than common thieves who used the Civil War as an excuse to pillage for personal gain. Funny how society can elevate some people and tear down others, even though both have committed exactly the same offense.

Evidence of the Civil War and its battlefields was surprisingly frequent in Missouri – much more than I had previously known. The Merrimack Caves had been used during that period to make gun powder and mine lead – a great combination to have in one location.

The caves were cool inside, which meant blessed relief for me in the heat of the day, but also for the hundreds of locals back in the 1920s, 30s and 40s who used to hold dances in the large hall near the entry. The floor had been made level and the spacious area was an ideal place for entertaining large groups of people.

The remainder of the tour took in features similar to many other caves – intriguing stalactites, stalagmites and formations of flowing stone caused by calcium and sandstone deposits. What was unique, however, was the addition of colored lights. There was a small theater where a video of beautiful nature scenes from all across the US of A was played on a waterfall of stone with "God Bless America" bursting through the speakers.

While setting up the tent that evening, in the twilight I noticed little sparks flying around out the corner of my eye. It took a while before I finally recognized them as fireflies. It was the first time I'd seen that phenomenon, and the tiny points of light seemed to introduce the night stars.

The further west I progressed, the more the land flattened and sparsely populated the trees became. The heat and humidity stayed the same as in Illinois. It's strange to dry off with a towel in 95 deg (35 C) heat and three hours later find that the towel is still wet. And me too.

I'd slowly been stripping down since leaving Chicago. First the gloves came off. Then the jacket was rolled up and tied to the top of my bags. After that, the helmet was removed and tied on top of my jacket. Leaving me clad in t-shirt and jeans, boots, sunglasses and a smile.

When I got to Springfield (another one), I fired off an email to my long-lost cousin Kim and her husband Troy to let them know I would soon be in Oklahoma and would like to stop in and say hi if they were around. Pulling into Carthage the next day, I received a response saying they would like to see me but had moved to Jefferson City, Missouri… a full 200 miles behind me. After ten minutes thinking about it, my decision was made. I would set off the next morning for a side trip back to see them. For variety, I would take different back roads, north and east of Route 66.

The campground I stayed at that night was adjacent to an outdoor drive-in theater. Now, it's been quite a few years since I've been to an outdoor theater and I was sorely tempted. In the end I decided against it because a kids' movie was showing and sitting on the bike without a backrest, staring up at a screen for an hour and a half would be less than comfortable. Although, I felt strangely guilty at letting the opportunity pass unchallenged. As I got set to ride the next morning, the campground owner reminded me to put on my helmet – it's required by law in Missouri. I'd just ridden the full length of the state without it! Oops.

The journey to Jefferson should have been 200 miles, but I took Interstate I-49 instead of I-44 out of town. There was a sign saying something about Kansas City, which set me off singing "Going to Kansas City" and not paying attention to where I was headed. Halfway to Kansas City, I realized my error. I turned right and set off cross country on back roads, changing the words of my song to, "Going to Jefferson City, Jefferson City here I come," for the remainder of the trip. Lest I forget my destination again.

But it was an enjoyable diversion, and not only did I get to see quite a bit more of the country, I also saw my first armadillo. Admittedly it was road-kill but it was mostly intact, meriting a stop to inspect. Afterwards I saw about 40 road-kills and the novelty wore off somewhat, so they must be pretty prolific. Perhaps their sex life is similar to the possums of New Zealand.

It was a great visit with Kim and Troy. I slept in a bed (my first one in several weeks), washed the bike and got my laundry done. The comforts of home and great company made it easy for me to stay another day before heading back on a different route to Carthage. From there, I picked up Route 66 to where I had left off.

As I headed west, I came to Joplin, the stomping ground of Bonny and Clyde. It would have been nice to spend a bit more time exploring, but being a Sunday, most things were closed. It had been a good location for robbing banks, since police couldn't cross state lines during a chase. Joplin has four state lines in close proximity.

Bidding Bonny and Clyde farewell, instead I carried on through to Kansas to look for Dorothy and Toto.

Kansas to Oklahoma

MD 143.7.30.23:11

July 30, 2016

Route 66 doesn't linger in Kansas, spending only about a hundred miles or so in the state. So I whizzed right through, making only one stop at an old gas station that had been converted to a 1950s-style diner. With a state motto of "As Big as You Think," I guess it didn't really matter how much of it I went through.

They served a mean hamburger at the diner. And the place was air conditioned, allowing me to cool down before moving on into Oklahoma. While I continued to cool down, a whole passel of Harley riders from somewhere in Asia arrived, followed by a support vehicle from the company that had provided their bikes. They wore all the proper gear and acted the part, but somehow didn't fit my image of proper bikers. Then I looked in the mirror. Once again, I was reminded that riding a motorcycle is a state of being. It's only truly appreciated by a select few – regardless of their race, sex, ethnicity, class or sect. Ride safe, brothers and sisters, and enjoy your trip!

It was clear the Disney movie *Cars* had made a big impact in this part of the country. Eyes had been drawn on the windows of all sorts of old vehicles. Tow Mater tow trucks, complete with buck teeth, Dock Hudson police cars and others had been popping up all over the place. Several of these were at the diner. They definitely brought a certain novelty and ambiance to the place.

Full of hamburger, it was time to move on, heading over the border to Oklahoma. Dorothy wasn't in Kansas anymore, and neither was I.

Well, it had to happen. It was about midday when I pulled into another diner for a break and bought a cup of coffee.

"That'll be $1.90 plus tax," said the waitress.

Shocked at the price, I said, "About an hour ago I bought a gallon of gas for $1.78."

She gave me an icy glare.

"I appreciate that you give free refills on the coffee," I stammered. "But try to keep this in perspective. A gallon of gas requires exploration, drilling to depth, pumping oil out of the earth, piping or shipping or trucking or a combination of all three from half way around the world to a refinery, refining the oil into gas, storing it in a tank, trucking the gas to a petrol station, storing it in underground tanks, and finally pumping it up again into your vehicle."

"Yeah?" she said looking confused.

"Which will power a Harley along the highway for about 30 minutes at 80 mph for 43 miles. All for $1.78 a gallon," I said, feeling my point had been succinctly made.

Deep in thought, she returned the coffee pot to the heater. Then turned and countered, "A cup of coffee, on the other hand, comes from bushes that have been planted on a hillside in the southern hemisphere where the berries are handpicked as they ripen, put in a bag, trucked to a storage warehouse, loaded onto a ship, unloaded into a distribution warehouse, trucked to a restaurant, roasted and ground up. Where one teaspoon is mixed with a cup of hot water."

"My point exactly," I said rather triumphantly.

"Which, will wake up and power the average biker to about 90 percent full mental and physical capacity for two hours. Four times as far as a gallon of gas. All for $1.90 a cup," she retorted.

"OK. You have a point there," I conceded.

I'm now watching closely as I've seen the price for a bottle of water approach that of a bottle of beer. Which is even more mind boggling, especially since the primary ingredient of beer is water.

The next day, the heat-wave continued to escalate and I heard several people had died from these conditions. Being wrapped up in a helmet and black leather, separated only by a narrow margin from the black pavement below, in 105 deg F (41 C) heat with 91 percent humidity, is not for the faint-hearted.

The heat could be seen rising off the blacktop in the form of a wavy distortion on the horizon. Mini mirages were created as water evaporated off the landscape nearly as fast as the wind whisked it off my skin. Perhaps it was the effects of the temperature, but a thought came to me as I rode along with my legs extended on the highway pegs. If the air had someplace to escape, it could blow up my pant legs further than my knee and cool me down. So, I undid the buttons on my 501s.

Shazam!

The wind whistled through my pant legs, out the newly created vent above my crotch and continued upwards, blowing my head backwards. The velocity was so great, my underwear billowed out of the opening like a spinnaker, giving me a wedgie that raised my voice three octaves.

Easily fixed at the next stop.

Afterwards, sans undies, I tootled on down the highway cool as a cucumber. However, I had to suspend this activity after an embarrassing incident later that day.

I passed through a highway improvement plan that involved planting flowers in the borrow pits along both sides of the road. A large number of insects traversed from one side of the road to the other. A disproportionate number of these were bees and it wasn't long before my legs were numb. I soon discovered that only about 90 percent of the insects that were sucked into the air intakes of my pant legs were actually making the appropriate turns and departing through the fly orifice.

During the middle of the day, I stopped for lunch at a family restaurant and had forgotten my fly was unbuttoned. As I was waiting to be seated (sans undies), a significant number of the "lost" insects discovered the exit and came crawling, hopping and flying out – much to the astonishment of myself, the hostess and the patrons seated nearby.

I'm not sure if the lifetime ban from Denny's is just for Oklahoma or nationwide.

Oklahoma was another musical I had been involved with during my university days. As you might imagine, I was singing all the songs as I made my way through the state, and I can report that the wind does indeed come sweepin' down the plains. So much so that they have installed wind turbines everywhere. Rows and rows of them. All good but it does change the landscape from plains to a kind of technological semi-forest in some places. Although, they don't look any worse than the oil wells and are a darn sight more user friendly when it comes to breathing fresh air.

The "Sooners" had a rough life here on the plains. Route 66 became the road of choice during the dust bowl years as people pulled up stakes and headed on west to California. The trip must have been nearly as bad as staying, since they had to cross the Mohave Desert and the Sierra Mountains on the way. In a slightly less desperate style, I was soon to find out.

I went to Kettle Grasslands Park where, once again, George Custer had been instrumental in the destruction of Native Americans. Man did that guy get around! He had been tailing a war party and, arriving at the wrong camp, killed the Cheyenne Peace Chief, Black Kettle, plus 160 others.

Custer's men also killed over 800 horses and burned the village as part of the policy of total devastation. The horses were, of course, instrumental to the Native Americans' way of life, like the buffalo.

Once things had settled down, and the "peace pipe" was smoked between him and the survivors, the ashes were spread on Custer's feet and a death curse was placed on him and all his men, should they ever attack the Cheyenne again. Looks like it worked.

By now, I had passed through a myriad of small towns, each with their own character, but also having strong similarities. They followed one of two basic formats. The first was the lineal format, which included a long main street. The highway typically passed through the center of town, with shops increasing in size and substance until the middle was reached. Then the number of shops slowly diminished until you were back on the highway again. The number of streets off to the side varied depending on the size of the city.

The second was the circular format, which had a central square. This square usually consisted of either a park or the county court house. Streets formed rings around the center. Sometimes the highway didn't enter the main square but passed by a block away. In a similar fashion to the lineal configuration, the size of the city was delineated by the number of rings radiating out from the central square.

Common to all, unfortunately, were the closure of large clothing and appliance stores, banks and old movie theaters. Boarded up display windows, second hand stores and small cafés, with an occasional museum, now populated the average main street. When I look back on my youth, I think that the loss of the movie theater was probably the worst part. As kids, we went to the Saturday afternoon matinees for 25 cents. It was usually a double feature western of some type. At least one of the two movies would have featured John Wayne, Hop Along Cassidy or Roy Rodgers. Afterwards, for the entire walk home, we would excitedly discuss our favorite parts of the film.

Adults would attend one of the two evening showings, and if you weren't there ten minutes early, you had to sit in the front two rows. It was a fantastic community event for socializing. Nowadays, everyone is at home in front of their own personal entertainment system. In their own little world. Such a loss.

One of the pop-up museums I stopped at was the Seaba Station Motorcycle Museum in Warwick. Inside, I was rewarded with an array of antique motorbikes, small in number but broad in variety. Until that day, I had no idea that John Deere had once manufactured bicycles. There was also a 1979 Triumph Bonneville, still in the crate. And there, hidden in the back, was a red Honda 250 Dream street bike, similar to my old black one. Memories flooded back.

I have to admit that one of the scariest things on this trip had been going into museums and seeing that items considered part of common everyday life in my youth were now considered antiques or historic points of interest.

But I couldn't not go, could I?

Feeling hungry and a bit parched, I pulled into a small one-horse town for some lunch and a soda. Afterwards, I saw an interesting building emblazoned with the name "City Meat Market" and covered in old signs for such things as Standard, S&H Green Stamps, Texaco and Goodyear Tires. Leaving the bike in front of the café to cool down, I took a wander over to take a photo.

A shirtless man adorned in a long grey beard, wild hair and bib coveralls opened the door.

"Come on in," he invited.

I wasn't prepared for what I saw next. All around were Pennzoil, Dr Pepper, RC Cola, Greyhound Bus and Berna Shave placards, along with a good couple dozen of Route 66 signs for starters. But hidden in amongst them were hundreds of other items – brand name guitars, juggling pins, flags, cheerleader's loudhailers, hats, ceramic ducks, nick knacks, and several open and half empty bottles of whiskey.

"Here hold this," said the character, handing me an old Route 66 sign that was corroded and beat up. "Give me your camera and stand right here."

Taking a photo, he then handed the camera back to me and said, "This is the very first Route 66 sign ever made."

"How do you know?"

"I have the paperwork to prove it," he answered, seeming a little offended that I'd ask.

I decided not to question anything else he told me. Although some things did sound a bit far-fetched. Every item had a story. Fearful that the stories would lead to sitting down with one of those half empty bottles of whiskey and the loss of the remainder of the day, I thanked him for his time and angled towards the door. In hindsight, that may have been a lost opportunity. But there you go.

Entering Arcadia, on the outskirts of Oklahoma City, I noticed a huge, round red barn. It was built that way so tornadoes would go around it. Not sure just how that logic works, but I suppose it was successful because it was never struck by a tornado. The round shape also allowed the upper floor to be built free of structural supports, providing one large open space. Once again, people quickly noticed that the open space would make an excellent place for dancing. And, so it did.

I love how folk socialized back then – dancing, parties, fairs, barn-raisings and people just generally doing things with other people.

Historic markers in the future will probably read something like, "In 2016, 22 total strangers were able to plug into the internet, charge their phones and check their social media pages at this location. And none of them had spoken to or knew anything about the person next to them when they left. Nor had they had any memories or recollection of being in the area afterwards."

The other end of Arcadia offered a more modern structure selling soft drinks and burgers. Rumor has it that this place dispenses over 650 flavors of soda. That should put Baskin Robins in the hot seat to get more creative. I was attracted at once by two key focal points: A 65-foot-high soda pop bottle formed out of horizontal pipes, including a straw sticking out the top. And a giant cantilever pipework structure, anchored by battered rockwork walls, rising out of the earth and stretching over six lanes of petrol pumps.

After dark, the large pop bottle lights up with LEDs completing the full effect of the marvelous attraction. All up, it was a brilliant example of both architecture and structural engineering perfectly complimenting each other.

Not to mention clever marketing and an exciting place to stop en route to the Texas Panhandle.

Texas

MD 143.8.02.10:17
August 2, 2016

Everyone knows that everything is bigger in the Lone Star State!

I wouldn't get to experience the full immensity of Texas on this trip, since I was only crossing through the panhandle, but I did see the world's second largest cross.

Rising up from the middle of a large circle divided into twelve stations, it's a lot more impressive than it sounds. Each station has life-sized sculptures depicting the story of Christ's crucifixion. One sculpture though, seemed a little out of place and, well, a bit weird. There was a Roman soldier holding Jesus from behind, and instead of the traditional Roman helmet, he was wearing a traditional chieftain's feather head dress. I have no idea of the significance of that sculpture.

Of all the states along Route 66, Oklahoma and Texas had the worst road signage. In some places, there was a Historic Route 66 sign about 200 yards before a Y intersection, with no indication of which arm of the Y was the correct one.

Other times there would be five to ten signs leading into the locality of a museum or some other attraction. Then all signage would disappear after you'd passed what they wanted you to see, leaving the hapless traveler in the tricky situation of heading off down various side streets trying to figure out how to get back to the highway. Which is how I wound up in a particular diner off the main road.

"Many a time, I've ridden for several miles down wrong roads or dead-ends or into shady-looking neighborhoods before I rediscovered the correct route," I complained to the short-order chef behind the counter. We were the only two people in the establishment. "I reckon these towns think they can make more money by letting the likes of me get lost so that we accidentally 'find' other things of interest."

"And yet here you are," he chuckled as he set my order of hamburger and fries on the counter.

"True," I said, suddenly noticing the irony of venting about getting lost to someone who worked in a business I'd discovered by getting lost. "Well, at least I get to see things I would never have made an effort to see on my own," I said taking a sip of my drink.

"Did you notice any laundry?" asked the chef.

"Laundry?" I said, confused.

"Yeah," he said. "Prior to the advent of dryers, most people would hang their clothes out on the clothesline in their back yard. Hanging laundry was a real social opportunity. Neighbors would talk over the back fence – keep informed about news, gossip, politics, recipes and how to raise kids."

"Come to think of it, I didn't see many houses with laundry out."

"Nowadays people just chuck things in the dryer and tune out. Isolated in their homes and bombarded by rubbish and propaganda on the internet and TV, they no longer know what their own neighbors think. There are no checks and balances with reality," he continued, beginning to hit his stride.

"Hmmm," I reflected as I dipped a French fry into the generous dollop of ketchup on the edge of my plate. Seems I wasn't the only one worried about the increasing isolation of modern life.

"With on demand TV, cable, the internet and radio, people can select only what they want to hear. Watch only sports or reruns of sitcoms. Listen to radio stations playing only rock music popular from 1960 to 1970, or a talk-back radio station that reinforces their own views. Never anything new – nothing to challenge their default opinions and ideas."

"That's true enough I suppose," I said finishing off the last of the hamburger.

"Meanwhile, in order to keep as many viewers as possible, the news has become generalized. It's nothing more than a series of headlines with no substance or depth to the underlying story," he observed.

As if on cue, the TV mounted above the end of the counter alerted us to an important announcement. "Stay tuned tonight at six when we cover the huge seven car crash on the Interstate this afternoon where two people died," said the cute, but serious-looking, female anchor while several aerial shots of the wreck were shown in the background.

"Those short five to ten second tidbits start about an hour ahead of the news program," said the chef pointing his thumb in the direction of the TV. "They treat news like a soap opera, instead of an information-providing service," he scoffed. "Now, how about a piece of blueberry pie?"

"Welcome to Channel 00 News at Six," said the TV. "Death and mayhem on the highway." Images of the crash appeared behind the two anchors. "Tonight, we report on a seven-car pileup on the Interstate on the edge of town where two people died. But first we have…"

I stayed to eat my pie and watch the 6 o'clock news.

"Stay tuned. When we return, our reporter on the scene, Jane Doe, will fill you in on the terrible car crash that claimed the lives of two people earlier today." More of the same images in the background.

"Funny how they have to advertise themselves after the show has started," chuckled the chef. "You know they're desperate if they're afraid you're going to change channels during the news."

"And now here's Jane Doe on the scene at the Interstate," says John the male news anchor, "with up-to-the-minute details about the seven-car crash that killed two people this afternoon. Jane?"

"Thanks John," says Jane Doe, looking down the camera with a serious look on her face that seems to have a touch of cheerfulness just below the surface. "Well, as you can see behind me, there was death and mayhem on the Interstate this afternoon. About 4:40 pm, seven cars collided with each other. Resulting in the death of two of the drivers," she says as she points off towards the road. For a two-second beat, the picture switches to the same images again, then back to the live feed. "I have Officer Smith of the Highway Patrol here with me. Officer Smith, can you tell me what caused the crash?"

"At this point in time, it's not clear just what the cause was. The Highway Patrol are continuing to investigate."

"Thank you, Officer Smith. Back to you, John," says Jane Doe.

"Thank you for that in-depth interview, Jane." John turns to his co-anchor, Susan. "A horrible situation. I wonder what the cause was. Any ideas Susan?"

"Well John, I've driven that Interstate and let me tell you, I've seen frisky possums on that road many times and I've had close calls trying to miss them. I'll bet it was the lookout possum."

"Right you are, Susan. I think the government should start a possum sex awareness program to prevent wrecks like this in the future."

The chef shook his head in an on-going state of incredulity. "And that's where people get all their ideas. All because folk don't hang out their laundry anymore," he reconfirmed.

A couple of customers walked into the diner just then. The chef asked, "Any of you hear what caused the wreck on the Interstate?"

"I heard possums," one said.

Giving me a knowing look and feeling justified, the philosopher-chef continued, "The other thing about laundry on the clothesline, is it's a subtle reminder that, really, underneath our clothes, we're all the same. We all wear socks and underwear (though some may be a bit frillier than others). We all have dresses, blouses, shirts and pants that get soiled and have to be cleaned. None of us are perfect."

I nodded. "As my old coach used to say, 'They put their pants on one leg at a time, just like us.'"

Over the years, the official Route 66 has been changed or improved. In some cases, the original road is now a frontage road, runs under one lane of a four-lane freeway, or in some instances, is just plain gone. But trying to stay true to the spirit of the trip, I made an effort to keep to the authentic route as much as I possibly could. At times, that meant riding down a portion of road that suddenly came to a dead-end, then riding back to the detour. Or driving back up to a dead-end from a detour, then back out again.

I had left the many shades of green behind a while back. Trees continued to became sparser as they were replaced by shrubs. Shades of brown, mixed with small patches of thin green grass, colored the plains to either side of the highway. Dead armadillos still populated the roads, and the heat still radiated off the asphalt throughout the day, though it had lost some of its punch as the humidity had dropped substantially. Many more wind turbines sprung up along the ridges of hills as I rumbled along my way.

One of the highlights of the trip came the morning after spending a night in a field next to a rest stop. I saw my first roadrunner! I looked around to see if Wile E. Coyote was coming after him. Beep! Beep! He was a neat looking bird but pretty shy when it came time to take his photo. I'm not a birdwatcher, but it's always a delight to see new and different creatures. Now I could add him to the list of other birds I'd seen this trip, like cardinals and bluebirds.

I almost blasted past the Cadillac Ranch, until I noticed a large number of cars parked alongside the road. Skidding to a halt, I turned around and sauntered back to a makeshift pullover carpark. About the distance of a football field away, through a struggling crop of corn, stood ten Cadillacs with their tails pointed to the sky. As I got closer, I saw they were buried nose down, at about a ten-degree angle, halfway past the front door, in a straight line. Over time, people had spray painted them with layer upon layer of bright rainbow-colored graffiti. The seasons have taken their toll, turning the vehicles into little more than molded chunks of metal. While tires still hung on most of their wheels, unless you knew what you were looking for, there was little semblance of their original Cadillac glory.

Rumor has it that these cars were set up as an art project by a group called the Ant Farm. The tilted angle is supposed to be the same as that of the Great Pyramid of Giza in Egypt. I don't have a clue as to what relationship a pyramid and a Cadillac have in common, but it works for me.

I suppose the main attractions of Route 66 advertised in all the videos and photos are pretty interesting. And I did try to visit them as they showed up along the road. But the real treasures were the surprises I didn't expect. Like a two-story service station in the middle of nowhere, with displays of old metal oil can opener/spouts, grease guns and metal five-gallon gas cans.

Or the barbed wire museum with its two 40 inch (1 m) diameter balls of wire on the entry gate. Who would have thought there were so many varieties of barbed wire? Not to mention post-hole diggers, steel fence posts and wire stretching devices – many of which I've used more often than I care to remember.

And then, there's the Second Amendment Cowboy. A 25-foot (8 m) statue of a cowboy standing behind a sign emblazoned with the entire wording of the Second Amendment to the Constitution of the United States of America. Always worth a reread. "A well-regulated militia being necessary to the security of a free state, the right of the people to keep and bear arms *shall not be infringed.*"

"A free people ought to not only be armed and disciplined, but they should have sufficient arms and ammunition to maintain a status of independence from any who might attempt to abuse them, which would *include their own government.*" Signed, George Washington.

Seems to me that people are always looking for better, faster and more efficient ways of killing other people. And that will never stop. Governments keep investing huge sums of money to develop not only more advanced guns but weapons of all types, under the guise of protecting the country. I accept that. What isn't clear to me is why they then give those newly developed weapons to other countries. Who in turn use them back on us, creating a need to have even more advanced weapons.

The other alternative is to make sure your opponent has no weapons. With the playing field continually changing from day to day as to who are the "opponents" and who are not, I think ol' George hit the nail on the head. It's best if everyone has their own weapons so they can then make up their own mind and protect themselves as required. Depending on someone else to come and rescue you doesn't always end in the ideal outcome. Police are mostly reactive, involved in the clean-up process or in determining what occurred after the fact, more often than stopping the act while it's still in progress.

Someone hell-bent on killing others will always find a way – like driving a vehicle through a crowd, for instance. I doubt people would support the removal or select ownership of cars. Giving up the right to own guns won't solve the problem. It will only give more power to those who still hold them.

Case in point were the Native Americans. "Give us your guns and we'll put you on a reservation and take care of you," said the government. Yeah, right! Once the guns were surrendered, there was no way to really protest when the "we'll take care of you" part fell to bits.

Rather than waiting in lengthy queues at the airport while security officials check each and every person to ensure that no one is smuggling a pair of toenail clippers on board, or a pair of knitting needles, it's my view that there's a much simpler way to go about things. I think everyone should be given a pistol after boarding – similar to the pair of headphones in the seat pocket in front of you. These would each have one plastic bullet, so as not to penetrate the fuselage, and would be good for only a single firing. Flight attendants would include a briefing about its use during the pre-flight take-off spiels.

"Exits are located to the front and rear of the aircraft. Note which one is closest to you now.

"In the event of turbulence and when the seatbelt sign is on, buckle your seatbelt by placing the two parts together as such.

"In the event of sudden pressure drop, oxygen masks will drop from the ceiling. Place over your face and pull draw string.

"In the event of a water landing, place the flotation device over your head. Pull cord to inflate. And blow into tubes as required to maintain buoyancy.

"In the event of hijacking, firmly grasp the pistol in your right hand, cock lever, aim carefully at hijacker and squeeze the trigger.

"Now, please place your seat in the upright position and prepare for take-off.

"Thank you for flying Constitutional Airlines." And so on.

Imagine some hijacker standing up saying, "We're taking over this plane in the name of (insert terrorist group du jour here). If you want to live, you will all do as I say."

To which the other 254 passengers grab their pistols, cock and take aim. I think hijackings would quickly become a thing of the past.

OK, OK. I'll concede there could be a couple of domestics over the course of time. Such as…

"Kick my seat on more time, asshole…" Or…

"I'm tellin' ya lady, end of the line and wait your turn for the toilet." Or…

"You mean, before the wedding, when you told me you…"

But overall, the total number of people who die from terrorists taking over airplanes would still have to be greater than a couple of mishaps. Not to mention the savings to the whole of society by avoiding the time consuming and personally intrusive security checks.

When I got to Adrian, I found myself between a rock and a hard place. I was at the halfway mark – 1,139 miles (1,833 k) from both Chicago and Los Angeles, smack-bang in the middle of Route 66. I really wanted to head due north, 733 miles (1,180 k) to the famous Sturgis Motorcycle Rally. And I really wanted to finish Route 66. In fact, I'd kept moving at a constant pace in the hope of being able to achieve both. But I now realized time wasn't on my side. I'd seen a lot, but the cost of my swift pace meant I was skipping or bypassing many other opportunities presenting themselves along the way. That seemed to be defeating the true purpose of the trip. It wasn't meant to be a race.

After some deliberation, I decided too many things in my life remained only half done. I had to finish this one. It was time to refocus on what I was doing in the USA. "Time to slow down and smell the roses," as Mom use to say. I'd have to skip Sturgis – set myself to enjoying the remainder of Route 66, then take a scenic route through the Rockies back to Miles City for my class reunion.

With no time like the present, I slowed down the pace at once, and stepped inside the diner beside the Route 66 halfway marker for a burger, potato salad and a bottle of soda.

And then, when I was good and ready, I sauntered on over to the Pearl, saddled up, started the engine and thundered on towards New Mexico.

New Mexico

MD 143.8.04.09:45
August 4, 2016

New Mexico became my favorite state since leaving Montana. The state motto, "Land of Enchantment," summed things up perfectly. It began with vast arid expanses where the sky filled the landscape. As I rode on sparsely populated roads in the late afternoon, giant billowing cumulonimbus clouds blossomed to titanic proportions. The sun protruded from around these towering formations, illuminating the striations of the earth's vivid rich reds, light reds, oranges, yellows, pinks and greys. The bold and subtle swirls of color in the sandstone positively glowed when struck by sunbeams.

Geology has never been one of my strong suits. But roadside information boards explained how sediments of sandstone, shale siltstone and the like, were carefully deposited from the Mesozoic Era through to the Cretaceous period. My imagination was sparked by the names given to the colorful layers: Navajo, Dakota, Schnebly Hill, Entrada, Dewy Bridge, Todilto, Summerville and others. I couldn't help but take an interest.

Throw in several thousand years of erosion, and the artistic result is glorious. A veritable feast for the eyes with colorful landscapes so vibrant they don't look real.

"The Bandelier National Monument of New Mexico is about 100 miles north of here," said the woman from the Albuquerque Chamber of Commerce as she handed me a handful of brochures. "It's a good example of the Hopi Indian cliff dwellings. And the park includes a one and a half to two mile hike around the valley floor, bordered by the cliff face."

"Thanks," I said, gladly accepting the information. "I've been curious about the Hopi ruins since my university days, and have a hankering to investigate." The excursion would take me off Route 66, but I decided to make a day trip north to have a gander.

Arriving at Bandelier, I joined a tour group led by a uniformed guide. "The Hopi took advantage of natural depressions in the cliff face and built walls to form enclosures," he said as we stared up at the ancient dwellings. "Flash flooding was always a worry and that may be why most homes were positioned as they are. As well as providing protection against animals and other humans, of course."

"How high up are the caves?" I asked following him to the base of the cliff.

"It's a 148 ft climb on the staircase to the lower caves," he said pointing. From there, a series of ladders continued skywards to the upper reaches. Easily doubling the height of the first staircase.

I was up for the challenge, and eventually I managed to crawl into several of the caves. People had lived there for thousands of years. There were fireplaces, shelving and beds carved into the stone. Holes had been drilled into the floor and ceiling for holding weaving sticks used in the making of cloth. Other holes drilled in parallel rows into the cliff face remained where timber roof supports had once protruded.

"What are those ruins down there?" I asked the guide, looking down from the top of a ladder.

"A small city was also constructed at the cliff base on the valley floor," he answered. "It was comprised of many attached dwellings facing toward the middle of a circle. Some were for storing food. There were no front doors, so entry was via a hole in the roof."

"After all these ladders and stairs, I've got a hunch that the settlement was a retirement village for the elderly," I said wheezing.

"Could be," he laughed. "In its heyday, this would have been a very impressive complex."

"Looking, for all accounts, like a cliff face full of swallows' nests for people," observed one of the other tourists.

"Cozy," I agreed. "But you wouldn't want to come home drunk. It's a long way to the bottom if you slipped off the ladders. And I think after the third or fourth time you spent the night at the retirement village, the wife might suggest you start digging out another enclosure further along the cliff for yourself."

All up, this was turning out to be a most enlightening trip, and as a bonus, Los Alamos was just a few miles further on. Taking the opportunity, I extended my detour to the place where Oppenheimer and his team had created the atom bomb. Strategically located on the point of a desolate plateau, with a single road climbing up to the site, anyone trying to sneak up and steal national secrets would have stood out like a sore thumb on the barren landscape.

The town itself was a lively little place. I only stopped for lunch after cruising around for a while, but I'd like to go back some day and spend a bit of time looking at the displays and museums. After all, the course of history was forever changed by the research done there.

One day, my dad and I were listening to a discussion on the radio about how terrible it was that the US had dropped the Bomb on Japan. My dad turned to me and volunteered, "I'm glad they did. I was aboard a ship on my way over. The Japanese were showing no signs of surrender. If they hadn't dropped it, I might not be here right now." Which of course meant, me neither.

Speaking of the Bomb, there's an interesting rumor about the Harley-Davidson Fat Boy. It was supposedly designed and introduced to counter the massive influx of Japanese bikes into the US, and was branded through an amalgamation of the names of the two bombs dropped on Japan: Little Boy and Fat Man. The original color options included gray and yellow – similar to the bomber aircraft used for delivery and the bombs dropped. The solid disk wheels were reminiscent of aircraft wheels. Newer models are peppered with 50 cal holes around the perimeter of the wheel disks. With the patriotic logo on its fat gas tank, the "Grey Ghost" has become immensely popular over the years. In 1991, Arnold Schwarzenegger, wearing sun glasses at night and riding a Fat Boy in *Terminator 2*, took cool to a new level.

Apart from being a secure location, another key reason for doing atomic research in the Los Alamos area was the availability of uranium. Once back on Route 66, I took a tour through a mining museum, where the whole lower floor was set up to replicate mine shafts, complete with the actual equipment used. The simulated setting was so realistic that it was easy to feel claustrophobic in the tight spaces.

After the museum, I passed through several hundred miles of countryside that had been mined for uranium. I didn't particularly notice the land glowing at night but decided not to set up my tent until well clear of the area. Just in case.

Long hours of holding the throttle open had caused soreness in my elbows. "Tennis Elbow," if you will – but without the tennis. "Contrary to popular belief," my doctor had advised some time back, "the quickest way to recovery is exercise rather than rest."

"What kind of exercise?"

"The best one is to hold a broom at arm's length, about midway along the handle. Rotate all the way through a 180 degree arc to the right and then back left," he said demonstrating the movement, "extending the broom end out further as your strength increases."

I don't traditionally carry a broom with me on the bike. But improvising with tent poles as a substitute seemed to alleviate the problem. Each night prior to setting up my tent, I'd hold the poles out at arm's length and rotate ten times with each arm. I would do the same in the morning as I repacked. It seemed to be working but was pretty boring. Walking around and singing while I did the exercise tended to help pass the time.

At first, I couldn't understand why people were so stand-offish in the campgrounds. Then it dawned on me. A man in back leathers with a Klingon ridge down his forehead, walking in a circle three times around a deflated tent while waving sticks over the site and singing incantations, was probably someone they didn't feel entirely comfortable about approaching. At least I wasn't drawing shapes in the dirt and lighting candles. That would really have given them cause for concern.

As I rode under a bridge on my way back from the campground to Route 66 the next day, I couldn't help but smile at the artwork. Blue roadrunners, green yucca plants and a red sun featured against a pinkish beige background. In the US, roading engineers and architects have put a lot of time into the patterns, colors and reliefs that decorate retaining walls, bridges and bridge abutments throughout the roading network. Each design is different. It all creates interest, reduces blandness, provides an opportunity to think about the meaning of the designs, and helps mark out points of difference to identify locations. Not to mention making traveling more fun. Thinking back on the hours and hours I'd spent trying to convince clients and engineers in New Zealand about the importance of artwork along motorways, I couldn't help but wonder if my counterparts here had had the same issues. I consider the artworks in the US and the subtle reliefs that have since begun to decorate concrete roadside structures in New Zealand a great success. Now, if I could just convince them to paint the ones in New Zealand.

On entering Navajo country, trading stores became more prevalent. I pulled off the road and dropped the kickstand in front of the Indian Market. The entire facade was adorned with signage bragging Rugs, Jewelry, Pottery and Fireworks. Another sign informed me I was standing right on the Continental Divide.

I was surprised to note that the Pearl and I had risen to 7,295 ft (2,224 m) above sea level over the past couple of days. That explained why the temperature had been so much more pleasant since leaving Texas. The steady drop in humidity had also been a godsend. From the 88 percent we'd experienced in Missouri, we were now down to 25 percent. Making the 80 to 90 deg F (26 to 32 C) days much easier to deal with.

"All our wares are handmade," the cute female proprietor at the Indian Market informed me. "You won't find original Navajo jewelry and pottery of this quality for a better price anywhere."

"They are beautiful," I agreed picking up and admiring several smaller clay pots. "These patterns are quite stunning."

"Those pots are wrapped in horse hair before being fired," she said. "That's what makes the intricate patterns. Each one is a one of a kind."

"Stunning. But as you can imagine," I pointed out, "there isn't enough room on the bike to take anything much."

"I did notice your beautiful bike," she smiled. "I have some very small fired clay pots over here better suited to your needs." Leading me to the back of the store she indicated a selection of miniature pieces. They were intricately carved and painted to the same detail as the larger vibrantly colored pots.

Dang, she was good. I wound up parting with some cash. The larger pieces simply had to remain on the shelf. And I think that's a good thing. Rather than collecting souvenirs along the way as prompts to remind me later, I was forced to remain in the moment and pay attention to what is going on in the now.

Back on the bike, with my newly acquired tiny clay pots safely packed in the Black Pearl's saddle bags, the earth formations around me continued to blossom and kept getting more and more beautiful as I headed west into Arizona.

Arizona

MD 143.8.06.07:32

August 6, 2016

So now I have a new favorite state (after Montana of course), and the jury will please disregard the verdict expressed at the beginning of the previous chapter – the landscape of New Mexico was but a prelude to Arizona. Things just kept getting better all the time.

The colors and shapes of the Grand Canyon State continued to expand on the display of God's amazing handiwork. There were reds, yellows, blues, grays, shades of beige and pretty much everything else you can imagine. Colors were interwoven across the cliff faces as if hand-painted with a giant brush.

Simply awesome. Made all the more appealing since I was now becoming more familiar with the geology.

"So, what's your impression of Petrified Forest National Park?" asked Gypsy. He had been leaning against his Springer gazing out across the barren landscape when I pulled in beside him at a roadside lookout.

"It's hard to think 'forest' looking out at miles of treeless terrain," I answered. But what we could see were thousands of fallen trees preserved through chemical and mineral interactions, that over the millennia, had replaced the actual wooded material to become stone. What looked like rocks across the landscape were really former trees.

"What I find interesting," he continued, "as they turn to stone, they still retained the weaknesses characteristics of the original tree. That's to say, they're weaker through the trunk than along the length. When they break into sections, they look like they've been cut and are now ready for splitting."

"Yeah, I see what you mean. You could be forgiven for thinking someone has taken a chainsaw, felled that tree and cut it into chord lengths." Pointing, I said, "And that one has broken down into what looks like wood chips."

He nodded and contemplated the scene. "The park is continuing to grow," he said, lighting a cigarette. "New discoveries of more petrified trees and fossils keep emerging every year."

"I've only seen one live tree," I said turning back to look towards the turnoff for the road we were standing on. "It reminded me of Rock Springs Forest in eastern Montana. Back in the horse and wagon days, travelers bound for Jordan from Miles City started taking a bucket of water with them to encourage the survival of a lone tree in the otherwise barren landscape. The sapling gained such popularity, they called it a forest."

"Funny," he smiled. "You know what else is funny? Trees are used to make paper. And paper is used in newspapers."

"So?" I asked bewilderedly. "I'm not sure I'm following you."

"Well, here we are looking over Newspaper Rocks. Published in a petrified forest."

"I get it," I said grinning. The Newspaper Rocks had acquired their name because of the number of hieroglyphics carved and painted on the edges of massive boulders that had fallen away from the cliff face. It's believed these symbols were used for communication and informing others about important events.

"Trying to decipher the meaning of those images is a bit of a challenge," he pointed out. "What do you suppose the giant stork type bird holding a man in his beak means?"

"Bikers, stay on the paved roads?" I guessed.

After Gypsy and I parted company, I passed the rusty carcass of a 1930s vintage car that had given up the ghost along the way. While the tires had long since vanished, the dry climate had preserved the metal body and timber-spoked wheels. It had been left there on the original Route 66 trail and stood as a monument to the hard times faced by the desperate travelers who had fought the elements on their way westward during the depression.

A storm was brewing as I continued through the park and it looked like it had hail in it. The single living tree now stood highlighted in a ray of bright sunlight against the ominous sky. Its slender white trunk and branches, thinly populated with vibrant lime-green leaves, coupled with the back-drop of dark purple clouds made it almost surreal.

Entranced by nature's beauty, I almost missed the implications of what a storm would mean for me if I was caught up in it. With all the trees petrified and lying down, I had no shelter. I opened the throttle, picking up speed in a race against time to reach the town at the park exit. My floorboards scraped the asphalt several times as I banked around the corners in my haste.

The town – all five buildings' worth – had a free campground at the edge. There were some plywood tepees for the kids to play in. These looked much safer than solely relying on thin nylon tent fabric to repel hail stones. Luckily, my tent fit perfectly inside one of the little structures. My first night in a tepee! Woohoo!

Being virtually alone in the campground, I decided it would be OK to take up a little more space. After some slight shifting of a picnic table, I pulled the Pearl under the adjacent metal shade canopy and parked her beside the table. I finished securing her cover in place just as the first dollar-sized raindrops began striking the overhead shelter. Then I scrambled back inside the safety and comfort of the tepee, just as the thunderstorm arrived in full force. The wind gusted and the rain bucketed down outside. In the dark, it was hard to tell how much of it was actually hail but, come morning, both the bike and I had survived in prime shape.

I had been singing "Take It Easy" by the Eagles all morning on the way to Winslow. Not sure exactly what I expected, but I definitely wanted to stop and stand on a corner and maybe, just maybe, see a girl slow down to take a look at me. A guy can dream, can't he?

It transpired that everyone in the entire city made famous by the lyrics of that song must have been thinking the same thing. Thus inspired, they had set up a particular corner in honor of the lines: "Well, I'm standing on a corner in Winslow, Arizona…" There was a real flatbed Ford parked there and all. The blank wall of an adjacent building had been painted to look like a storefront. Images of the Ford were painted as reflections in the windows. A sculpture had also been erected to honor songwriter Glen Frey of the Eagles. I'm not sure why, but the place had a kind of magic and I really enjoyed myself. Perhaps because it was unexpected.

And no, I didn't see her.

About 58 miles (93 k) further on, with a stop-off along the way, I reached the college and ski town of Flagstaff. There seemed to be a big festival in progress, with bands in the street and dancing in the town square. I ran into a couple of Native American lads after dismounting.

"There's a festival like this about once a month," said the Navajo youth pointing to the dancing. "You should take a look at the Navajo cultural extravaganza they're holding at the museum over the next couple days though. It's only a once-a-year thing."

"I'll do my best to make it," I said. "Are you from these parts? You looked more Sioux to me," I said turning to his friend.

"I am," he admitted. "My dad grew up on the Sioux reservation near Hardin."

"Small world," I said. "I'm from Miles City. He and I probably competed against each other in sports when we were in high school."

"Have you seen any of the sights around this area?" inquired the Navajo.

"Just short of Flagstaff, I stopped at Walnut State Park to look at the cliff-dweller city." Where the dwellings in New Mexico were entered from the valley floor up, these were from the cliff top down.

"That city dates back over 7,000 years," he said.

"What I want to know," I stated, "is who hauled the drinking water up to the dwellings from the valley floor below? I mean it's a long way down to the bottom via all those switchbacks."

"They most likely caught the water as it ran down the cliff face during rain storms."

"Ooookaay," I said, the light bulb switching on. Sometimes the simplest solutions are not the most obvious.

Riding around later, I accidentally discovered a frontage road near the edge of town that dead-ended in a thick clump of trees – a perfect place to pitch the tent for the night. In the light of day next morning, it became apparent I was right next to the Williams Cemetery.

While many cemeteries have areas of shady trees to create a sense of restfulness, these tombstones were set in amongst the thick forest of pine in any position they could fit. Headstones tilted this way and that from the force of tree roots. Everything was so compact, it would have been hard to walk around the trees without stepping on the graves.

Refreshed from a nice cool sleep in the forest, beside very quiet neighbors, I rode up to inspect the local ski field before the cultural event at the museum was scheduled to start.

"I noticed your Montana license plate," said a young man as he came over to introduce himself. I had been sitting on my bike in the carpark gazing at the mountain ski runs. "I'm from Seeley Lake, Montana," he told me.

"What are you doing here?" I asked, shaking his hand.

"I install ski lifts," he said. "It's a great job with lots of travel. I've just come back from New Zealand."

"I live in New Zealand now!" I exclaimed.

"Yeah, I noticed the Auckland patch on your jacket. I worked on Treble Cone and Mount Hutt in the South Island."

"Imagine that. I've skied Mount Hutt several times."

This world just keeps getting smaller and smaller.

The cultural event was excellent. There were a number of competition divisions for things such as jewelry, beads, painting, dancing and pottery, and the skill involved was perfection personified. My favorite was the graphic artwork, and I was fascinated by the weaving demonstration. Finger dexterity was unbelievable and the wool shuttle, moving back and forth, a blur.

The museum collection included several large dramatic oil paintings of the Grand Canyon. They looked so real you could climb over the bottom frame and go for a hike. The artist had captured the light of sunrises and sunsets, highlighting precipices, outcroppings and vegetation contrasted against the dark recesses of the eroded gullies. I sat transfixed, admiring the paintings for a big portion of the afternoon.

On paper, the trip towards the California state line appeared to be a quick one, but as is so often the case with Route 66, the surprises just kept coming up to delay progress. One was a car show in Seligman.

I parked the Black Pearl, ditched the heavy leathers and took a nostalgic walk down their main street. I had arrived towards the end of the show, but there was still much to investigate. The time and energy people put into restoring fine old vehicles is incredible. I recognized distinctive models from my youth – Chevrolet Belair, Corvette and Impala, Plymouth Duster, Roadrunner, Ford Thunderbird and Mustang. These faithful restorations were accompanied by heaps of roadsters modified from old bodies of various makes.

And to think that if I had kept the '69 Mach One Mustang I'd once owned, undriven, in a garage for the last 45 years, I could have sold it for over a quarter of a million dollars! Mind you, 45 years of insurance and garage rent would have taken a chunk out of the profits. And I'm of the belief that things are made to be used; I would have struggled to keep it undriven all that time.

Approaching Kingman, towards the western border of Arizona, there was nary a campground to be found. Which, didn't bother me too much. But I couldn't find any place I felt reasonably safe to pitch the tent either. Hot and tired and with dark thirty coming on fast, I acquiesced and took a motel room. It would be a first for this trip. But I confess, I was looking forward to the air-conditioning.

My plan was to leave right after an early church service and keep a move on to avoid the heat of the day in the upcoming Mohave Desert. However, my body clock was used to a sunshine alarm to drive me from my tent. With curtains drawn in the cool dark room, the plan suffered a serious setback as I slept on.

It was nearly 2 pm by the time I saw the "Welcome to Oatman" sign announcing the last stop before crossing into California. The temperature had already climbed to a blistering 105 deg (40 C) as I motored past Snob Hill into the town center and backed off the main road to drop the kick-stand in front of the Oatman Hotel.

Oatman is an old mining town that has refused to die. They started mining gold again in 2010 after closing down in the 1990s. Wild donkeys roam the streets. They have a Fourth of July egg frying using the heat of the sun on

110

Main Street every year. Now that we were approaching the end of July, it was even hotter and I think they could have fried up a mean steak if they'd wanted to.

I was disappointed because my delayed departure from Kingman meant I'd missed the gunfight held every day at noon. There's nothing like a good shootout to bring people out of the air-conditioned shops and bars. Then I made the mistake of chewing on an apple as I roamed around town. Soon I had a small following of donkeys who seemed to think that they had every right to my apple. I understand they can be quite aggressive at times. In the end, I compromised and we shared.

After drinking three Gatorades and a Coke to rehydrate myself, and strapping down two three-liter jugs of water on top of my luggage, I left to cross the desert. Erroneously thinking the "heat of the day" had passed and that the afternoon temperature would cool down as I traveled westward.

California

MD 143.8.09.17:23

August 9, 2016

So, like, you know, I finally arrived in the Golden State.

The temperature just kept rising after I left Oatman and continued into the Mohave Desert. How did anyone complete this passage in the old days? Or the Sooners, and wagon trains before them? Even now, for that matter? The amount of water they'd have needed to carry surely left no room for anything else.

I kept taking photos of the bike's thermometer as it continued to rise. It stayed at 115 deg F (46 C) for a long time, then about 6 pm, just as I thought things would be cooling down for the night, it went up about three octaves to 120 (49 C)! This is officially the hottest place I've ever been.

To clarify, the use of "octaves" in temperature works like this: from "Man, that's hot," to "HOT DAMN!" is roughly three octaves.

I've also heard of a method for determining the air temperature that involves counting the number of chirps a cricket makes in a 14-second time period, then adding 40 to get the temperature in degrees Fahrenheit. Unfortunately, all the crickets in these parts had died of thirst and heat stroke, or had left for the coast a long time back, leaving me unable to test that procedure.

I was constantly passing signs advising me not to proceed if flooding was in progress. It's hard to comprehend flooding when you can spit and the moisture doesn't even reach the ground. Perhaps the ground wasn't porous. I would have performed a test to see if urine soaked in or not, or whether it even reached the ground. The only problem was, no matter how fast or how much I drank, it never filled my bladder. There was nothing to let out. And I surely wasn't going to waste any water from my drink bottle.

Huge piles of sand adorned the sides of the road from previous flood-clearing operations, like sand dunes along the ocean shore. These seemed to continue for a couple of miles at a time. There didn't appear to be a river bed so much as a broad expanse of hillside on a gentle slope. The quantity of rain must be astounding when it comes. The image of an inland tsunami came to mind and generated all kinds of visions of riding a tidal wave across the desert on my motorcycle.

Surf's up!

The road began to deteriorate terribly. I don't think this portion of Route 66 had been repaved since the 1930s. Crevasses four inches wide and three inches deep crisscrossed the road forcing me to slow to 10 mph. Bouncing along set my teeth to chattering as if I was suffering from hypothermia. When I came to the sign that said "Rough Road Next 10 miles," I confess I took the new adjacent highway.

The daylight was in the final stages of defeat when I arrived at Amboy. Not keen on riding at night, plus wanting to see the countryside during the sunshine hours, I set up the tent, without the rain fly, off to the side of the road and went to bed. But sleep was another issue altogether. Trains ran continuously all night and their whistles wafted across the desert plains. They were taking advantage of the "cooler" weather.

"Cooler" is a relative term. It was still 110 deg F (43.5 C) at midnight. The heat radiated from the ground. With no breeze, it was stifling in the tent. The humidity was down to nine percent. I used the mattress as an insulator and just lay there naked and sweating. Even though I drank all the water and sweated profusely the entire time, everything was dry as a bone come morning.

I stopped at the Daggett Pioneer Cemetery where, in stark contrast to the green pine forest of Williams Cemetery, white timber crosses poked out of the sand in and amongst sparse olive-colored sage brush leaves and tumble weeds. Stone borders outlined some of the graves. At first, the size of the place wasn't apparent because the sage height and density camouflaged the crosses, but little flecks of white timber kept catching my eye and it became apparent that hundreds lay there. The desolation of the place implied that those buried could go no further on their journey west. But actually, reading the inscriptions, most of them came from Daggett itself (now a ghost town), the railroad and the surrounding community. Nonetheless, I had no desire to join their number, so I took another long drink of water before moving on.

After two more jugs of Gatorade and four cups of coffee for breakfast at a petrol station, I set off to find the day. I found it close to Victorville, where someone with a great imagination and a lot of time on their hands had built a forest of sculptures out of everything you can imagine. Most were poles that had prongs like branches welded to the main supports, which in turn supported bottles of various colors slid over the prongs. The tops were adorned with radiator fans, rifles, gears, yokes, sewing machines and whatnot. Together this unlikely collection formed a forest of glass-bottled trees. It was a delight to wander around the grounds and simply enjoy the fruit of a creative imagination.

Most of Route 66 was pretty well marked in California… at least until I got to Pasadena, where I planned to spend the night in a motel. All the campgrounds in Los Angeles were fully booked, and the hotel was pretty low-end. But for all I cared, I could sleep on the floor. Security for me, my bike and my meager possessions was my primary consideration.

With a little daylight remaining after I took my gear off the bike, I thought I would make a run for the end of the route. But I lost the signage just after leaving Pasadena, and try as I might, I never could recover it. I must have been on it part of the time as I traveled every street along the way until finally arriving in Santa Monica right at sunset.

There were thousands of people leaving the beach and others arriving at the pier for the nightlife. I took a photo of the setting sun, then headed back to the hotel.

First thing the next morning, I made another futile attempt at locating Route 66 and this time arrived at Santa Monica Pier about 9 am. I followed a service van through the entry gates and found the End of Route 66 sign located halfway out on the pier. I'd officially made it.

I was positioning the Black Pearl under the sign to record my accomplishment for the ABC competition when a guy stopped and started admiring the bike.

"I see your Montana plates. Did you really ride her all the way from there?" he inquired.

"Actually, I've just finished Route 66. Would you mind taking a couple of pictures for me?"

"Really?!" came the surprised response, "Sure. Happy to take a photo. The whole of Route 66, huh?"

That's when a third voice joined the conversation. "Hey! What are you doing out here? It's illegal for vehicles to be out this far on the pier," advised a police officer stomping towards me. "Move it now or get a ticket!"

"He's just finished riding the whole of Route 66," admonished my photographer. "I reckon he's earned this photo, so just back off a minute!"

"Be quick about it then."

"Thank you," I said gratefully to the officer. "Dumb place to put a sign if you're not allowed to ride to it," I added under my breath, but nothing could spoil the moment.

ONE

Route 66 had been way more enjoyable than I'd thought it would be. Yes, it's the "Main Street of America" and "The Mother Road" – large scale and vast – but it was also a very intimate, up-close experience. Before and after riding down the main streets of each town, you ride through residential areas and look into people's front yards. In some places, folk still sit on their porches and laundry still hangs in the backyard outside in a few. It's a real personal glimpse of American Life.

Riding the Harley had been a perfect way to see the sights. As ever on a motorcycle, you're aware of everything. The smells, the texture of the road and, yes, the heat. There's always that uplifting sense of freedom. And parking is a breeze. Plus, people had been constantly drawn to the shiny chrome and paint of the Black Pearl, leading to all kinds of interesting conversations.

Older people often amazed me with their comments.

"I used to have a Harley after the war," said one old codger. "Them was good times, my friend."

"My boyfriend had a Harley, and oh the places we used to go!" an elderly lady quietly confided as she gave me secretive and knowing glances, after her husband had moved along.

"My friends all had Indians. I couldn't afford a motorcycle," lamented one guy. "But if I woulda gotten a bike, it woulda been a Harley."

Conversations with middle-aged people frequently followed a theme.

"I'm jealous you're out traveling while I have to work," said a typical man in a suit carrying a briefcase. "But ... someday," he said as he looked on listlessly. "Yeah, someday I might just up and go," he reaffirmed. "Someday."

Young people and kids were always fun. They usually wanted to sit on the bike and would ask a thousand questions.

"Watch those pipes. They're hot," I cautioned. "Hold here and there and climb on up."

I'd usually position them onto the gas tank so they could reach the handlebars and then say, "Look there at your mom and dad so they can take a photo. But don't smile. Can you sneer? That's the way."

After the photo I'd tell them, "Push that button right there." The horn would honk and we'd all jump at the sound.

Once I let a kid push the starter button. But never again. I couldn't get the little rug rat to let go and get off the bike.

After Santa Monica Pier, I headed back inland to the La Brea Tar Pits to see the saber tooth tigers and mastodons. The reassembled bones of many creatures found in the pits were on display in the museum. Some were covered with hides to replicate what they may have originally looked like. Let me tell you, those mastodons were *huge*!

"Unlike most discoveries of prehistoric creatures at other geological locations, the tar from these pits not only preserved a large number of animals in a concentrated area, but also meant that what we have here are the actual bones of the animals and not just fossil replicas," spouted the guide. "Furthermore, the plants, seeds, insects and a whole myriad of information about the life these guys lived were preserved adjacent to each critter."

When we were outside, he continued, "These tar pits are a work in progress too – still every bit as capable of capturing hapless victims. One day the wind took my hat and I stepped over the fence to retrieve it. Even though it was very shallow, I got stuck."

"Oh oh," I said.

"Yep," he agreed. "It took two other guides to pull me out. If pits like these were out in the middle of nowhere, and I hadn't been able to attract attention, I could well have died of thirst in a couple of days. Followed by ground predators coming to eat me. Who would, in turn, get stuck. Followed by scavenger birds. Who would get stuck. And so on. I'd have probably wound up on the table of some archaeologist some 2,000 years in the future," he concluded. "Along with my hat."

"Reminds me of eastern Montana gumbo," I said.

He gave me a slightly puzzled look, but obviously decided not to ask.

After the tar pits, I took a ride down Rodeo Drive. I found a parking spot at the halfway point of the retail area and strolled around a bit. There was a sculptural exhibition extrapolating Salvador Dali's paintings into immersive three-dimensional art experiences. Almost as surreal were the facades of all the high-end shops. Gucci, Tiffany, Tissot and Louis Vuitton – each boasting of their prestige and struggling to make a statement more ostentatious than the others.

Before long, I'd had my fill of people and it was time to escape the multitudes. On a meandering route that would eventually take me to my class reunion back home in Montana, I headed east into Angeles Forest. This turned out to be the most beautiful ride with abundant turns and grand vistas as I climbed to over 7,000 ft (2,134 m). I stopped often until LA's smog got so thick, I could make out neither ocean nor city.

I spent the night at the top of a ski hill in pine trees. It was snowless in the summer months, but for the first time in weeks, I had my sleeping bag zipped up to stay warm. It was heaven, and I slept like a baby on a bed of pine quills.

Descending to the valley floor the next morning, I found myself looking at the largest Joshua Tree forest in the US. Sighting these unusual-looking succulents is always a good indication that you've entered the Mohave Desert. Which in fact I had. They look like a yucca plant stacked on top of a tall cactus trunk. They don't conjure up your typical forest image of tall, closely spaced trees, but they are impressive – especially when backed by the deep blue desert sky.

Not long after I passed through Joshua State Park, I arrived at Ivanpah and saw one of the world's largest solar thermal plants. Talk about surreal. Salvador Dali had nothing on this place. In a vast site area of 3,500 acres, beams of light rose up from ground-mounted mirrors to three 459 ft (139.9 m) tall collection towers that simply glowed. Unfortunately, the visitors' information center had closed ten minutes before my arrival. I would have dearly loved a tour but settled on reading the information panels instead.

Using 1022 deg F (550 C) heat generated from the sunlight reflected by the mirrors, the three towers produce steam to drive a series of turbines, generating a gross capacity of 392 megawatts. I reckon with the 340,000 plus mirrors, you could stand on one of these towers and get one heck of a tan in about two seconds!

The Nevada border could be seen from Ivanpah and I think perhaps even the lights of Las Vegas if it had been dark. Vegas probably uses this much power and then some. Even during the day.

Nevada

August 12, 2016

"Well sir, I've been to two county fairs and a rodeo, but I ain't never seen nothin' like Las Vegas before!"

Drunks passed out on the streets or in the gutter. Women naked from the waist up advertising shows. Hawkers handing out flyers for prostitutes. People dressed up like Transformers, Chewbacca, The Hangover cast, Batman and Robin, and a host of other characters, charging money for customers to pose with them. Artists drawing caricatures. Buskers of all types. People selling sodas, water and even beer from coolers on the footpath.

After the solitude of the desert highway, it was all a bit overwhelming walking amongst the throngs of people from all around the world.

I did take in the *Jersey Boys* theater performance, since I'd missed it when it was in New Zealand. I got a good seat, for a reasonable price, purchased on short notice. It was a grand show, and I spent the remainder of the evening strolling down the main drag singing Frankie Valli and the Four Seasons'. "Sherry, Sherry baby (Sherry baby) / Sherry, can you come out tonight ..." I sang as I made my way through all the strangeness of the Las Vegas Strip.

The architecture was extravagance for the sake of extravagance. Harley-Davidson had even joined in, with a giant motorcycle bursting through the wall above the entry to their restaurant. I wandered through most of the bigger casinos just to gawk and look at the grandiose edifices. Out of all of them, I think my favorite was Caesars Palace. Huge caryatids supported the upper floors around the open mezzanine hall. The main causeway meandered through the shops, simulating the feeling of wandering outside in a Greek agora in the early evening with dark blue sky overhead.

Since each casino was set up in such a way that you could easily wander around and lose yourself for a whole day, there were several that I never got to see.

As an architect, I couldn't help but be envious of the design briefs, challenges and budgets my colleagues would have been given. "Let your imagination run wild, make it more grandiose than anything else here, and don't worry about cost. Now, knock yourself out." Where do I sign up?

And, yes, I placed a bet, and lost a dollar. My gambling limit for a day. Money comes too hard to throw it away.

Ultimately, the activities, novelty, excitement and extravagance wear off relatively quickly, leaving a sadness of pretense. People are in the middle of the desert pretending they're in Paris, New York, Egypt and other places. Pretending they can afford to throw their earnings away. Pretending they can afford to shop at top-of-the-line retailers. Pretending they're part of the in-crowd. Pretending they can win. Pretending the pain, suffering and activities of those around them are OK. Pretending they're happy.

Maybe they *are* happy. But it wasn't really my cuppa tea.

Because Vegas is a large city, I took a room in a motel. A strain on my poor budget to be sure, but I took full advantage of the benefits. Only four blocks off the main drag, the accommodation was centrally located enough for me to walk everywhere with ease, and then cool off in the pool afterwards. The Pearl was parked in a secure place around back. And I could do my laundry.

This chore took place in the shower, where I put on my clothes, soaped up, rubbed vigorously, dropped them to the tub floor, then tread on them while I put on more clothes and repeated the process. I rung my washing out and hung it over the outside railing. The air was so dry, my clothes were ready to wear by morning. Sweet. Although the ring around the tub is probably still there.

As I was leaving, I discovered there was a free washer and dryer just down the hall. Story of my life.

Sitting in a Harley-Davidson dealership, sipping a cup of coffee a few days later, I began contemplating the crossing of several more deserts and the numerous hot days ahead. After my bug-related restaurant experience in Kansas, I was reluctant to let the air up my pant legs again.

"You're looking pretty deep in thought there," said a tidy-looking biker. "They call me Slick."

"Hey Slick. It's this heat. I was thinking there has to be a way to travel cooler."

"Have you tried the hydro-vest?" he asked stroking his neatly trimmed mustache.

"Never heard of it," I said surprised.

"You soak it for five minutes in water, lightly squeeze off the excess, and wear it under your leather jacket," he informed me as we headed over to the clothing section of the shop. "The water slowly evaporates over four to five hours and keeps you cool. They're the absolute best thing in desert heat."

"Sounds logical and scientifically sound," I said.

I bought one on the spot, and headed out in the 99 deg F (37 C) heat, full of hope. It was horrible! After about 30 minutes I knew how a lobster feels when you throw him in a pot of boiling water.

My face was red and sweat was running down off my head, body and legs. I couldn't take the heat any longer. As I started to unzip my jacket, a geyser of steam erupted out of the collar and fogged up my visor. Luckily, I was going slow and pulled off to the side of the road without incident. I was ranting and raving and ready to turn around and demand my money back, when Slick came riding by. He saw the steam and stopped to see if I was OK.

Turns out, wearing the hydro-vest inside out doesn't allow the water to evaporate properly. Vest thus reversed, off I went again.

This time it worked a treat! The rest of the day I cruised in cool comfort. Fine-tuning was achieved by unzipping the sleeves and the front zipper to regulate airflow and control evaporation.

Before I left the next morning, I soaked the vest as instructed. Thinking I could improve on the evaporation situation, I also soaked my pants, socks and gloves. Enthused, I then took the new "I Rode Route 66" blue skull cap I'd purchased in Santa Monica, drenched it in water and put it on to be worn under my helmet. Of course, that made the fit of the helmet even tighter and I figured the ridge down my forehead would be bigger than ever. But I thought it would be worth it to be cool.

Then into the desert I went!

Because of direct exposure to the wind, the pants and gloves dried out almost immediately. A replenishing system was required.

At the next gas stop I tried filling my boots with water and tucked my pants into them to act like a wick.

Even though it was now 105 deg F (41 C) out, I felt pleasantly chilled. After about 70 miles I pulled into another service station. When I stopped the motor, the humidity and temperature difference between me and the surrounding air caused a dense fog to materialize around my entire body. People gathered as I fumbled about trying to find the pump nozzle in the diminished visibility, until I thought to open my visor and remove the helmet.

When I went in to pay, I overheard a kid say, "Dad, there's a blue Klingon at the counter." Checking in a mirror, I discovered that dye from the skull cap was leaching out and my head was now a bright shade of cobalt.

They didn't have a water spigot at the pumps, so I soaked my gloves and filled my boots with windscreen washer fluid instead. And back on the road I went.

Later that afternoon, a cloud appeared and blocked out the sun. It was then that I realized the sun and the water had been working in a symbiotic relationship to maintain a comfortable body temperature. I also discovered the humidity level was so low that evaporation was continuing at a high rate no matter the temperature or time of day.

And I had been steadily climbing in altitude.

Without the sun to balance everything, I was now getting downright cold. The windscreen washer fluid probably contained some alcohol in it since it was evaporating at a much faster and therefore colder rate. Ice began to form on my gloves and pant legs.

The next city was still some ways off as the sun sort of slipped beneath the horizon. My body started turning the same color blue as my head. I began to get seriously concerned when my hands could no longer open and close to operate the clutch or brake.

I could see the newspaper headlines: "NEW ZEALAND MAN FOUND FROZEN IN DESERT". "Detectives are baffled as to how the victim had sustained frostbite over 80 percent of his body when temperatures have not dropped below 90 deg in three weeks. Foul play suspected."

Luckily, the windscreen washer fluid ran out a short time later and I began thawing before I arrived at the campground.

122

"Do yous know howda turn soup inta gold?"

This question was addressed to me by a short man in a white t-shirt and dress slacks at an adjacent table. I was in a dusty, sparsely populated, greasy-spoon diner and had just sat down to eat my sandwich. I turned to look at him with the sandwich stopped halfway to my mouth. He carried on before I could answer.

"Yous start wid a couple ah potatoes an ah onion. An den yous add ya salary and stir ovah heat. An finally yous add 24 carrots!" he completed triumphantly.

He was from New Jersey. His car had broken down and he was waiting for his son to come collect him and repair the vehicle. He told me his life story while I ate and he waited. It included the loss of his father, whom he'd adored. How his father had scrimped and saved and given him his life's savings so he could buy himself a house when he got married. And how his wife left him after she manipulated the sale of the house and all of their money into her hidden bank account. How she took their kids and moved to the west coast with her new lover. How he left his job and struggled on, making his way to the west coast to be close to his kids again. And finally, how he loved his kids who, now grown, were finally back in his life again. I listened engrossed throughout and barely uttered a word other than an occasional, "Uh huh."

When at last he'd finished, he paused and reflected, "I got no regrets. If I hadn'ta gotten married, I wouldn't a had my sons. But," he concluded, "I do have remorse."

That was one of the most astute statements I've ever heard.

When I stood to leave, I went to his table, shook his hand and said, "May God be with you."

"Yous wonna forget will yous? How ta turn soup inta gold?" he asked as I left.

"No," I promised. "I won't forget."

How could I forget 24 carrot soup? Every event in my life, good and bad, had shaped me and been a stepping stone to my arrival there at that point in time. And how could I regret that?

123

Arizona Revisited

MD 143.8.13.14:52

August 13, 2016

After leaving Nevada, the "All for Our Country" state, I decided to back-track a little and check out the more interesting features I'd missed while adhering to Route 66 – places like the Grand Canyon and Navajo National Monument. So I headed back into Arizona.

I went across the top left hand corner of the state, just over the Utah border, then through the city of St George, which offered up another surprise in the form of a fascinating wildlife museum, with stuffed animals from all over the world displayed in natural lifelike settings, all tucked away in a nondescript metal building. Viewing all these animals in close proximity made it easier to understand their relative sizes. Springboks are tiny compared to a mule deer.

Dipping back down to Arizona, one of the first things I came across was the Pipe Spring National Monument – a natural spring out in the middle of nowhere that provided water for wildlife and livestock and grew to become a Mormon outpost. It was pretty well restored and maintained, and the tour group consisted of two people – the guide and myself – meaning I received a fairly in-depth historical explanation. The early settlers had piped spring water under their houses, creating a cooling effect – an effect so efficient that it actually kept goods from spoiling in the kitchen. An early refrigerator, if you will. Reminded me of my hydra-vest.

It was an arid part of the country, with long rides through sage and dry grass until suddenly the topography changed to include forest as I approached the Grand Canyon National Park.

I set up camp at Jacobs Lake and rode into the park's northern entry, arriving towards late afternoon. The Grand Canyon is so vast and intricate that during broad daylight it's easy to overlook the scale and detail of the spectacle. With the shadows and low angled light of day's end, a whole new world emerges.

An orchestra had set up on one of the lodge terraces and began to perform just before sunset. Several classical pieces were played (after "The Star-Spangled Banner," of course) as I and many others sat looking out across the ever-changing twilight landscape. Spectacular views set to spectacular music.

Unfortunately I had to leave, before the performance ended, to avoid riding back to my tent in total darkness. Darkness is a concern in these parts, due to the number of deer and buffalo along the road. I traveled at about 20 mph over the last 20 minutes and stopped every 10 minutes as kamikaze deer sprung out in front of me.

Bound for Navajo National Monument Valley, I was surprised to discover a place called Marble Canyon. I turned off and took a short detour. There is so much splendor around this neck of the woods that it boggles the mind.

Along the way, several huge boulders had broken away from the cliff face, rolled down towards the road, and come to rest in various, precarious positions. Some appeared overly top heavy – like an ice cream cone – and looked ready to tip over at the first strong wind. But they must have been that way for a long time, because people had built walls up towards the overhanging bits to utilize them as roofs for their dwellings. Insurance adjusters would have a heart attack at the possibilities.

Next, I came across a group of people just launching inflatable rafts to float down the Colorado River through the Grand Canyon. Their boats were robust and it looked like it was going to be a fun trip. These excursions can last up to several weeks, depending on how far you want to go. Tempting as it was, I couldn't discern any way to load the Harley onto a raft and keep it dry, so I gave it a miss.

Another place that demanded I stop for the night was the Navajo Monument Indian Ruins, which included another impressive collection of Hopi cave dwellings. I put my name down for a free five-hour guided tour that started at 8 am the next morning, then retired to the picnic table by my tent to watch the sun playing with the vibrant desert colors as it descended into twilight across the desert.

Next day, it turned out that there were only three of us on the guided tour, including the guide.

"I'll be your guide today," said a young Navajo. "Be sure to save some energy hiking down into the valley as we have to hike back up at the end," he cautioned.

He was an informative guy, explaining the various nutritious and medicinal uses of the plants along the way. But then he said, "These cave dwellings were discovered by the Wetherill brothers in 1895."

"You mean the Navajo who had been all over this country for several hundred years had never seen these structures?" I asked shocked.

"Well, actually the Wetherill brothers were led here by a Navajo guide who had been here often," he responded.

"'Discovery' seems to be a relative word," I admitted. "But it must be very difficult to give your spiel knowing full well your ancestors did the actual leg-work and don't get the credit."

Throughout the hike we were treated to the ever-changing shadows across the cliff face as the rotating earth allowed the sun to peek into the huge cliff overhang, slowly drawing the earth dwellings out into the light.

The guide called our attention to a number of interesting hieroglyphics carved quite high up the walls. "Since we already know who made them, considerable speculation has been spent on what, how and why," he said. "What was their significance? How did they get clear up so high on the wall? And, why were they put there in the first place?"

"Perhaps they were just graffiti by some of the young punks of the time," I theorized. "I mean, I've seen some spray-can hieroglyphics in locations that defy the imagination as to how they were applied. No one seems to really know what they mean or why anyone would waste so much paint and effort to put them up, knowing full well they'll be removed shortly afterwards."

"You're right," he laughed. "At least the park service knew it was the Hopi who put these ones here. The police seem mystified about the identity of taggers."

"Perhaps the tags will get painted over, and in 800 years or so, someone will 'discover' them," I continued. "Then archaeologists will get their knickers in a twist trying to research, decipher and catalog them. And tour guides will have to speculate on who, how and why."

"Job security guaranteed," he offered.

The land formations of Monument Valley are incredible. The vertical shafts of rock that made this area famous project straight up in the middle of an otherwise flat landscape. Red and orange colors define these pillars, and each one has a character of its own. You could ride for 15 minutes then stop to behold an entirely new vista.

And I did. Often.

Then suddenly I had completed my dip down into Arizona, I was crossing the border into Utah.

Utah

MD 143.8.16.16:15

August 16, 2016

Well, Utah turned out to be a diamond in the rough. "Life Elevated" is the state motto. And aptly named.

Monument Valley spills over the state border and carries on for some time. My route was like a huge undulating serpentine trail coming back on itself. But I actually only traveled over the same highway once for about 50 miles. Rock formations, like Mexican Hat, added surprise and delight to my ride. The "Hat" bears a resemblance to an upside-down sombrero. Surely it will topple over any day now.

I took what I originally thought would be a paved road through the Moki Dugway between a couple of national wilderness areas. Flat country opened out before me all the way to the distant cliffs. Since it was just me and black pavement for as far as the eye could see, I opened up the throttle. Yahoo!

Unfortunately, I accelerated so fast I missed reading the small print on the sign… "Three miles of 10% grade gravel switchbacks. Use extreme caution!" I became transfixed with wonder as the giant cliff wall loomed higher and higher in front of me. But this emotion turned to concern when no apparent passageway could be seen. The pavement seemed to just run in a perpendicular line, straight into the base of the cliff.

It transpired that the pavement did indeed end at the base of the cliff, but the road did not. It made a sharp 90 degree turn to the right, then continued forward on gravel, with a series of narrow, steep, windy stretches that seemed always about to come to a dead-end, before a tight 180 degree switchback would miraculously appear and the road continued on. At no time could I ever see any portion of the road ahead, or where it would eventually wind up, until I reached the top. It was a buzz to look back down and see where I'd been. Great fun! At the top I came across a couple of German ladies who were as amazed as myself. In fact, they were making the trip again. Just because.

I couldn't really understand why someone would go to the trouble of carving a road up the face of that cliff – other than for people like myself and the German women, who would ride it just for the sheer thrill. I'm filled with gratitude to those people who go beyond the ordinary. So often real enjoyment comes from the simple, unexpected things in life.

Natural Bridges National Monument consisted of – wait for it – natural bridges! Eons ago, the river had wound through the canyon, carving out those giant natural architectural wonders. There were many trails that allowed explorers to hike down to them, under them and over them. But I elected to sit on a bench and observe the magnificent views from the turnouts.

The day was coming to an end as I shot along through Fry Canyon. I wished I'd been there earlier as I would have stopped more often to observe the intricate erosion patterns of the canyon walls. But as it was, the low angle of sunlight cast dramatic shadows and created stunning drama by highlighting the texture and color of the countryside.

With a little imagination, you could recognize one standalone mountain as a castle carved out of stone, complete with fighting platforms, turrets, battlements and battered walls. I half expected to see an army of knights riding horseback across the plains with standards flying.

All different, yet all wonderful.

The woman at the information center had told me the route through Boulder and Fry Canyon was one of the most scenic routes in the USA. Ha! She had no idea of the places I'd been. Actually though, she was pretty close to right.

But my daughter and sister had told me that Bryce Canyon was their favorite National Park. It was close by, so I made that my next destination, and it was beyond spectacular. The oranges, creams, whites, reds and a myriad of subtle shades of each, colored the vast natural earthworks. Erosion had whittled away at the earth until impossible spires remained, reaching up to the sky like arthritic fingers. Canyons, tunnels and pylons appeared, disappeared and changed shape constantly as I took a short hike down into the core of the eroded hillside.

Unbelievably, I was able to secure a campsite in the middle of the park. This was fortuitous because it was late in the day when I arrived. I quickly erected the tent, then shot up the road with short stops at all the pullouts to view the scenery in the dwindling light. All this was preparation for the next morning's sunrise ride when, hopefully, I could witness the best sights again in the early morning's soft angled sunlight.

Later that evening, I went to a lecture by a Dark Ranger. Actually, he was a park ranger who had a great interest in astronomy, and an incredible ability to present that evening's topic – "The Creation of the Universe" – in a way that engaged the entire audience, young and old alike.

It's wonderful when you find people who love their work so much that they pass their enthusiasm on to everyone they come into contact with. And yet, we each have the opportunity to do just that. By sharing our excitement about our interests with others, we may just inspire someone who hasn't yet set their course in life. Excitement is contagious. It's really a matter of simply developing an honest fascination and keeping ourselves excited about what we do. Just think of it – a workplace where there's a whole office of people excited and happy to be there, to share and learn. A whole community like that. A whole country.

Next, I trundled on down to Zion National Park and, just before the entry, pulled into a trading post carpark. Bad timing. It was lunchtime and four tour buses and two Harley tours, with about 25 bikes each, had arrived a mere five minutes before me. It was a real zoo as everyone competed for toilets, souvenirs, snacks and drinks.

One of the Harley tours was made of up bikers from Taiwan. I know this because one of them came over and gave me a patch signifying a ride in Taiwan. He spoke no English. He just presented the patch to me with both hands and a slight bow of his head. It was a very nice gesture and a big honor to receive. There was no way he could have known I had recently been to Taiwan and therefore how much more that patch meant to me. I'm still not sure why he picked me.

I posed dutifully as we had our photo taken together. There was a lot of smiling and hand shaking. Suddenly remembering my language skills, I said "Xie xie" (thank you in Mandarin). It created quite a stir. Gaining in confidence, I followed up with, "The next stop is the Zion Information

Center," and then, to cap it off, advised, "Mind the gap when alighting to the platform." This aroused the attention of the entire group and they all rushed over. After many more photos, lots of smiles, handshakes and waving, they all rode off in a thunderous roar of Harley smoke.

The ride into Zion Park started with a series of short tunnels, then a long one peppered with penetrations in it, similar to the Taroko Gorge in Taiwan. That similarity, combined with having just met the Taiwanese bikers and hearing Mandarin spoken again, suddenly transported me back. And, just for a moment, I was able to reach out and caress a happy memory.

Zion Park was dramatic and beautiful in its own way. Private vehicles were not allowed up the canyon and a bus service was provided instead. I elected to skip the main valley, and alternatively rode up a lesser known valley on the other side of the park. The sheer scale of the peaks was mind boggling.

I'd become almost desensitized with the constant beauty that had assaulted my senses over the last few days. I'd run out of adjectives and superlatives. Everything had become just ... amazingly awesome!

The immediate impact of the landscape's beauty is one thing, but having the awareness that it is continually changing and always different, heightens a sense of wonder at the amazing creativity of God. I could go back there next year and it would be totally different, while being every bit as beautiful as it was the first time I went. And again, in a hundred years. Always the same. And always different.

How do you top all that? I don't know exactly. I quit taking photos for a while and just rode along with my mouth agog until I swallowed a couple of bugs. Those bugs were a sure sign the desert was behind me – with the return of moisture comes living creatures again. It was such a novelty that I didn't even mind the minor task of cleaning the windscreen and helmet visor of bug-splatter at frequent intervals.

Somewhere towards the Colorado border, I pulled into a small one-horse town and stopped for a nice lunch at the only café.

"Howdy. What can I get for you?" asked the waitress as she poured me a cup of coffee.

"Well, a burger and a piece of that blueberry pie sounds about right," I said staring at the pies on the counter.

When she set the plate in front of me, I asked, "Is there someplace close by where a guy might get a haircut and beard trim for a reasonable price?"

"Cross the street, take the first alley you come to and continue on till you see the green garage. Sally works out of her garage. If she's not in there, knock on her back door."

With the blueberry pie settling nicely in my stomach, I motored the bike over as directed. I knocked on the back door and a dark haired, middle aged woman in a house coat appeared tentatively at the screen door.

"I understand you cut hair and trim beards," I said.

"Yes, I do," she said studying the leather clad biker in front of her for a moment. The door opened a bit as she leaned out to take in the bike. "How did you hear about me?"

"Why, I've heard about your services and skills at every stop since Flagstaff, Arizona."

Which earned me a toothy smile and a small discount. We had a great talk and I discovered that at 38 years of age, with a husband and three children, she had only ever left town for a short while to attend a nearby university. And had never left the state! Nor had she a desire to do so.

Some people have all they need and want right in front of them. Others need to explore. It's wonderful how each one of us is so different. And still the same.

The next morning, I felt refreshed and groomed for success as I headed for Colorado – the "Centennial State" – on the frontage road paralleling the freeway.

Colorado

MD 143.8.21.17:39
August 21, 2016

Singing "Rocky Mountain High" and all the other John Denver songs I could remember, I rumbled along towards a state that embodies the heart of the Rocky Mountains. The landscape continued to change, until it had become something I was more familiar with. Tree clad mountains and crystal-clear waters. And bugs!

With the super dry, arid land and low humidity now behind me, the thriving insect life became more and more obvious. Every time I stopped for gas, the number of bugs splattered on the windscreen, and my helmet and pant legs increased. Due to the heat, I'd gotten out of the habit of wearing my leather chaps. From the knees down, my jeans had collected a fair amount of dirt through the desert, and dust when I'd passed through a long cloud of cement and lime powder generated by road works. Now that layer was added to with a mixture of wings, exoskeletons, legs and various shades of green and yellow innards. It was looking like it was time for a laundromat at the next town.

As luck would have it, I happened to run into a brief rain shower, which provided just enough water to make me damp all over. Then the sun came out and baked me back to normal before my arrival late that afternoon. Fat, dumb and happy, I carried on oblivious to the implications of what had just happened.

My conventional method of doing laundry on the road (rather than the shower method employed in Vegas), consists of taking all my clothes (three shirts, a pair of jeans, underwear and socks, swimsuit, towel, hat, glove liners and tennis shoes) and tossing them all into a washing machine in order to make up a full load. Usually that leaves me barefoot, wearing only my leather pants and a shy grin.

The problem arose when I couldn't bend my jeans to fit into the machine. The shower of rain had caused the dirt to mix with the cement and lime and set, with the various bug parts acting as reinforcing. Resulting in concrete! My jeans were as hard as rock.

Wedging each leg between the dryers, I leaned back hard. This had varied results. The right pant leg slowly bent to about 90 degrees. However, the left pant leg broke clean off about four inches above the cuff. Not the best outcome, but at least the jeans would now fit in the washer. About two hours later, I was ready to set off again. Happy, except for one pant leg being shorter, though quite a bit cleaner.

I'd taken to the freeway to get to Glenwood Springs as quickly as possible because the tread on the Black Pearl's rear tire seemed to have disappeared. It was another reminder of how far I'd actually traveled this trip. Being a Friday, I was moving flat out to get to the Harley dealership by late afternoon. By the time I reached Green River, the tire had run clean out of rubber. Luckily, the Harley dealer squeezed me in on short notice and promised to have me back on the road before closing time.

After some ribbing, followed by a detailed explanation of why one leg of my pants was shorter than the other, the new rubber was installed and I headed out in search of a campground. I was hoping to make it to a site near Frisco along the Dillon Reservoir. But unfortunately, the days had been getting shorter and night fell too quickly for me to make it that far.

An app on my phone showed two campgrounds in Eagle. Regrettably, the first "campground" was actually an office complex. The second one was a private house in the middle of a block of private houses. They'd clean missed the boat on that one.

Trying to find my way back to the freeway, I pulled over to the side of the street to see where I was and regroup. It was now well after dark. Rain began to fall. The app showed no other campgrounds less than two hours away in any direction. I exhaled in frustration and turned off the phone. And in so doing, happened to look over towards the house on my right.

With windows cracked or missing, door ajar on a broken hinge, and grass overgrown, it was in a sorry state. An abandoned house! Turning my head further to the right sat its twin. Another abandoned house!

"Any port in a storm," I said with elation.

I pushed the Pearl in between the two houses, where she was almost totally concealed in the tall grass. After moving a length of broken guttering and a couple of bricks from the space behind her, there was sufficient room to pitch the tent. A short reconnaissance of the houses confirmed I wasn't intruding on another squatter's domain. Shortly thereafter, I crawled into the tent and fell asleep to the musical pitter-patter of rain on nylon.

I took Highway 6, which was mostly the frontage road for the Interstate, until it veered off around Dillon Reservoir outside of Frisco and I suddenly found myself going over Loveland Pass. What a lovely surprise! Rising up and up to 11,900 ft (3,627 m) and over the continental divide, I went into the clouds and well above the snow line. Then there was a nice long road snaking back down to the valley. The hardest part was navigating the turns while rubber-necking to take in the mountain peaks and stunning scenery.

I traveled onward to Denver, spending a couple of days visiting an old friend, then out the other side to the Garden of the Gods Park. It was a fabulous day to be in the park. As the name implies, this park is really a huge rock garden. Dynamic protrusions erupt from the ground, reaching for the dark blue sky. Large boulders the size of houses sit precariously balanced on rocky platforms. I couldn't help noticing something familiar in the rock structures and colors. At one place there was a jagged outcropping of deep burgundy rock, and directly adjacent was a similar vertical outcrop that was limestone white.

These were nothing more than the same geological layers I'd observed throughout New Mexico, Arizona and Utah. The only difference was these layers, having been pressed together by the tectonic plates pushing up the Rocky Mountains, were now vertical instead of horizontal. Having previously seen these colorful strata as horizontal rows of hills in New Mexico, then stacked upon each other when viewed in the Arizona Grand Canyon, angled up through the foothills and finally standing vertically on edge in the heart of the Rockies, I felt a deep sense of completeness settle in. An understanding.

While I may not know the exact nomenclature or the scientific details, I can see a plan. A perfect plan. Continuity. And with that comes a sense of peace. Everything is well thought out and under control.

I'd seen so many things, the days and experiences began to blend together. Now, heading generally northwards into the chilly mountain air, I arrived at

Hot Sulphur Springs around noon and took one of the last two available campsites. Once everything was unloaded, erected and secure, I grabbed my togs, towel and a book and strode on over to the hot springs.

The hot springs development tumbles down a hillside with a series of small pools interconnected by boardwalks. Each pool has its own unique character and temperature.

"Didn't I see you at the campground on a motorcycle?" asked the robust middle-aged guy in the steaming pool as I set my towel down.

"Yeah," I replied. "It's been on the cool side these last couple of days. Figured I needed a good soaking and a warm up. Summer's not going to be with us much longer," I said sliding into the hot water beside him.

"You should be riding down south in the desert heat," he advised.

"That's where I'm coming from," I responded slipping into reminiscence for a moment. "But the scale and rugged beauty of these mountains and canyon roads are breathtaking and worth the cold. I've extracted nearly all my clothes from the saddle bags and bundled up for the challenge."

"Where do you stay? he queried.

"Usually in my tent. Campground spaces are plentiful lately but I've noticed lately many have restrictions against tents due to problems with bears. Also, with colder nights in the high altitudes, I'm thinking I'll start riding the mountains during the day and pitch the tent in the lowlands at night."

"There's a plan. Sounds like you've been riding a while," he observed wiping the moisture from his face. "Where've you been?"

I told him of my ambitions and the areas covered so far on my adventure. "The state highway map highlights scenic roads with a series of dots and dashes. I'm enjoying my riding time in the mountains immensely, and I've decided to continue to serpentine my way up north to include as many mountain passes as possible," I said climbing out of the pool to cool off in a reclining chair.

"Which passes have you gone over?"

"Loveland and then Uta Pass over towards Cripple Creek." There'd been a biker festival going on with hundreds of bikes returning to the city. It was fun riding with so many motorcycles commanding the roads in both directions.

And crossing Independence Pass at 12,095 ft high (3,686 m) is, I believe, the highest pass I've ever ridden over. Chilly up there above the snow line, but what a view!

"Any bad weather?" he asked as we entered another pool – a natural rock dish carved out of the hillside with a hot, aqua-green, murky waterfall dropping into one end.

"Outside of Buena Vista the clouds settled down for what looked like a really nasty rain squall. I ducked under a store canopy just as the first few large raindrops hit."

"Lucky."

"Another biker joined me moments later. But he soon became impatient to leave. I pointed out areas where I could see hail in the clouds and said there was no hurry to move on. Undeterred, he donned his stocking knit hat and took off. About a minute later, the pea sized hail hit."

"Ooohh. I hope his knit hat was enough protection."

"Me too. It's times like those that I really love my helmet," I said climbing out again to sunbathe on the deck.

"There are two larger pools under cover," he pointed out.

"I know, but why would you want to go inside with all that scenery begging attention?" I asked gesturing with my arm.

"A lot of our history is intertwined with mining and the gold rushes. Like Leadville and Aspen," he said a little later, changing the subject as we moved along the boardwalk to a small blockwork pool.

"Yeah," I said. "I went to that bar in Leadville. The one that's been around since 1879 serving the likes of Butch Cassidy, the Sundance Kid and Buffalo Bill Cody. Inside looks like it hasn't changed since their day. And, if it was good enough for them, how could I not sling my leg over the bar stool and order a beer?"

"Good for you. Some of the old gold mining areas like Aspen have moved on and blossomed under another type of wealth – skiers and tourists."

"That's for sure. Colorado is ski hill country all right. I made a point of seeing as many ski hills as I could. Even if they were all still green from summer," I told him, as we climbed out of yet another hot pool and moved down to the next one along. "Breckenridge, Copper Mountain, Beaver Creek,

Vail and Steamboat Springs. Oh, to have my knees back and be able to ski again," I lamented.

"I have a timeshare amongst the condos, impressive homes, hotels and little villages that have sprung up in every flat space available on the valley floor," he informed me. "And let me tell you, it's not cheap. Hikers and cyclists come in the spring, summer and fall. Hunters arrive in the fall, and skiers in the winter. It really is a year-round endeavor now."

"I did notice a separate bicycle road paralleling the freeway all the way from Denver to access these areas for people unable to afford motorcycles," I pointed out with a smile. "A nice touch."

"We do our best to please," he laughed. "Well, my cows aren't going to milk themselves," he said, crawling out of the steaming hot water and drying off. "Enjoy the rest of your trip."

"Thanks. And thanks for the conversation."

"Oh," he paused, "you'll want to go through Rocky Mountain National Park to see the Never Summer Mountains."

"Funny, I have never even heard of that park."

"Not as dramatic as Glacier National Park," he admitted, "but it's every bit as beautiful."

After he left, I soaked for a while longer, climb out and read on the deck chairs until I cooled down. Then moved to another pool to soak, read and repeat. I wound up in the hot pools for six hours! Reeking of sulphur, but clean as a whistle and medium well done, I sauntered back and melted into my tent for the night.

I awoke to a thick coating of frost that covered everything. Summer was definitely on its way out. But warm, relaxed and rested, I headed out for the Rocky Mountain National Park.

Hiking on the numerous trails there would have been heaps of fun, if I'd had the time. But riding over another mountain pass above the snow line, with glorious views of the Never Summer Mountains, was more matched to my physical abilities. Half of this range had been caused by uplift and the other half by volcanic activity. The Never Summer Mountains are usually covered in snow, but this year most of it had gone. *Even so, I probably still wouldn't call it summer*, I observed to myself with hands cupped around a hot coffee in the visitors' center.

I began to feel a bit guilty about just riding through. Then I spotted a lake within easy walking distance and I parked the bike for the short hike. It's good to stretch the legs and get closer to nature once in a while. And I was treated with yet another magic view.

As I departed the park, I witnessed a moose and her calf wandering down to the river for a drink. Moose are notoriously hard to find in the wild, so I pulled off the road to watch for a while. Talk about a tall drink of water – these guys stand six feet at the shoulder. With their long legs, they can effortlessly step over a five-strand barbed wire fence. Hitting a cow on the highway will mess up your front bumper and hood. Hitting a moose with a car will just cut him off at the kneecaps as his body continues to pass through your windshield to join you in the cab, up close and personal. I could probably just pass underneath on the bike, but I had no intention of testing that theory.

The golfers at Estes Park, further along the road, faced a different set of challenges. A herd of about 25 elk had bedded down in the rough just off the fairway around the sixth hole. Two golfers walked gingerly by the six-point bull on their way to the green. You wouldn't want to fall short on a chip. Add to that the hundreds of people watching from the road and waiting to see what would happen if the elk did take exception to the game being played around them, making par was probably a hard ask. I was told that in the winter, the main herd of 200 to 300 elk will often come down and take over the entire course.

Arriving at Loveland, in the north of Colorado, I noticed a sign for the Benson Sculpture Gardens, and took a side detour to investigate. Good choice. Over 130 bronze sculptures, of various sizes and subject matters by a range of talented artists, were strategically placed along footpaths and waterfronts throughout the park. The gardens continually evolve when annual funding allows for the commissioning of more works. With plenty of benches to sit on, it was a great place to relax and ponder.

I pondered on what it was going to be like in Wyoming. Then decided the best way to find out was to leave the Centennial State and go see for myself.

Wyoming

MD 143.8.26.10:40

August26, 2016

I moseyed on into the "Forever West" state. In this part of the world there's often only one road between towns – be it an interstate, highway or dirt road. But the paved roads are all in pretty good condition and it's easy to make time if that's your objective. Recently I'd had problems going very far without stopping for a photo or to read information and historical markers. Therefore, making time wasn't a bad thing.

Laramie was pretty much a case in point with regards to being a distraction. The old Territorial Prison, which is now a museum, is located there. As well as housing a number of infamous characters like Butch Cassidy, the prison was a fascinating study in architecture and business models.

The place was well known for the manufacture of brooms. This industry gave inmates a skill towards rehabilitation and employment once they were released. Over the years they also tried taxidermy, woodworking, leather working, and many other trades. Usually, these opportunities arose when a criminal was brought in with the requisite skills, then dropped again once he was set free.

Modern society has recognized the "unfairness" of using the incarcerated to do jobs that are socially redeeming and help pay for the cost of housing them. Nowadays they are able to watch TV, use the internet, run their outside syndicates by phone, network with fellow inmates and figure out ways to improve their crime skills while reducing the chance of getting caught once they are paroled.

Interesting note, Butch Cassidy was let go shortly after his stay at the Territorial Prison because it was his first offense and the judge thought he should be given a second chance to lead a productive and prosperous life. Which he did, I guess. In his own way.

Following the Sand Creek Massacre Trail, I wound my way through the valleys and along the base of the mountains to Shoshoni. The massacre was a low point for the American Military in which the inhabitants of a Cheyenne village were slaughtered and mutilated on 29 November 1864. About two thirds of the occupants were women and children.

There were portions of several other trails I followed through Wyoming, including the Bridger Trail, Overland Stage Route, Original Pony Express Route and Chief Joseph Trail. All were a wonderful opportunity for imagining the adventures and hardships endured by early travelers.

Picking any one of these trails and following it from beginning to end, while learning as much as possible about the times, conditions and people along the way, could be an exciting and informative ride. If sufficient signage was installed and towns joined in the spirit of the trail by restoring aspects of their early history, the experience would be every bit as engaging as the roadside attractions encountered along Route 66. And possibly spawn a stronger sense of local identity and pride. Not to mention generating additional revenue and historical awareness. I, for one, would certainly be keen for rides like that.

But then again, any excuse for a ride.

I expected the number of mosquitoes to diminish as the weather turned cooler. However, the only discernible difference I noticed was that, after the blood fest from the night before, their motion was even slower as they lumbered around in the cold morning air. This allowed for greater ease in smushing them against the tent walls. And the little red spots had continued to multiply over the course of the previous couple of weeks.

Because the increase was only at about the rate of four to six a day, I hadn't paid much attention to the total number of red dots, until I heard a little girl at the campground talking with her father.

"Daddy, can we get a polka dot tent?"

"I don't think they make them, honey."

"That funny man over there has one."

"He's a Klingon, sweetheart."

"Is that why his pant legs are different?"

141

"I'm not sure, pumpkin. But I think those dots might actually be blood."

"Oh… Then I don't think I want one."

Kids say the darnedest things!

A wrong turn on the way to Cody took me across the plains to Greybull instead of along the mountain foothills as I had planned. Another happy mistake resulting in a pleasant ride – proving that, ultimately, there are no wrong turns. And eventually I arrived in Cody just the same.

The town is named for one Colonel William F. Cody, otherwise known as Buffalo Bill, and the museum has an entire wing dedicated to the history of this amazing man. It also has four other wings dedicated to gun collections, artwork, Native American artifacts, and natural history exhibits. I spent nearly the whole day inside that fascinating place.

Bill Cody was a most charismatic character. Realizing that the American West and his lifestyle were changing, he switched gears and decided to become an entertainer. He set up the Wild West Show. It included sharp shooters, Indian attacks, trick riding, and other performances. The show toured the country and later through Europe, and he carried on performing well into the final years of his life.

Turns out, not only did ol' Bill educate the audience as he entertained them, he was also a great humanitarian who treated people equally and with respect. By including the Native American way of life into his shows, he gained respect from the tribes and all who worked with him.

Feeling properly educated as I exited the building, I headed towards Cook City to go over the 10,937 ft (3,333 m) high Beartooth Pass. I went over this pass when I was a kid, and the snow was as high as 20 ft (6 m) on the side of the road. It was like going through a tunnel without a roof. But by this late in the year, all the snow should be gone to runoff. Right?

The Chief Joseph highway demanded my full attention as I climbed and dropped thousands of feet, going over passes with dynamic views at every turn. I lost myself in the superb scenery, vistas and smells of the mountains. Then came the pinnacle peak of Beartooth Mountain in the distance. Framed between the pines. Enticing me onward. It became a focal point for hours of riding. Maybe it was just one of those days when all seems right with the world and my opinion was biased, but this ride seemed to have everything and I simply loved it. I felt like contacting the information lady back in Utah and telling her this ride eclipses Fry Valley. And she shouldn't just take my word for it – she should travel it herself.

Downshifting through the gears, I pulled into the Top of the World Café carpark for a soda and chocolate bar lunch. Then I reclined out on the veranda and basked in a happy glow, just enjoying the scenery while soaking up the sun, and warming up from the chilly ride. Two bikers pulled in and dropped their kickstands next to the Pearl. One was on a Fat Boy and the other on an Ultra Glide.

"Howdy," said the stout man in leathers leaving his helmet on the Ultra. He had a narrow swath of white to the right side of his otherwise black hair. "Name's Streak. And my buddy admiring your bike's artwork back there, is Spider."

"How's your day going?" I asked.

"Brilliant. We're just on a day ride from Cody to here and back," he said taking the seat beside me. "I never get tired of this ride."

"I can see why."

"Looks like you're on a longer ride," said Spider as he came up the steps and shook my hand.

I gave them an outline of my travels, and they nodded with approval. Soon we were talking about the things I'd seen and done over the last few days while following the various trails.

"Did you stop at Hell's Half Acre, one of the hideouts and meeting places for the Cassidy Gang?" asked Streak. "Hole in the Wall was another one."

"Yes, I did. Very rugged country full of switchbacks and blind-ended canyons. There is so much Wild West history around here, you could easily spend a whole summer just following up on different bits of it. Then I rode from Shoshoni to Thermopolis via the Wind River Canyon Road."

The road ran beside Boysen Reservoir and then along the river through a beautiful canyon.

"It may be an optical illusion, but I swear that river runs uphill the wrong way alongside the railroad tracks," said Spider.

"Thermopolis is a great place to spend the day soaking in the hot springs," declared Streak.

"It was already a hot day, so I didn't go in – though I spent a whole day soaking at Hot Sulphur Springs back in Colorado. Besides, I was having fun observing the beautiful chemical deposits caused by the hot water and the algae growing on the edges of the water flows." The results had included a two-story dome shape of whites, grays, oranges and greens that looked like the top of a melting double scoop ice-cream cone. Overland flows and deposits of chemicals mimicked the flowing forms you would normally expect to see inside a cave. The formations looked strange outside, but the colors were beautiful.

We all sat saying nothing for a while, ruminating and enjoying the sunshine, before I made another observation. "I noticed a lot of wind generators throughout the prairies."

"Yeah, the breeze blows pretty well all day long in these parts," Spider responded.

"When I was a kid in Montana, we used to make kites out of two sticks and some string with the funny pages stretched and glued over the frame," I reminisced. "First thing in the morning we would hoof it on down to the corral, launch them into the wind and secure the bitter end to the fence posts. Once airborne, they would fly until evening when the prairie winds died down for the night."

"The energy has been there for the taking for years. Good to see it finally being used, in my opinion," said Spider.

Again the conversation fell silent for a spell.

"Pronghorn antelope herds have certainly diminished over the years since I was a kid," I said. "Instead of seeing herds of 40 to 60, most I saw so far were about four to six. And those were pretty sparse."

"They must have been something to see back in the 1800s," admitted Streak. "Did you know they are the second fastest land animal in the world? There's only a one mile per hour separation between them and the cheetah, which can sprint up to 60 mph (98 kph). Those little critters can run."

"One reason I always ride at least 70 miles per hour," added Spider.

Refreshed and hyper from the sugar content of my lunch, I bid Spider and Streak a safe ride home. Then saddled up and headed out for the final climb over the pass and down the multitude of switchbacks that descend into Montana. The pass is well known for its fabulous views and scenery, and I was looking forward to numerous photographic opportunities.

Ominous dark blue clouds had been following me all day, yet the sun and I had always managed to stay in contact with each other and just ahead of them. They appeared to have been restricted to the other side of the ridge line I'd been riding parallel to. But now they had turned the corner and moved to the ridge in front. They obscured the sun, forcing the temperature steadily downwards until it was now well below 40 deg (5 C).

A few snowflakes started falling just short of the top of the pass. *Now I'll be able to say I rode in the snow on this trip!* I thought to myself. *Hot Dog.*

As I cleared the crest of the pass and started downwards, a cloud descended on me. Then the few flakes turned into a thick flurry and, within the length of a football field, I found myself in two inches of snow. It stuck to the windshield and my visor, rendering visibility to zero. At the same time, the Black Pearl's rear end did a little swish and I went into a lovely pirouette. *Ok, here is where I drop the bike.* But, by steering in the direction of the skid and continuously pumping the rear brake, I managed to recover and slowed the bike down to about five miles per hour. When I was finally stable and able to let go with one hand, I raised my visor to improve my vision.

It didn't make much difference. I was in a virtual whiteout. Eventually, I made out a pullout to my left, so I slid off the highway onto the gravel, which provided enough traction for me to stop. Just over the guardrail, everything dropped away to … forever!

The snow began falling even more thickly. *I may have to spend the night here.* I'd camped out in the snow many times so I wasn't too worried about that. But knowing Montana, it could easily continue snowing another two feet (600 mm), and then not melt off for several days. Or weeks.

In my younger days, when I was building a house outside of Bozeman, we received a dump of two feet in the middle of September that stayed there until the following April. And that was down at lower altitudes! I might be able to walk out in three feet of snow, but the bike would be completely buried and frozen in until spring, when the snow plows open the road.

Thus motivated and inspired, I thought it best to keep going. I walked over to the road to check the surface grip. Two cars had passed by, cutting tracks down to wet pavement. If I followed those lines, I might be able to maintain traction.

Just then, three motorcycles magically materialized out of the fog of snow, passed by in single file, following the tire tracks at about five miles per hour, then evaporated again into white on white like a dream.

"Right. If they can do it, so can I!" I shouted.

With white knuckles and legs spread out ready to jump off if she went over, I edged the heavy bike back onto the road.

Soon I passed another motorcyclist on a Gold Wing, pulled to the side of the road with his pillion standing beside him like a snowman. A few minutes later, the other three bikes rematerialized ahead. They had since pulled over once courage failed them and common sense had taken hold. All three stood accumulating snow under the "Welcome to Montana" border sign.

I was thinking that maybe I had better stop again too, when I discovered that my wheels were no longer turning as I slid by the little group. Not wanting to show fear, I gave a small nod of knowing confidence and continued sliding down the mountain. Luckily, I was on a moderately long, straight stretch at the time.

Because this highway is so steep, it wasn't long before I had dropped enough altitude for the snow to change to rain, and I was back to rubber on wet, but ice-free, asphalt. I exited at the next pullout to remove the accumulation of snow, unwind, regroup and give thanks for my safety.

Soon the other bikers emerged out of the cloud and pulled up alongside. "Well, we saw you go by and said, 'Right. If he can do it, so can we!'" one of them cheerfully explained.

What had got us down that slope was actually our mistaken belief that it was possible – bolstered by false courage and the bravado displayed by each other as we leapfrogged our way down the mountain. I guess that's what they mean by "the blind leading the blind." Yet, once again it reminded me that so many achievements in life are based on the belief that something *can* be done.

What an exhilarating, adrenaline packed day! Even though the cloud cover prevented me from seeing the fantastic views and taking photos, I felt very much alive and very grateful for that fact.

And it was good to be back on home ground in the Big Sky State.

Montana Idaho Washington

MD 143.9.07.12:55

September 7, 2016

Still semi-frozen from the snow storm up on Beartooth Highway, I was keen to continue on down the valley for warmer climates. I only stopped in Red Lodge for gas. There was something going on with motorcycles because hundreds lined Main Street and the side roads. Finding a campground might prove interesting if not impossible.

Turns out the Honda Gold Wing Rally was the source of all the commotion. For the next few days there were large herds of Gold Wings roaming the highways, and a lot of them had trailers.

Deciding on whether to ride with a trailer is a tough call. It would be nice to have some extra space. However, in talking with a couple of the bikers while fueling up, it seems they were carrying certain things "just in case." When pressed, they admitted they never actually wore most of the clothes they had brought along.

With my limited wardrobe, and a sparse use of laundry facilities, I've always found it easy to get a seat in restaurants. People just seem to be leaving soon after I arrive. Seriously though, on this trip, I'd never really been in need of more than I had. And if I really did need something, I could drop into a store and buy it. Compared to what airlines charge for extra weight or an additional suitcase, I could easily afford to purchase another outfit and discard it before I headed home.

With Route 66 done and dusted, and my meandering trip back to Montana and then Washington nearly completed, the other big item on my "to do" list was just around the next bend. After a quick overnight stop in Billings to visit a couple of friends, it was on to Miles City for the All-Seventies high school reunion.

Amongst the bustle of greetings and getting reacquainted, I was surprised to see how old many of my former classmates had become, while I'd hardly aged at all. However, in this digital age, the obvious was undeniably presented to me via someone's high resolution iPhone camera, showing me that, dang, I too have aged. A lot.

One nice thing about a reunion that covered the entire decade of the 1970s was the opportunity to meet up with people a couple of years younger who I hadn't seen for many years. Which is also one of the bad things about this kind of gathering... I'd forgotten the names of half of them. The worst part was talking to someone for 20 minutes knowing that I knew them, and them knowing that I can't remember who they are, and them not telling me, and me too embarrassed to ask; them knowing that and me knowing they know, but not being able to do anything about it. You know?

Four women switched name tags. When I was talking with them, the faces were familiar and the names were familiar. It just wasn't the correct match-up. They derived great pleasure at my errors. Some people can be so mean. But fair enough – there were five guys with "Daryl" on their name tags.

My brother Allen and his wife Becky also made the reunion. Unfortunately, my sister and other brother didn't, which was a pity because we could have had a nice sub-reunion of our own.

A dance was held on Main Street while through-traffic was diverted around the block. People spilled out of the bars on either side of the street, had a dance or two and then flooded back inside for more refreshments. I rode the tidal surge in and out several times as required to keep the thirst quenched and my legs moving. I watched the spectacle and breathed fresh air outside. And breathed the smoky, alcohol-laden air inside. Danced and became part of the spectacle. And so it continued, until the wee hours of the morning. Although, as confirmation that I'm not as young as I use to be, I retired just after midnight.

Ok, ten o'clock.

The next day we had a BBQ in a city park bordering a lake. A portion of this lake had been roped off and framed with docks, delineating a swimming pool area for use in the summer holidays. With school now back in session, it had closed for the season two days previously.

Even so, two former female lifeguards from my class decided to go for a swim. I agreed to go with them but needed to collect my togs first. Impatience got the better of them and they went on ahead. They took great delight when the police called them out saying they had received word there were a couple of teenagers fooling around in the lake! Perhaps some have aged less than others.

For the last 40 years, I'd had personal belongings in storage either at my parents' house or my siblings' houses. It was now time to ship these remnants of my life in America back to New Zealand.

My grandfather originally homesteaded land near Fallon, about 48 miles to the north east of Miles City. He later sold this to purchase a farm in the same vicinity. Three generations later, that property is still in our family and I'd spent many a happy time there. It was also the location of some of my belongings, so I hired a pickup and made the journey to begin the retrieval and sorting process.

The old barn now stood like a drunkard just before the fall, but the grain bins I'd helped build were still standing resolute.

It was hard work, requiring many breaks over the three days of sorting through memories of the past. But to just step outside and feel the prairie breeze on my face, and smell sagebrush and recently harvested wheat lightened the load immensely. Finally, the culled remains were loaded into the pickup and brought back to Miles City where they were shifted into my brother's van and shipped off to Spokane. And I was back aboard my two-wheeled steed ready to continue west.

"The Interstate Highway system sure is a wonderful invention and feat of engineering," stated the salesman in the pinstriped suit as he finished ordering the lunch special. He'd engaged me in conversation from a nearby table in a diner just out of Forsyth. "Did you know, if you had a big enough gas tank you could travel from New York City to Seattle, Washington, without stopping?" He seemed happy with that fact.

"As it is, people tend to just nip off the Interstate at an off ramp, pump some gas, visit the toilets, grab a quick bite to eat at some fast-food outlet and back on the road again," said the waitress. Her name-tag read "Dorothy." "Hardly anyone comes all the way into town here to eat anymore."

"It's a very shallow way to travel," stated the old farmer with the red "Murdoch's Ranch & Home Supply" hat. "There's no opportunity to see how people in the towns actually live."

"No opportunity to eat at local diners and sample the local specialties," Dorothy continued as she proudly set a plateful of the lunch special before the salesman.

"Or visit and discover what others really think, and question the accuracy of the artificial polls presented in the media," I threw in for good measure, gaining some respect from the locals.

"The back roads take longer," protested the salesman, between shoveling mouthfuls.

"But there are historic markers where you can pull over and learn about the areas," I countered. "You can tell when you're crossing a river because the older bridge structures are often above you. The winding roads demand your attention and reward you with little surprises around the corners."

"Albeit, sometimes the surprise is a cow in the road!" laughed the farmer.

"The trees and hills and fences are close enough to reach out and touch at times," I continued. "And you gently arrive into small towns and big cities by driving through the outskirts and houses first."

"It's definitely a much more intimate and rewarding way to travel, explore and understand the country," Dorothy chimed in.

"More often than not, there's hardly any traffic," added another woman, from the end of the counter.

"In the past I've traveled more than my share via Interstate Highways or the fastest, shortest routes to get to my destination. Even when it wasn't necessary. But I have no remorse on taking alternate routes when time was not truly pressing," I added.

"I've driven the back roads and I can't tell you the number of times I've had to backtrack due to dead-ends or undriveable conditions," complained the salesman. "Time is money."

"Maybe true," said the farmer. "But time should also be spent living. And life is on the backroads."

Traveling up through central Montana brought me back into Harlowton – an end terminal for me during my years on the Milwaukee Railroad. The highway follows the tracks on and off, again bringing back memories and a

151

smile or two. Eventually the road diverged and I broke off the main line around Two Dot to ride through the Little Belt Mountains.

More memories flooded in, and an even broader smile, as I thought back to riding through these mountains on my Honda 250 in 1969. I was a lot older now, but some things don't change – like the honest sense of freedom experienced when following the desire to travel on two wheels. And then I suddenly realized that the dream I'd had back then of riding around having adventures on a Harley like Bronson had actually come to fruition.

A new dusting of snow lay over the Spanish Peaks, Absaroka's, Crazy's and Mission Mountains, reiterating that fall was here and winter comes early in this part of the country. Best to keep moving.

The cloudless blue sky I'd been enjoying over the last few days packed in just before Missoula. I rode into town in one of the few really heavy rains of the entire trip. In New Zealand, riding my Super Glide, rain came over the handle bars directly and struck my helmet visor. The wind speed then continued to push the rain off the visor, maintaining a relatively clear field of view. In America, the windscreen on the Heritage caused the wind to create a little vortex between myself and the handle bars. The rain still struck my helmet, but without direct wind to push it away, collected and remained, obscuring visibility. The only way to clear the visor was to lean far out to the side into the slipstream of direct wind. Of course, the shift in body weight required counter-balancing by leaning the bike over in the opposite direction. I was reminded of the old movies in which the Indians hung off the side of their horses to shoot under the neck at the cavalry. With no enemy to aim at, the soldiers would pull back in confusion. As did the surrounding motorists as I rode by.

High tailing it up to Kalispell, I stayed with Allen and Becky while the bike went in for another scheduled maintenance. I love it that Montana has no sales tax, so I try to do as much servicing and purchasing there as I can. I also collected more of my personal belongings from storage at their house. It's hard to believe how many things (read, "junk") we accumulate over our lifetime.

From Kalispell I headed back to Missoula – probably the coldest ride of the whole trip. My late departure to visit an old mate that morning meant there was no time to stop halfway for a cuppa and thaw out. Luckily, the afternoon warmed up and once again I took to the old highways and frontage roads as much as I could between the mountain passes. The leaves were just starting to turn, bringing shades of sap green and lemon yellow into contrast with the dark green and blue greens of the forest. Perfect.

Autumn sends the trees of the northeast into frenzied eruptions of vibrant reds, yellows and oranges, resulting in a multicolor carpet draped over the hills. The northwest, however, retains a blanket of dark greens and blues with intermittent explosions of brilliant yellows and oranges. They are a delightful surprise each time they appear.

When Mr. Hershey was asked why there were so many brown M&Ms in each package, he said, "The ratio of brown M&Ms in the mix ensures the colored ones stand out and look brighter." And so it is with trees.

The shorter days meant that dark arrived sooner. I cleared Fourth of July Pass and descended on down into the "Famous for Potatoes State" of Idaho with the impending twilight. Then though Coeur d'Alene along the lake in the early evening, where the calm waters reflected a deepening purple sky. And finally, back into the "Evergreen State" of Washington, to Liberty Lake just off the Interstate, arriving at my sister Judy's house about dark thirty.

Black Pearl's previous owner offered to store her for me over the winter so I could come back and ride the following year. What an opportunity! I washed and shined her up like new and we stowed her in the large shed under a tarp. The real reason for the offer became apparent when he advised he would start her up once a month to keep the engine happy. I think that made all three of us happy.

My last couple of days in the USA were spent finalizing the shipment of my belongings and trying to make myself useful doing odd jobs around the house to earn my keep.

And resting. I had no idea I was so tired. I think I needed a holiday.

Then, suddenly, it was time to board the big silver bird back home to New Zealand and put this adventure to bed.

So I did.

Book 4
New Zealand 2017

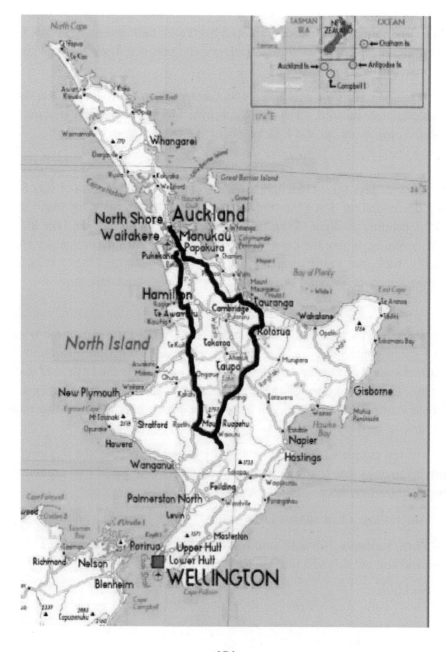

Filling in Time

MD 143.11.18.15.27
November 18, 2016

My trip along Route 66 and around the USA had been a real gasser. I'd ridden the emotional high of starring in my own movie for over three months. Life was in full Technicolor with Sensurround Sound and I felt so alive when I arrived back home in New Zealand. Unfortunately, without constant stimulus, it doesn't take long to lapse back into the mundane. Life settled into a routine. Sounds became muted. Things began to fade to black and white.

"Quit moping round," scolded Tristin. "We need to do something to liven things up. Let's take advantage of the good snowfall this year and go skiing at Whakapapa before the season ends."

"Great idea!" I said enthusiastically – and the weather agreed, offering up one of those rare weekends of crisp spring snow and near cloudless skies.

As you grow older, I think there's a disconnect between the brain and the body. The brain insists that the body can do things because it used to do them in the past. Perhaps the connection goes with the hearing, I don't know. But whatever the cause, the message isn't getting through.

> Brain: Oh wow, look at those moguls on that black diamond run. Let's go down there.

> Body: Hold on a minute. Those are pretty big moguls. I don't think we can handle it.

> Brain: What? We used to do much bigger ones than these all the time.

> Body: Key words here are "used to." I'm telling you, we've aged. The back and the knees are just not up to it anymore. Let alone the muscles. You're not in shape for this either.

> Brain: Awww, quit being a wimp. Here we go. Yeehaa!

About halfway down, my thighs were screaming bloody murder, and then I took a really impressive tumble.

Body: Owww. Ohhhh. Man that hurt, I told you! I told you! But would you listen? No.

Brain: Told me what? I don't know what happened there. I thought I could make that turn. Let's try it again.

Body: You're crazy. Are you even listening to me?

The upshot was my knees packed in about midday and I herniated a disk in my neck not long afterwards. That slowed me down a bit.

Since "slow" is not a speed I'm comfortable with, and the injury didn't present a problem for riding the Harley, I decided to tackle some more ABCs. I finally took a moment to properly read through the rules. Turns out, I'd been wasting my time taking photos in some areas (big things in the USA didn't count), while completely ignoring other areas that actually offered credits. I was further behind than I thought.

A short study of the map indicated a route whereby I could collect all nine points for big things in New Zealand, add another Harley-Davidson dealership, and collect three more regions, over a three-day counterclockwise ride around the North Island. The end of the year deadline was quickly approaching, and there were already plans for the Christmas holidays a mere four days away. Dare I say the saddle bags were packed and I was off the next morning?

Spring was in full swing and summer right on her heels. Deciduous trees were still in their new growth and flowers were abundant everywhere. The air was fragrant with their sweet smells. The bike roared like a lion as I accelerated, and purred once I reached cruising speeds.

I stopped at Ōtorohanga to visit the Kiwi House. The kiwi, New Zealand's national bird, is a shy little guy. The species' nocturnal nature means they're not seen too often in the wild. The Kiwi House have set up an internal room reminiscent of the bird's actual habitat, then fiddled with the lights to make the kiwis think it's night when it's actually day. They trundle around digging for bugs and grubs with their long beaks in the low-level lighting, right in front of one-way glass. Oblivious to the prying eyes of the tourists. At night their lights come on and they go to sleep when we do.

Afterwards, I stopped at a café for a cup of coffee and struck up a conversation with some people at the counter.

"Where you off to on that big bike of yours?" asked the older farmer in gumboots.

"Taking photos of big things for a competition," I said. "So far I've got the Big Apple at Waitomo, the Big Sheep and Dog at Tīrau and the Big Kiwi here."

"Well, there's also the Big Sheep Sheerer in Te Kuiti, the Ohakune Carrot, the Taihape Gumboot and the Taupō Trout," informed the younger farmer in a black singlet. He looked as if he'd been in an accident. His right eye was dark purple and swollen about halfway shut. On his forehead was a scrape with a rather large lump underneath, and he had a fat lip.

"Yup," I said, "they're on my list for tomorrow. But I had to stop to see the Kiwi House first."

"Did you like it?' asked gumboots.

"Yes. I found it especially interesting that the kiwi lays an egg that is 80 percent the size of herself!"

"I pointed that out to my nine-month pregnant wife last week when she was complaining of discomfort," said black singlet.

"How'd that go?" I asked surprised.

"Limited success," he lisped through his swollen lip.

And so here we are at last, where this book started. Riding the curves and bends on that sunny morning, I'd been feeling pleased with myself for ticking off so many mission objectives; I was chirping Christmas carols and on a high from my camping experience amongst the snow-effect of the flowering cottonwood trees in the Mangaokewa Scenic Reserve.

But that's when I'd seen that darn *Welcome to the Waikato Region* sign out of the corner of my eye, and felt the need to add it to my photo collection. Which had led to the fateful, ill-executed U-turn, and now here I was lying under the bike, on a logging truck route, in the middle of a narrow road, on a downhill slope, on a curve, with my left leg pinned under the motor, as the last couple of years of my life flashed before me.

Since it wasn't my whole life flashing before me, I figured I wasn't going to die. Nonetheless, dawdling about in retrospection or feeling sorry for myself wasn't the way to salvation.

Pushing with my right foot, I wiggled the other one out of my boot. Then, standing up and filled with adrenaline, I lifted the bike in one swift motion, turned it downhill, hopped on and coasted to the safety of a graveled area beside the road. Five minutes later, while I was still coming to grips with everything, a logging truck came barreling down the road and nearly ran over my fugitive boot. Thank you, Lord!

Since my leg and boot had provided a cushion, there wasn't a mark on Black Beauty. The few scratches on the boot could be polished out. A valuable lesson learned there. I never turn around on the highway anymore. Always at a turnout.

On the last leg of the trip, I passed through Matamata. Both *The Lord of the Rings* and *The Hobbit* trilogies had used this area as the location for Hobbiton. The visitor center has been given a makeover to make it look more like a hobbit tavern, including a round door and thatched roof. Just outside of town is the original film set, largely preserved and intact. And they're more than happy to take your money if you'd like to have look. I decided I would.

The countryside reeks of the Shire, with its green rolling hills and lush vegetation. Wandering around Hobbiton's lake and the offshoot trails to the underground hobbit houses made for a pleasant and relaxing afternoon. *The Lord of the Rings* magic was all around and I kept expecting to see Gandalf coming around the bend.

The hobbits themselves are actually a nice lot. Once you get them away from the touristy bits, they seem happy to open up and tell stories. Boy, can these big footed little guys put away the beer!

I'd obeyed the pull of the road, but I was also sensing the pull of the sea. That desire is never far below the surface. My plan to get out sailing more frequently during the summer months started off tentatively, then fizzled out altogether.

Although probably not helped by lying in the middle of the road, pinned by my bike, I thought my injured disk was more or less under control when I headed out into the Hauraki Gulf on *Bontekoe* with the intention of taking several days to reach Great Barrier Island for a week of R&R. But while raising the anchor on the second day, I felt a slight twinge once again. Followed shortly after by warning signs in the form of my left arm going numb and my neck not turning all the way to the left. Kind of hard to ignore. So regrettably, halfway to the Barrier, I did an about face and headed back to Auckland.

"Why me?" I queried forlornly. The winds were very light and I was more or less just bobbing along, trying to read a book and wallowing in self-pity. When I heard the first whoooshhhh….hiiisss, I raised my head. It sounded much bigger than a dolphin. I put down the book and stood up. Suddenly, just in front of me, the water changed texture and moments later a whale broke the surface. Whoooshhhh….hiiisss. Spray shot into the air right off the bow. A very *large* whale. Easily one and a half times the length of *Bontekoe*. And it was only a boat-length away! Due to the color of its skin, the shape of its dorsal fin and the sheer size, I believe it was a blue whale. My first ever sighting in all the sea miles I'd covered over the years.

It's hard to mope after being privileged with a sight like that. My mood immediately became buoyant as I sailed back to Oneroa Harbour at Waiheke Island. With lovely weather, I stayed at anchor there convalescing for several days, just reading books and watching the various antics in the busy anchorage. Float planes, stand-up paddle boarders, and dinghies choc-a-block with crew members commuting to and from shore.

The remainder of the summer was spent on short motorcycle rides around the Auckland area. Most of these were club rides with the HOGs. Within 30 minutes, riding south you can be out of the city and in the beautiful Hunua Ranges. Steep roads twisting through heavy forestation dropped us out into long straight stretches of flat marshland, before we headed back north on coastal routes with dynamic views out across the sparkling Waitematā Harbour and her islands. The shoreline changed between a mix of sandy beaches and rocky outcrops. Pōhutukawa trees lined the coast and often formed tunnels over the narrow roads.

The pōhutukawa is sometimes referred to as New Zealand's Christmas tree. Blooming from late November through to early January, each flower has a multitude of red stamen with bright yellow ends. While the flowers are a bright vibrant color when viewed up close, the overall effect from a distance becomes a dark, almost blood red, swathe that lines the coast.

Rides to the north of the city often ended at Puhoi.

Puhoi is home to the Puhoi Pub, which is a proper bikers' tavern. On any given weekend, several hundred bikes will be parked around the pub and up the side streets. Bikers spill out across the grass or stand under umbrella-shaded barrels out front. In less clement weather, they crowd around the pool tables under all sorts of memorabilia that hangs from the ceiling and plasters the walls.

There's no shortage of good biking in New Zealand.

Eventually, late summer arrived with more settled weather and it was time for the Iron Run to Queenstown in the South Island. The official rally started on the weekend of the 17th of March, but I thought leaving on the first of the month would give me more time to explore. "I want to make sure I get a good seat," I told people.

Another Beginning

North Island Start

MD 144.03.03.10:18
March 3, 2017

Come the first of March, I was shooting down the motorway at a good clip. Passing cars like they were standing still. Singing "Born to be Wild" at the top of my lungs. Open roads and blue sky in front of me. Blue sky above me. Blue and red lights behind me. Oh crap!

Turns out, it's illegal to sing on a motorcycle in the bus only lane.

Well, actually, singing on anything other than a bus in the bus only lane is illegal. And singing while on a bus, in my experience, is usually received with less enthusiasm than I would prefer.

"It's a bit confusing as to when bikes are allowed in the bus lane and when they aren't," I explained to the officer.

He suggested, "If you don't understand that the *BUS ONLY* sign means buses only, maybe there are serious considerations about having a vehicle license in the first place." And suddenly things were much clearer.

Then he said, "By the way, your warrant of fitness has expired. Typically, there's a one-month grace period."

"No problem," I replied cheerfully. "I'll get it today."

"I pointed out the one-month grace period because it expired two months ago," he said humorlessly.

Still singing, "Born to be Wild" under my breath, I hoped he would realize he was dampening my vibe. Maybe take the hint and get caught up in the spirit. Although, it's surprising how few of the younger generation have seen *Easy Rider* or heard of Steppenwolf.

Right! Get a WOF. Piece of cake.

The AA testing center couldn't do it because their motorcycle guy was out sick. The NZTA center could only do up to 250 cc. That left me about 1,300 cc's short. Two hours later I finally found a testing station capable of certifying me. And you can imagine my surprise to find the front brake pads were worn and the rear brake light sensor was out. Arriving at the Harley-Davidson dealership at 5:02 pm, I was too late. Oh well, you've got to give them marks for punctuality.

Long story short, two days later with a considerably lighter wallet, I was ready to set off again. Once more singing "Born to be Wild" in a soft voice as I loaded the bike.

Then came a phone call from Tristin's boyfriend, Jordan, requesting a coffee meeting. Seems there's hope for the younger generation yet. While he didn't know of Steppenwolf or *Easy Rider*, Jordan certainly knew how to impress by asking for permission to marry my daughter.

I had known this day was coming for some time. I gave him every argument I could think of to talk him out of it. But even when I pointed out the fact that I would be his father-in-law he wasn't dissuaded. So I definitely knew he was serious. Of course, I was overjoyed to have him join our family and gave my enthusiastic consent.

I agreed to hang around a couple more days so he could pop the question to an unsuspecting Tristin in a romantic setting, and I would be available to act surprised when she told me, see the ring, and hear how it all went down. It went down wonderfully!

While I was sitting around waiting, I spent some time on the internet looking up a few geography facts about New Zealand. I thought they might come in handy for emails to friends about my trip.

New Zealand is roughly three quarters the size of the state of Montana with a population of about 4.5 million to Montana's 850,000. But what's not immediately obvious in these statistics is how long and skinny the country is.

San Diego, California, is 34 deg north while the top end of New Zealand, Cape Reinga, 34 deg south.

Tacoma, Washington, is 47 deg north against New Zealand's southern-most tip, Stewart Island, at 47 deg south.

So basically, over the length of its three main islands New Zealand is roughly the length of the US west coast. South of the Auckland city center, the North Island narrows down to just over the length of three football fields wide.

Cook Strait separates the North and South Island with enough distance to provide a proper ocean sailing experience. I'd be taking the three and a bit hour ferry ride across with the bike on my upcoming trip.

There are miles of coastline and the prevailing southwest winds make for superb sailing. One of the main reasons I still live here. New Zealand has a proud sailing history. At the time writing, we have won the America's Cup four times.

Including the Southern Alps, there are twenty-some mountain ranges to be crossed or skirted when moving around the country. Several peaks are in the 9,750 ft (2,970 m) range with Mt. Cook being the highest at 12,218 ft (3,724 m).

Captain Cook explored much of this land from the sea, so everywhere you turn, his name is bantered about. Just like Lewis and Clark in the northwest of US. Except Cook also explored quite a bit of the Pacific Northwest coast as well.

The indigenous people are the Māori. They called this country Aotearoa - land of the long white cloud. Their language, Te Reo Māori, is spoken quite commonly and accounts for many of the names of the towns, streets and such. The wh is pronounced f. Wai means water, so you see it appear often for the names of rivers, bays and harbors. "Kia ora" means hello.

And did I mention that the *Lord of the Rings* and *Hobbit* trilogies were filmed here? If you enjoyed the scenery in those movies, you can't help but love New Zealand.

This was my third trip to the South Island aboard Black Beauty.

I had two key destinations in mind for the adventure – Queenstown for the rally, 1000 mi (1600 km) from Auckland, and Bluff, a further 124 mi south, to reach the bottom of the South Island. Then home. The rest I'd figure out on the way and I expected to treble the standard distance by taking shortcuts, back roads and scenic routes.

My big push for HOG ABC points just before Christmas had paid off. I'd secured third place and a $500 prize. The first Kiwi to win a prize. With the start of a new year, the ABC competition restarted, and I figured I could do better.

I really enjoyed the contest. It was like a yearlong scavenger hunt. The real beauty of the competition lies in discovering items off the beaten track. Previously, I'd passed through so many small towns on the main streets and highways without really stopping to see what else was there. Usually, the sign or object I needed to find was one or two blocks off the main road. And while searching, I'd found all kinds of interesting things I hadn't even known existed.

Besides the challenge of finding the items, and therefore providing some direction for my trip, first place carried a prize value of $1,000. I was motivated. Now that I knew what I was up against, I decided to go all out in 2017 with a focused intent to win.

All in good sport. With a carrot at the end to boot.

Now, if I could just get underway.

North Island from the Top

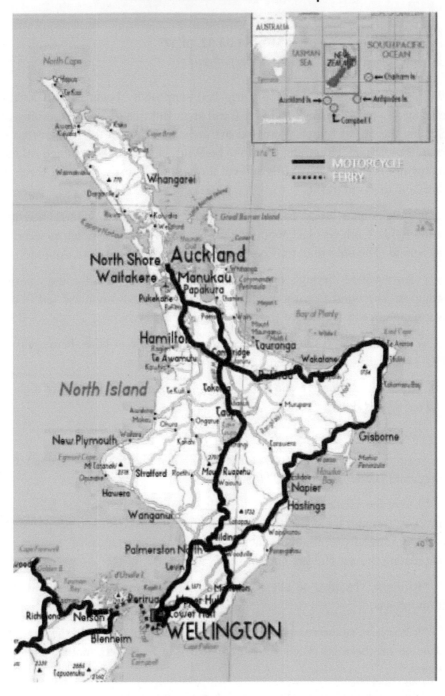

March 7, 2017

Well, in the four days since my trip had supposedly begun, I still hadn't managed to pass the Auckland City Limit sign. But finally, on the morning of Sunday the 5th of March, I crossed the invisible line... in the regular traffic lane, I might add. Humming, "Born to be Wild," I immediately turned off the motorway at the Bombay Hills and cut through back roads, weaving through farmland to avoid traffic.

In Auckland's "food basket," windrows of harvested onions lined the onion fields. Corn was just about ripe for harvesting, and the potatoes weren't far behind. The only rural traffic was an occasional tractor or ute. And me.

I downshifted through the curves and opened up the throttle on the straights. The wind flowing over the handlebars against my chest felt like a warm embrace as it caressed the leather against my body.

When I arrived in Gisborne, I recognized a couple of bikes belonging to HOG members and backed into the carpark next to them.

"Hey Poet. Rabbit," I said nodding to the brothers as I pulled out a chair and sat myself down.

"Good day for it," said Rabbit. "Which way did you come?"

"Every day is a good day for a ride," I smiled. "Came through the Fitzgerald Glade, Rotorua and Hicks Bay."

"I love the Glade," said Poet. "It feels so intimate the way the hilly road traverses through the dense forestation of ferns, underbrush and ponga. Such a warm, friendly feeling of enclosure. And the fragrance of evergreens permeating the air. Hmmm hmmm."

"Riiiiight," I said. I do like how the tree branches span over the road and form tunnels.

"Yesterday, sunbeams penetrated the occasional openings in the canopy. Dancing on the road. Then we plummeted right back into another emerald tunnel."

"Did you go to the hot springs in Rotorua?" inquired Rabbit.

"No. I just stopped to take my ABC photo." The thermal activity in Rotorua is a lot like Yellowstone Park, so seeing the geysers and bubbling mud wasn't that much of a novelty for me. "I was planning on stopping at a campground on the lake but I missed the turnoff and wound up carrying on in the dark to a wetlands reserve campground at Matatā."

"So, you came around East Cape today?" asked Poet.

"Yeah. Last year my rear wheel bearings went out when I tried to round East Cape, so I felt a sense of obligation to complete what I had started," I explained. "Perfect day for it. And the views out to the ocean were stunning as I powered up and purred down the Raukūmara Range. Blue on blue on blue."

"Bet you had a good view of White Island today," said Rabbit. "Could you see any steam?"

"Sure did. It looked a lot closer than 50 kilometers (30 miles) away too."

Tristin and I had anchored at this live volcano en route to our circumnavigation of the South Island some years before. By morning, orange sulfur ashes had covered our boat. The oranges, reds, browns and yellows of the rock and soil were so dramatic, I'd faced aft looking at them until they blended together as we sailed away. The memory was still strong enough to bring the colors vividly back to my mind.

"We've just arrived from Wairoa via the back road," said Poet. "It has everything you want. Scenery, hills, curves and twists. And vacant of traffic!"

"Yeah, I highly recommend you take that route," added Rabbit.

So I did.

Traversing this country must have been a real challenge back in the old days. The highway rolled gently up and down the hills as you would expect. But that gave a misleading impression of the nature of the terrain. Suddenly there was a gorge, cutting sharply down about 325 ft (100 m), and only 65 ft (20 m) wide. People would have had to backtrack forever to find a crossing point. That's typical of New Zealand. Nowadays it certainly makes for interesting bridges and stunning views.

There are two primary wine belts in New Zealand. One is positioned between Gisborne and Hastings. What corn is to Iowa, grapes are to this area.

I located a couple of the vineyards that make some of my preferred wines, which adds a level of enthusiasm and enjoyment, because I can now picture the vineyard as I drink the product.

Just before I arrived in Napier, I witnessed an odometer milestone event. Firstly, the turning over of 99,999.9 km. Followed shortly thereafter by 100,000.0 km. Woohoo! I pulled over to take a photo and all the cows came to the fence to see what the yelling was about. That's a pretty good distance to have traveled on a bike. And I still had four to five thousand kilometers, or about three thousand miles, left to cover on this trip.

In 1931, Napier was destroyed by a magnitude 7.8 earthquake. In the great tradition of the Kiwi "can do" spirit, the townspeople decided to rebuild as quickly as possible, and it just so happened that the event occurred right in the middle of the Art Deco era. Therefore, the majority of the buildings follow that design vernacular. Government bureaucracy wasn't well established, leaving people to get on with recuperating, rebuilding and life in general. Within two years, 110 buildings had been rebuilt. Keep in mind that no high-tech building equipment was in play, and that most of the work was done by hand. There was minimal insurance back then. People had to just bite the bullet and move on.

The town is famous for its Art Deco Festival in the summer month of February, with vintage vehicles coming from around the country, and people dressing in period clothing. It's also become a destination stop with things like Host a Murder Mystery weekends, where the whole community joins in the fun. At the least, it's always a vibrant place to pause and have a cup of coffee.

Heading south, out of Woodville I watched the rain clouds descend from the Ruahine Ranges, and then in the pass to Palmerston North the sky began to look ominous and threatening. After only 20 minutes of riding in the rain, I stopped and set up camp for the night. The campground was nothing more than a field behind a community hall. But they had the nicest hot showers.

By midmorning the next day, the wind had blown the clouds away and continued to blow as if it wanted to make sure they didn't come back.

Located between the Tararua and Ruahine Ranges, wind generators relied on a steady wind funneling though the pass. The single solar panel and wind generator on my boat puts out enough power for me to live on, if I'm conservative. These puppies take care of 39,000 households.

Carrying along to the west coast, I arrived at the small town of Bulls. "Bulls" seems a strange name for a town and I'm not sure of its origin. But they have a Big Bull constructed of timber, which I intended to photograph for my ABC points. I was delighted to discover that the whole town had taken to playing on the name. The police department was identified by the sign "Const a Bull," the library was "Read a Bull," the public toilet was "Relieve a Bull" and, my personal favorite, "Soci a Bull" for the Town Hall. I mean the whole thing was Laugh a Bull. I went Bull is tic.

Sometimes I crack myself up.

Hanging onto the handlebars for dear life as the wind continued to build, I made my way down the west coast as far as Greys Road, where I turned inland, up over the mountain range to Upper Hutt. Cut into the side of the mountain, the road offered spectacular views to the ocean. Unfortunately, the wind was blowing so hard, it had not only blown the clouds away, it had already pushed in the next batch. Consequently, three quarters of the ride wound its way up in a light drizzle on wet roads. But nothing could take the shine off this very beautiful, narrow, twisting, scenic ride. Bikers' heaven.

It seemed like every few kilometers I passed signs related to *The Lord of the Rings*. So many scenes from the movie were filmed in this area, including the park next to the campground where I stayed along the Hutt River. After a while, it becomes a bit like the "George Washington slept here" mania in the US. The trilogy was, after all, very long. So there's plenty of mileage to be gained from it.

The Cook Strait ferry lay in her berth awaiting our midday passage as Black Beauty and I arrived in New Zealand's capital, Wellington, on yet another blustery day. After purchasing my ticket, I still had enough time to travel around the bay to Eastbourne. Yes, it was to get the letter E. This was one of those occasions when I undertook a ride I'd never have made ordinarily. Yet it was remarkably invigorating and rewarded me with a completely different view of the city and harbor.

With the crossing imminent, and another ABC point under my belt, I felt like I could slow down and relax. I'd really enjoyed getting into the spirit of this trip. Starring in my own movie again as I traveled down the North Island.

Looking up at the high sides of the ferry as it rested at the dock, I smiled and squinted my eyes until everything faded to black.

"Cut!" I said, opening my eyes. "That's a wrap."

South Island

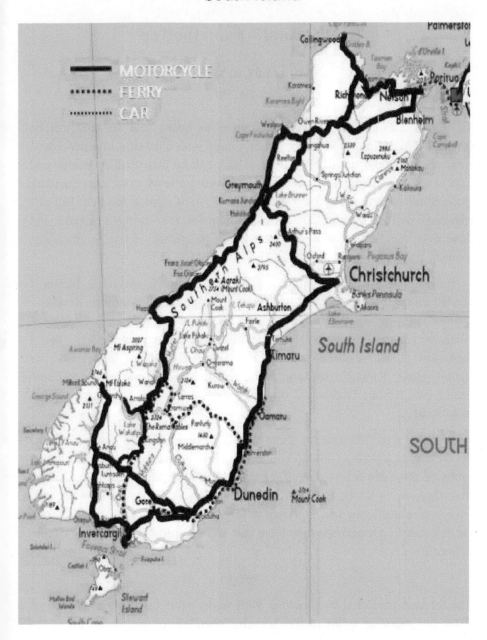

South Island – From the Top

MD 144.03.10.15:22

March 10, 2017

The Cook Strait ferry allows motorcycles to board first so they can be strapped down. I motored up the loading ramp with a handful of other riders. After disabling our anti-theft alarms (which can be activated by bumps and rolls at sea), we all trundled on up to the passenger level as the cars boarded. Cook Strait can get pretty hairy when strong winds oppose the tide. But this crossing was fine, over mild seas of six to ten feet (two to three meters), and downright majestic once we entered the calm waters of the Marlborough Sounds.

Releasing the tie-downs on Black Beauty once we arrived at Picton, I headed off on the Queen Charlotte Track, through the Marlborough Sounds – another fantastic curvy road that follows the shoreline with occasional rises where you can pull over and look out across peaceful bays and inlets. Have I mentioned that New Zealand is a wonderful country? Especially for motorcyclists. Fantastic scenery. Good roads. Minimal traffic. Even better once I got off State Highway 1 (the main road that travels the length of both main islands).

I located a pullout near the shore with a gravel beach and pitched my tent for the night. A young German couple did likewise and proceeded to enjoy a romantic interlude before dark. Then again, just after dark. And then again at least three more times, before the grand finale just after sunrise. I suppose once you're inside the tent, it's easy to forget that sound travels right through the thin fabric. Or perhaps they were just showing off the wondrous vitality of youth.

The forecast predicted bad weather with heavy rains for the next few days. After my morning swim in the Sounds, I headed for Nelson to await the passing of the storm, rest up and explore the city.

It rained so hard that the hundreds of red splotches from all the mosquitoes I'd killed back in the States were nearly washed away. Rain in

New Zealand doesn't mess around. It's not unusual for 150 mm (six inches) to fall in the space of two days, yet still leave lots of blue sky between the heavy bouts.

Between deluges, I managed to scoot into town for a movie – a recent remake of *King Kong*. It was fairly good but kind of funny that it was set in the early 70s. Oddly, I don't remember hearing anything in the news about a giant gorilla on an island back then. But my mind might have been elsewhere in those days. Anyway, using that time period allowed them to introduce helicopters and modern weapons to help keep the storyline at bay, while also discovering more creative ways to blow things up.

"Be sure and go all the way out to the end of Cape Farewell and see Farewell Spit," said the cashier at the petrol station. "When the tide's out the beach is enormous."

"Hundreds of whales have run aground there," added another local standing nearby.

"What causes that?" I asked

"I suspect it's because it's so shallow for so far, they get confused trying to determine which direction offers escape," he speculated.

The Tākaka Hill crossing was an exhilarating ride with switchbacks, vistas and scenery. The entire ride was spent playing peek-a-boo with the rain clouds. From there on, the road followed the coast all the way to the campground at the end of the spit.

Farewell Spit lived up to all the hype and on the way back I saw a sign saying "The Source." Intrigued, I took the diverging one-way metaled road to investigate. From the carpark, there was a beautiful little walk up alongside a swift stream overflowing its banks. Then before me appeared the Source itself – a fully-fledged gush of water spewing right out of a rock face at ground level. It was remarkably like the Eternal Springs I had visited in the Taroko Gorge in Taiwan. Yet another of those unexpected and impressive surprises.

While trying to set up the tent in the Department of Conservation (DOC) campground at Lake Rotoroa, I was visited by the South Island's most unwelcome inhabitants. Sandflies! These little buggers are half the size of a mosquito and pack a much more annoying bite.

Where a mosquito is like a modern water drilling rig, her long proboscis making a clean hole in search of blood, the sandfly comes in chewing away like a thirst-crazed idiot with a pick and shovel, wreaking devastation and destruction to the whole area.

Starting at the feet, they work their way upwards looking for any available opening. They are attracted to heat, odor, color, shape, movement and sound. And are most active between the hours of 12:15 pm to 11:59 am. I've heard they don't like windy days and perhaps that's when they rest and recuperate. However, in an unscientific test, I once accelerated up to 72 kph (45 mph), before the six attached to my hand finally let go.

Within five minutes of getting off the bike, I looked like my favorite polypropylene nightshirt after the time I mistakenly washed and dried it with my new flannel sheets. Approximately 3.62 bazillion black spots were scattered randomly over the whole of my being.

Each one was aggressive. And they were relentless. Getting into the tent and zipping it shut without letting in a swarm of 3,000 was a challenge.

The upshot of this was a campground supporting 20 spaces populated by only four tents, three RVs and two cars, with everyone sheltering inside. Tourists would arrive, jump out of their car, run over to the lake – which was absolutely stunning, by the way – take a photo, and run for their very lives back to the safety of their vehicle. This is the main reason photos on brochures look like it would only be you enjoying this pristine undiscovered mountain lake. Because, if you were standing out there, you would probably be the only human there. Notice I did not say you would be alone.

"I'm going to file a complaint," I told the DOC worker as he stepped out of his truck to inspect the campground.

"Why?" he asked with a concerned look on his face.

"You have let these poor sandflies breed beyond their food source. They're so famished they will eat anything that moves!"

He laughed gently. "Yeah, they're hungry little buggers," he said with what sounded like a hint of good-natured affection.

"It's inhuman," I reiterated while rapidly retreating back to safety of my tent, slapping my exposed forearms.

The Punakaiki Pancake Rocks are located in Paparoa National Park along the rugged West Coast highway. Besides being a fascinating rock formation, looking – as the name suggests – like stacked pancakes, there are blowholes and a turbulent cauldron to see. The best activity occurs during high tide when the sea is rough. And today it was. Water spewed high into the air as it shot out of the blow holes. Usually preceded by a deep *barooommmm* as the waves reached the end of a tunnel and looked for a place to expend their energy.

The West Coast is known for its rain and, unfortunately, the weather hadn't cleared as forecast. The stunning road and coastline weren't at their best in the dank conditions. But then I'm not at my best every day either. It was still beautiful.

I spent the night in Greymouth, gateway to Arthur's Pass, instead of carrying on in the rain. Arthur's Pass is such a beautiful ride, and I would much rather see it on a nice day. Sleeping on the beach, I listened to the surf roar all night. In the early morning mist, the rain began to clear, and the full moon, just above the horizon, played peek-a-boo amongst the clouds. Sunrise painted the clouds yellow and orange. I basked in the glory of it all as I took my morning walk along the surf-line, recharging my soul.

It all reminded me why I love to travel. People who live in an area, witnessing the same thing day in and day out, might become numb to the splendor and not really *see* their surrounds. Whereas everything is new to me as a visitor, and I'm more apt to really *see* and appreciate. Couple those fresh eyes with the tactile awareness of weather on the motorcycle, after a day riding in the rain a sunny day is like ending a fast and sitting down to a feast.

South Island – The Middle Bit

MD 144.03.13.12:42
March13, 2017

Waiting for the rain to clear before attempting Arthur's Pass was a wise decision... a real blessing, since I make so few.

Arthur's Pass is another brilliant place to ride. The weather started out cloudy and more than a little windy. Not to mention quite nippy. *I'll wear my thermals starting tomorrow*, I promised myself while stopping for a cuppa to warm up and wake up. Then off I went up the lovely winding mountain-pass road.

There is a bridge near the top called the Ōtira Viaduct. In 1999, the viaduct replaced a narrow two-lane road that used to snake down one side of the steep gorge and up the other. Rock slides had posed a continuous danger and caused road closures. Portions of the old road can still be seen below from the vista point overlooking the valley, along with areas completely covered by rock slides. In its day, it must have been a great bike ride.

After the pass, I came to a place called Castle Hill. Another filming location for *The Lord of the Rings*, the rock formations there appear really striking from the road and I'd always wanted to stop.

So I did.

It's a popular place for picnics. Flat grassy spaces are surrounded by huge stones providing a sense of privacy. Trails meander throughout the hillside. Walking around each corner exposed a new and different vista. They are just limestone rocks, but their shapes and placements are in such a fashion as to create awe-inspiring views. Some were arches and others formed narrow passages between eroded forms. I'm sure the Hopi would have quickly filled in the voids to make a small city in no time.

I whizzed right along after leaving the park, as I was beginning to feel the time pressure of getting down to Invercargill and back to Queenstown in time for the rally, stopping only to collect a few letters like Y at Yardhurst – the only Y in New Zealand.

Christchurch, the largest city in the South Island, had been struck by a 7.1 magnitude earthquake in 2010, followed by a 6.2 the following year. Similar to Napier, there were deaths and major destruction in the city. In the advanced age in which we live, city councils, insurance companies and lawyers have become well ensconced in society and have had sufficient time to prefect their bureaucracy. And thus, for no apparent reason, are able to prevent people from moving on and rebuilding.

Five years after the second quake, rubble was still piled high around the city center and the city's namesake cathedral. Public officials, insurance companies and owners had argued over who was responsible, who'd pay, who'd approve new works, and most importantly, who'd get the lucrative new building contracts. Substantial parts of Christchurch weren't even at the stage where reconstruction could commence. A significant number of people had homes that were deemed unfit to live in by council, but the insurance companies had prevented demolition until inspections had been reviewed, and so on. Meanwhile the people were in limbo with no place to live. Many just deserted the city in frustration.

I rode around looking at the cavernous voids between the remaining buildings and a couple of new construction projects finally getting underway. The differences between Christchurch and Napier, the two historical periods and the social expectations of the times, were simply astounding. With modern materials, technologies and equipment, the rebuild should have been long since completed with only the finishing touches being applied.

One interesting bit of architecture was the new "Transitional Cathedral" designed by the Japanese architect Shigeru Ban, who employed large diameter cardboard tubes to quickly construct a new building. Perhaps the new structure will have a shorter lifespan, but it was completed and up and running by 2013, providing a significant symbol of hope for the community.

On the way out of town, I paused for a quick stop at the local Harley-Davidson dealership for another ABC point. They were hosting a BBQ for participants in the Iron Run, cheering them southwards en route to Queenstown. It's always a joy to hang out with other bikers. After a beer and a couple of sausages it was decision time. Any more beer and I would have to stay. I decided I could still make Timaru before dark, so I said my thanks and goodbyes then took to the road again.

I don't think I was 15 minutes out of town when a light mist set in, which changed to drizzle, then became full-on rain showers. I decided that reaching Timaru for the night wasn't worth the effort.

Apart from the hazards mentioned near the beginning of this book, riding in the rain is an interesting experience when it lasts for a long period. Initially you're all bundled up, warm and dry. Visibility is an issue, especially at lower speeds when, without a slipstream, the face shield retains splattered water droplets. Like driving without windshield wipers. You can sort of see but not very well. And, it's annoying.

Then there comes that moment when water finds its way in around the collar. It's perceived as a cold spot on the side of the neck at first. Then it collects until there's enough for a small trickle. It works its way down along the side of the chest and then the stomach until its progress is finally arrested by the belt. Resulting in little shivers.

Water's persistence means it doesn't take long until it finds another weak spot and continues on downwards. As more moisture continues to enter, it follows the known route at first. Then the wet channel from the neck down slowly spreads wider. Gently cooling the body. Only slightly in the beginning.

But it's not until you feel the cold trickle along the side of the left testicle that a major shiver is sent up your spine. When that cold trickle makes the final part of its journey into the crevice between the buttocks, it becomes obvious that all is lost. Shortly after, your cotton underwear wicks the cold wet throughout the entire crotch area until complete saturation is achieved. And ultimately, total immersion.

My rain gear is of advanced design. With no less than six seams culminating between the legs, the rain is able to bypass the neck entry completely and head directly for the crotch. It only takes 17 minutes for the rain to find this point of access. I'm not sure why the designers of rain gear insist on so many seams all culminating in this region.

The hardest part is going into a restaurant or campground office to book a tent space looking like you've just wet yourself. Of course, I feel the need to explain, "No really! It's the design of the pants!"

178

And then – the wise cracks, "If you're incontinent, maybe you're too old to ride?" And other insinuations of this nature.

Worst still, is the silent treatment which begins with *the look*. Then averted eyes. Followed by a slow shaking of the head.

Besides the fact that sitting on a bike with a wet crotch isn't much fun, knowing there won't be dry clothes to change into once you arrive doesn't help... let alone the knowledge that tomorrow, no matter what the weather, the day will start with that same cold, wet crotch.

I am sharing all this with you so that you'll understand my frame of mind while in the parking lot outside of Starbucks, watching the dark moisture-laden nimbus clouds rolling in up ahead. In a moment of enlightened desperation, I decided I would beat Mother Nature at her own game. Rather than suffer the anticipated dread of that first cold wet trickle, I pulled out the elastic waistband of my rain pants and poured the remaining half cup of warm coffee into my lap. Laughing gleefully. The end result and indignation would be the same, but this way, I would get at least 30 minutes of warmth at the beginning. Ha! Gotcha!

It felt marvelously warm.

However, I had neglected to consider the woman in the car parked next to me. She was a nurse on her way to work at Happy Dale Home, just outside of Timaru, and long story short, she turned out to be a nice and understanding lady.

"You look like you could use a dry place to sleep and we have a spare room available," she offered. "Follow me, it's just up the road." And waved me on as she departed.

Their facility was warm but fairly bleak. And for some reason the door handle was missing on the inside of my room. No worries, it was nice to dry out as I placed my clothes on the radiator.

"Come along," she invited, opening the door the next morning. "I'd like to introduce you to some of my doctor friends."

The four of us had a long and slightly perplexing conversation over a nice cuppa. Finally, I said, "Thank you so much for the room and coffee and, ahh, interesting discussion, but I'll just be moving on now."

"Oh, but this has been so interesting and there is so much more we would like to ask you," said the doctor in the white coat. They seemed rather reluctant to let me go and kept encouraging me to stay and talk some more. But I can only drink so much coffee.

"Thanks, but I really do need to get to the rally," I explained as I skirted around the table, grabbed my helmet and managed to buzz myself out the front door.

When I reached Black Beauty, and readied myself for the next leg to Dunedin, I noticed a big irregular dark shape under the bike. *Uh-oh*, I thought. Then I looked down and there was one underneath me too. It took me a few moments to realize it was a shadow. It'd been that long since I'd had sunny days.

With luck, the rain was gone for a while.

I waved farewell to the slightly concerned-looking little group that had gathered outside Happy Dale to see me off, and then I was away.

South Island – To the Bottom

MD 144.03.20.16:43
March 20 2017

At a rest stop before arriving at Dunedin, I noticed another dark spot under the bike. Unfortunately, this one was not a shadow. I figured the oil was from a leaking seal. I decided it would probably be best to address the issue in Dunedin as that would be the last time I would be near a Harley-Davidson dealership for a while.

"The good news is it's not the seal," said the Harley service manager.

"And the bad news?" I asked flippantly.

"A bearing has gone in the transmission," he replied gravely. And your belt is due for replacement.

"And?" I asked suspiciously.

"And the parts will have to be ordered from Australia." He paused as I began to absorb the severity of the situation. Then he made the dreaded statement, "And won't be here until after the rally."

One of the worst things a biker can do is show up to a bike rally without a bike. When they told me I couldn't take my bike to the rally, I panicked for a minute, then remembered my cousin's age-old wisdom: "The main thing is... never get excited." I managed to calm down, get hold of myself and tried to stay objective and focused. It wasn't easy. In addition to the disappointment, it was all going to be *very* expensive. Bugger!

The only viable option was to hire a car and drive to the rally. How embarrassing.

Dispirited, leaving Black Beauty in the care of the Harley dealership, I followed the path I had planned to ride down to Bluff and collected my patch for reaching the southern tip of the South Island. The nice thing about being in a car was that I could listen to music and buy lots of junk food. The downside was having to pass all the ABC stops along the way. I'd have to come back later with the bike to collect my points.

Of course, now that I was sitting in the comfort of an enclosed vehicle, the weather had cleared and the days were filled with a brilliant blue sky. I grudgingly noticed that the refreshed landscape was especially green and vibrant. At that point I think I would have been happier if it was raining.

Bluff is known for its oysters – and they were in season. While not cheap, they were fresh and *ohhh sooo gooood*! I bought a six pack that came in a box on ice, and sitting on the rocks looking across the bay, savored them one at a time in the warm sun.

While technically not the southern-most point, Bluff is considered the end of the South Island. And similar to Cape Reinga in the far north, there is a signpost showing the distances to various places. The South Pole is a mere 3,000 miles away. On such a glorious, calm day, Stewart Island (Rakiura) can easily be seen in the distance across Foveaux Strait.

There is a sculpture on the mainland at Bluff consisting of a clevis pin with giant chain links attached, which run down into the water. At the entrance to Rakiura National Park on Stewart Island, the other half of the sculpture has the chain links coming up out of the water and attaching to another pin. One school of thought suggests it's keeping Stewart Island from drifting away. Another is based on legend in which the South Island is a giant waka and Stewart Island is an anchor.[3] In any event, it's a very clever artwork.

Heading back almost due north, I stopped for a picnic lunch alongside the lake just outside of Queenstown to relax and absorb the beauty of the landscape. The mountains just to the east of the lake are known as the Remarkables. Descending right down into the lake where the Devil's Staircase road winds along above the shoreline, they truly live up to their name.

The festivities of the Iron Run motorcycle rally started in earnest the day after I arrived, with registration, demo rides, clothing sales and thunder rides. I signed in and set out to explore.

---

3. According to Māori legend, the demigod, Māui, hauled up a giant fish, Te Ika-a-Māui (the fish of Māui – the North Island), using his canoe, Te Waka a Māui (the waka of Māui – the South Island), with Rakiura, also known as Te Punga o Te Waka a Māui (the anchor of the waka of Māui – Stewart Island), as his anchor.

My first action was to put my name down on the list for a demonstration ride. The short cruise along Lake Wakatipu to Closeburn helped satisfy my craving to be back on two wheels.

"Well, what do think of the Fat Boy?" asked a biker in buckskin leathers with fringed sleeves and chaps. I immediately recognized him as a fellow member of the Auckland HOG chapter.

"Hey Donkey," I said dismounting. "It's a nice ride. But not quite what I expected."

"How so?"

"I rode the Street Glide earlier this morning and was pleasantly surprised," I explained. "And I can't help but compare." I kept thinking of the heated handgrips and how nice they were on the chilly ride. And the large GPS screen showing the road ahead. And the way it seemed to hunker down around the curves.

"Definitely the best way to understand bikes," Donkey concurred. "Same day, same weather, same route and the same mental attitude."

"True enough. I feel like I got an honest comparison."

"So, will that be cash or charge?" asked Donkey with a smirk.

"Hey, no pressure there!" I laughed. "Luckily, since I'm already the owner of two Harley-Davidsons, I'm going to have to give it a miss." *At least for the time being*, I thought to myself.

"See you tonight then," he said walking over to another biker who'd just completed a demo. "So, what do you think of that Sportster?" I heard him say.

That night was the St. Patrick's Day main event which, as you would expect, carried a strong Irish theme. I'd purchased a green top hat at the Two Dollar Store to blend in. There was live music, several food stalls and, of course, the required green beer. Everyone seemed to be enjoying themselves. I was drinking and laughing and drinking and singing and drinking and telling stories and drinking. Hell, I even thought I was dancing until someone stepped on my hands.

Somehow almost everyone was able to navigate their bikes to the main Thunder Run by 10:00 am the next morning. Cradds, the director of the Auckland HOG chapter, noticed my forlorn look and offered to take me along as a pillion. It was the first time I'd ridden pillion on a Harley since the impressionable age of 16. On that occasion, I'd nearly fallen off while riding behind my buddy Pat on his brother's Electra Glide when he opened up the throttle. Cradds' bike wasn't equipped with a backrest, and some things never change, as I nearly fell off again.

Crowds gathered around the hundreds of bikes parked next to each other. Anticipation built as everyone mounted their bikes ready to depart. Then the air literally vibrated with the sound of the engines. Exhaust fumes and the smell of leather filled the nostrils. Marvelous!

HOGs typically ride in a staggered formation – two seconds behind the bike in front and one second behind the bike to the side. That set-up allows time to react to changes in traffic and emergencies. It also prevents unwanted cars from entering into the formation. The flow of bikes numbered over 1,200 on this ride and Cradds and I were about 200 back from the front.

Once again, the streets and highways were lined with young and old alike. The entire procession took nearly 45 minutes to pass by, bike after bike, testing both the patience of some of the motor vehicles on the side roads and the stamina of my arm as our bike's designated waver. After a while I developed a technique similar to the Queen's wave – a minimal rotation of the wrist from the 12 o'clock to 2 o'clock position directed at those on the right hand side, then switch and repeat to those on the left. When we crested a hill or took a long curve, there were motorcycles ahead as far as the eye could see. Similarly, looking in the rear-view mirror or turning my head revealed headlights back to... forever.

The last of the riders were leaving Queenstown just as the leaders arrived at our destination in Arrowtown. Bikes were directed to park down the main street, where cars had been prohibited for the day. Even parked handlebar to handlebar on both sides of the main street, two side streets and a large carpark were soon filled to capacity.

When not overrun with hundreds of motorcycles, Arrowtown is a quaint old gold mining town. I returned again once the rally was over to spend some time in a more relaxed style. Included in the preservation and restoration of the main town, a replica settlement of the type built by Chinese miners was positioned along the riverfront. Most of the buildings were simple lean-tos against the cliff face or small cabins constructed by stacking flat rocks for walls and topped with a corrugated roof. Several also used corrugated metal for their fireplace chimneys. Since the primary focus was on getting gold, becoming rich and leaving again, it's easy to understand the temporary nature of the structures and their design. In some respects, the dwellings were similar to those of the Hopi, only using more modern materials. During its heyday in the 1860s, Arrowtown was a thriving little community and would have been something to witness.

Next, I drove up to the Cardrona ski field for the view. From there you can see another ski hill across the valley high up in the Remarkables, and the switch backs of the access road rising upwards. The road appears deceptively innocent from a distance, but having ridden the ski bus to the top with Tristin in the past, I can vouch for the validity of my daughter's anxiety when looking out the side window and seeing nothing between us and the valley floor below.

There was no snow on Cardrona just yet, but it wouldn't be long.

The Rockies may be higher overall, but these mountains rise from an altitude not far above sea level, making them quite dynamic and impressive in appearance. Taking the Crown Range highway to Wanaka lifted me up above the valley floor towards the pass with inspiring views. From the top, I watched Airbus A320 and Boeing 737-800 passenger airliners landing at Queenstown. Their precarious-looking descent followed the valley, which placed me high above them. It's strange to be standing on the ground looking down at a large jet aircraft flying below.

The next day I arrived on the east coast and drove to Moeraki just south of Oamaru to see the famous Moeraki Boulders. A couple dozen round balls, between four and six feet in diameter, lay scattered and half submerged in sand along the beach. An incredible creation of nature, these seemingly perfectly round stones appear out of the sandy hillside, roll down onto the foreshore and slowly migrate out to sea. With no rocks or rock outcrops along this stretch of coast, they seem totally out of place on the smooth sandy beach.

I shot up to Oamaru and spent the afternoon just wandering around the Old Town area. Most of the town was, and still is, built from the local sandstone. Appropriately known as "Oamaru stone," it's a soft cream-colored material that's easy to carve. The old architecture felt comfortable, warm and welcoming, and it encouraged further exploration. I felt lighthearted wandering around through the markets, art galleries and novelty shops. And there I ran into an elderly Kiwi sheep shearer.

"Where're you from?" he asked detecting my accent.

"Montana originally."

"I used to shear sheep in Montana and Wyoming," he informed me. "Half the year here and half the year there. Very pretty country."

"Really? Small world," I said.

"I reckon I've shorn over a million sheep over the course of my life," he announced, squinting with one eye as if to calculate the number.

It's easy to get inundated with big numbers nowadays. But when you stop to think about it, the process of grabbing an animal, sitting it up on its bum, running the shears over its body until all its wool is gone, and turning it loose, constitutes a bit of work. Then one million becomes a very big number indeed. So much so, I decided this sheep shearer was pulling my leg.

"A million is a pretty big number," I responded skeptically.

"Yeah, but when you're talking 500 to 600 sheep a day, it adds up fairly fast."

"500 to 600 a day!" I stammered in surprise.

"Yep. I believe the record is 731 over nine hours," he recalled. "And 45 seconds for a single sheep."

"Wow! That is impressive." I thought for a moment. "So how come my barber takes 15 minutes? And I'm mostly bald on top."

We spoke a while longer, and when I told him I was interested in art, he suggested I visit the Steampunk HQ.

What a remarkable experience it proved to be! Very large metal sculptures constructed from old buses, steam engines, smokestacks, earthmovers, tractors, and I don't know what all, filled the interior and yard of the old three-story stone building. I clambered aboard Chopper Holland, a ten-foot-high motorcycle, for a photo. This impressive piece of machinery sports tractor tires for wheels and requires operation from a standing position.

But the most thrilling artwork of all had to be the infinity room. Not much larger than a toilet stall, it had mirrors on all the walls, ceiling and floor. Strings of small fairy lights were suspended from the ceiling. Reflections upon reflections gave a sense of looking off into infinity in every direction – like I was floating in space surrounded by stars. Music was piped in and the lights changed in color and intensity. I stayed in there for nearly two hours. Not necessarily because it was that enthralling, but because I couldn't find the door.

At mid-morning the next day, my Harley parts finally arrived in Dunedin and, with luck, I expected to be back on the road by early afternoon the following day.

South Island – On the Road Again

MD 144.03.22.12:20
March 22, 2017

Finally, after seven days in a car, I was reunited with Black Beauty late in the afternoon.

"Your clutch cable is sticky," the service manager said. "You may want to replace it soon."

"OK, that's strange," I said. But 15 minutes later I was back at the shop because the clutch was way too tight. After some adjustments, I was off again.

Singing "On the Road Again" by Willy Nelson, I headed southwest. I decided to visit Bluff again because it's close to Invercargill and I still needed an I for my ABC points. Besides, I was obligated to make the ride because I'd accepted the patch the previous week. And then there were the oysters, you know.

While in Invercargill, I ran into Joe 90 and Bugsy, a couple of other riders I knew, heading into Hammer Hardware.

"Here to see the motorcycles?" inquired Joe 90.

"Yeah, I've heard there's a collection worth checking out."

"You're in for a treat," he said. "It's more than just a motorcycle collection."

Now, you wouldn't ordinarily expect to see motorcycles in a hardware store, but this is no ordinary hardware store. It's more like a museum that also happens to sell hardware. It's sandwiched between an outdoor camping and clothing store, and a household giftware store. All three are connected by a causeway through the middle, allowing internal flow between them. While the motorcycles predominately reside inside the hardware and camping stores, there's an impressive car collection in the giftware store. A clever idea for when men and women are shopping together.

Burt Monro, of *The World's Fastest Indian* movie fame, was born and bred in Invercargill. To say people here are into racing their bikes is an understatement.

"Burt Munro's original Indian is just towards the back," said Bugsy passing me as I stood studying a 1930s Italian motorcycle above a display of specialty hammers.

"Be right there," I said. "These hammers are hilarious. Look, this one has a 90-degree bend for hammering around corners."

"My favorite is the double handled one for two people," pointed out Joe 90 laughing.

Munro's original Indian motorcycle and fairing shells were on display, along with some original items, such as shelves full of failed attempts at creating the perfect piston.

"Wow," I said. "It's the original sign, 'Sacrifices to the God of Speed,' I saw tacked to one of the shelves in the movie."

"They've set up one of the fairing shells for people to climb in and have their picture taken," said Bugsy. "In you go. I'll take your photo."

"Burt must have been a much shorter man than me," I said as I squeezed into the skin-tight space.

"Smile." Click.

"Thanks for pulling me out," I said as we walked over to a '57 T-Bird. "Everything in here is fascinating."

"Wait till you see the Norman Hayes Engine," said Joe 90.

"Wow, it's difficult to believe this is actually a motor," I commented looking at the unlikely components.

Signs warn, "This is NOT a Briggs & Stratton" and "Would-be industrial spies are warned that this machine is protected by world patent rights." The square-shaped motor was more or less the size of a one cubic-meter box.

"Look," said Bugsy pointing to various parts, "a bedpan, garden hose tap, brass toilet cistern, timber piston rod and a pressure cooker. And there's a preserve jar behind the tubes."

In addition, chains, sprockets, bare copper wires, exposed nuts and bolts and the like, protruded outwards in all directions.

"Do you think it actually works?" I asked.

"Sure does," said the store owner from behind me. "We just have to be careful we don't set off the smoke detectors."

I watched in fascination as the owner cranked the wheel around a couple of times. Adjusting the hose bib, he gave another crank. Then, with a belch of smoke and short burst of noise, she took off under her own power. I was gobsmacked.

Rube Goldberg couldn't have improved upon the design.

The previous few days had been a little wet, but the weather had cleared again and I was lovin' it. I rode into Fiordland, skirting the base of the Southern Alps, towards Milford Sound. I noticed the clutch was tight again. I dug out my tools and adjusted it, but 15 minutes later it was the same. Soon I found I was able to shift without using the clutch! Something was definitely wrong. At Manapōuri, I reluctantly turned back towards Dunedin. The next day was Friday and I could just see the weekend slipping away again. I decided to make the 180 mi (290 km) ride straight through and be at the dealership first thing in the morning.

It was a bitterly cold night and I rugged up with nearly everything on the bike. By the time I arrived at the campground in Dunedin it was 11:30 pm. That night was the coldest of the trip to date, with the temperature just above freezing. I pried my fingers off the handgrips (thinking of the Street Glide I'd demoed in Queenstown), squeezed my thighs against the engine until my legs thawed enough to get off the bike, and stiffly, I somehow managed to crawl, fully dressed, into my sleeping bag.

After much arm waving, finger pointing, gnashing of teeth and protests, I headed out from the Harley dealership late Friday afternoon with a, once again, repaired motorcycle. In so much as I could, I'd tried to take a different road each trip out. However, all roads seemed to funnel through the small town of Clinton before they diverged again. By now, the locals and I were now more or less on a first name basis.

"Look," someone said, "there he goes again!" Waving as I passed through.

With a deficit of 24 hours and four tanks of petrol, I arrived back at Manapōuri about the same time I'd been there the day before. It was like

190

hitting the pause button on the video while you get up to relieve yourself, grab a beer or pizza, and come back later right where you left off.

Fortunately, the weather continued to hold as I pushed on into Fiordland National Park.

The trip to Milford Sound is stunning even at the worst of times. The morning clouds burned off quickly, leaving a flawless sky, as I crawled out of the tent to make my morning cuppa coffee. Sun rays peered over the mountains and into the valley while I struck camp. It knew it was going to be a great day.

Since there are no petrol stations along the way, the big challenge was to ride to Milford Sound and back on a single tank. The total distance is almost exactly equal to Beauty's maximum range. I fueled up in Te Anau, the last town, and I hoped to make it by accelerating slowly and coasting down hills to reduce fuel consumption.

It was a superb ride. The cold snap seemed to have set the trees off in the higher altitudes and the colors were starting to come out.

The Mirror Lakes were my first stop. In the calm of the morning, these sheltered bodies of water produce a near perfect mirror reflection of the mountain range behind. Close to shore someone had mounted a sign bearing a mirrored impression of the words "Mirror Lakes." Because the words read correctly when reflected, a photo of the lakes and the sign only looks correct when rotated upside down. If you manage to capture a flying duck in the picture, you can really confuse people.

At several stops there were small flocks of kea. Kea are the only mountain parrot in the world. Standing at about 19 inches high and with a powerful body, these pesky little buggers love to tear things apart. They will extract the rubber strips from the windscreens of cars, windshield wipers, and anything else they can get their beaks around. When they saw my motorbike with its shiny buckles and straps and cables, they immediately flew over to investigate.

Full of fear, I began running around flapping my arms and shooing them away. Meanwhile, they flapped their wings and hopped along just ahead of me. I'm sure I closely resembled a seagull protecting his turf. I'd no sooner chase one off than another would come in from the other direction. I soon realized they were working as a team; by moving just ahead of me and drawing me away from the bike, their cohort could come in and attempt to dismantle something behind me.

Jabbering tourists were all the while scrambling around trying to take pictures. I'm not sure whether it was the birds or my antics they were photographing, but finally, both tourists and birds left me alone.

A short hike took me into the forest and alongside a stream that had carved its way down through the solid rock over the years. The swirling water created a deep gorge through softer rock and filled it with boulders of impossible shapes. These white forms, filled with holes, twists, half arcs, and rounded tops, gave the illusion of water flowing through a pile of bleached bones. Often times the stream disappeared from view but the throaty roar let you know it was still working its way through more rock below.

The road to Milford Sound continued to lead me upwards through Eglinton Valley, bounded on both side by high mountains. Stunning to look at and so majestic, they were just like the Rockies. The highway wound its way up and up to the mountain ridges until I was about 300 m (975 ft) below the peaks at the end of the valley. Then I was faced with a massive vertical rock wall in front of me. And a stop light.

The one-way tunnel ahead had been cut through solid rock during the Depression. Cars, buses and motorcycles take turns heading to or returning from Milford Sound. The light turned green, and leaving the intensely bright sunshine, the tunnel seemed unbelievably dark. The beam from Beauty's headlight was immediately absorbed by the rough-hewn walls and the uneven partially paved floor, which I soon discovered was littered with shallow potholes. With only a pinhole of light from the distant exit in front of me, it felt like I'd been swallowed alive. Since I couldn't distinguish the sides from the gloom ahead, it was extremely disorienting and I was afraid I'd run into the tunnel side at any minute. Random water drops continuously fell from the ceiling throughout the passage. Because there was no snow on the peaks directly above the tunnel entrance, and we are passing through solid rock, I was baffled as to this water's source.

Once through, and into the welcoming sunlight, the descent was quick, along a series of steep switchbacks, until arrival at Milford Sound. The road runs parallel to a short runway used by sightseeing aircraft, then continues on down to the waterfront, revealing an information center, café and hotel, all nestled amongst the snowcapped peaks of the Southern Alps. High-speed tourist boats run people out to the ocean mouth of the fjord, stopping along the way to view seals and too many waterfalls to count.

Front and center in the panoramic view from the café, Mitre Peak rises from several hundred feet below the surface of the sound, right up to 1,700 m (5,560 ft) above sea level. It dominates the landscape and is probably one of the most photographed settings in New Zealand.

So I did.

South Island – West Coast

MD 144.03.27.19:45

March 27, 2017

Diligence, coupled with miserly use of the throttle, paid off as I arrived back in Te Anau with a whopping quarter liter of fuel remaining in the tank.

Brilliant weather always makes for a grand day of riding. Skirting the Remarkables alongside the lake, I bypassed Queenstown, and continued on to Arrowtown for the third time. You might get the sense that I like the place.

I'd stopped to read most of the historic markers along the way. It's amazing how most of the roads started as trails carved through impossible terrain to enable ox- and horse-drawn wagons to deliver people and goods to the gold fields. Towns sprang up to support the prospectors, then the trails were developed into roads, providing access to such places as Arrowtown, Greymouth, Queenstown and Blackball, and a whole passel of other locations in the South and North Islands.

In fact, I reckon if gold hadn't been discovered, half of New Zealand would probably still be unexplored wild wilderness. I mean, why would they build a road through inhospitable terrain if there were no towns to go to? The entire population would still be living along the coast.

Then I got to thinking about the US and imagined what it would be like if no gold had been found in California or Montana. At the very least, the Black Hills would still belong to the Sioux.

The leaves of deciduous trees were just beginning to hint that fall was in the air. For a few minutes over my cuppa, I contemplated the numerous photos that showed Arrowtown under a brilliantly colored canopy of autumn trees and wondered what it would be like to live here during those months. Perhaps I could take up residence in one of the old miners' shacks against the cliff. Surely there was some gold left in the banks along the river. Enough to squeeze out a meager existence for the winter. Who knows, it'd been so long since they'd mined the place – perhaps more gold had washed down the river by now. Maybe there was even a new mother lode lying in wait to be discovered!

Recognizing the symptoms of gold fever, I quickly finished my coffee and headed up over the Crown Range to Wanaka, then onwards toward the West Coast.

After pausing for another quick stop at Cardrona to wet my whistle, I passed a lengthy fence covered in thousands of bras. All in different colors, shapes and sizes. It was called Bradrona, and had been set up to raise awareness about breast cancer. I'm all for going bra-less, but with the cost of bras, I couldn't help but think, *That is one expensive fence*!

Highway 6 skirts the edge of Lake Hawera and Lake Wanaka. A huge sign warning "HIGH MOTORCYCLE CRASH AREA" greets the rider. *No worries, I'm not in any rush. I'll just take the ride a little slower.*

This road is a bikers' dream, with hills, curves and turns galore. And the scenery is stupendous. Heavy clouds hung in some of the valleys, while others were entangled with the trees above the cliff faces. Snowcapped peaks occasionally pushed up through the lower layers, while distant ranges sometimes appeared through breaks in the cloud cover. All this was reflecting off the perfectly calm waters of the .... "OH CRAP!"

So that's why it's dangerous! Too easy to get caught up looking at the scenery and forget to pay attention to the road. A mishap narrowly avoided, I focused more on Black Beauty and where we were headed.

By 10:00 am the weather had settled into a consistent pattern of drizzle, rain, clear, drizzle, rain, clear. It was OK as I was still on a high from the day before and happily singing "Let it Rain" by Eric Clapton.

Which it did. Tentatively at first. Then in abundance.

Seeing as the weather wasn't cooperating and I've ridden over Haast Pass several times before, I only stopped at my favorite places. The Blue Pools were one of them. A relatively short hike took me through the wet bush and across two cable suspension foot bridges. The glacier-fed pools below were so crystal clear that it was difficult to identify the water level against the giant boulders. Fish appeared as if suspended in air above the gravel bottom.

Several boys were on one of the huge boulders bolstering each other's courage to jump in together. Even though it was raining, the air was fairly warm. But I don't think they understood the meaning of "glacier-fed." Their knowledge level increased significantly the moment they hit the water. Luckily it was only a few strokes back to shore.

People had built hundreds of little stone monuments along the river bank, consisting of semi-flat stones piled one atop the other, with the bigger ones on the bottom and slowly getting smaller as they grew higher. Most of these cairns were five to seven rocks high, but several were up to 15. Each time I'd visited, there seemed to be more stacks. This is noteworthy, because for all the work erecting them, I'm sure they are washed away each spring by the snow melt floods.

The rain was getting heavier by the minute, so I continued on up the West Coast without really stopping. Poor visibility meant I couldn't see much, and I skipped the Fox Glacier entirely. I rode up to the parking lot of the Franz Joseph Glacier, but the conditions meant that a viewing was impossible. Signs along the entry road denoted the glacier's retreating boundary at various times in history. When Captain Cook first saw it in the 1700s, it reached nearly as far as where the main highway is now. Even between my previous two visits, the recession had been noticeable. I was curious to see how much more it had withdrawn in the last five years. But that would have to wait.

New Zealand is known for its one-way bridges – especially in the South Island. In Fiordland, the wettest part of the West Coast, the rainfall varies from one to eight meters (four to 26 feet) a year. Runoff from glaciers and rainforests produce wide alluvial fans as the rivers bring debris down from the mountains. Some of these washout areas along the coast are extremely wide and require exceptionally long bridges. With the possibility of these being wiped out during springtime floods, it's both a practical and economical decision to make them single lanes. Longer bridges are equipped with pullouts along the way to facilitate movement in both directions.

However, the most fascinating bridge I've ever come across is just out of Greymouth. This extraordinary structure has one road lane with train tracks down the middle. What you wind up with are trains, trucks, cars, motorbikes, bicycles and pedestrians all competing for use of the narrow bridge. One direction at a time. No contest as to who has right of way.

My goal for the day was to reach the old mining town of Blackball by nightfall. The place was primarily known for coal mining but some gold as well, and it had a rich history with respect to unions winning rights for workers and such.

I pulled up in front of the aging two story hotel, killed the engine and looked up at the hotel's name. "Formerly, The Blackball Hilton Hotel." *Ok, this should be interesting.* I dismounted, climbed the steps and passed through the double doors into the entry foyer.

"Curious name," I said to the manager as I took a seat at the bar and ordered a beer.

"Yeah," he said. "It was originally called the Blackball Hilton... you know, as a bit of joke. But the Hilton Hotel chain got word of it and told the owner to change the name."

"As they would do."

"'No thank you,' he said. 'We don't pose any threat to your hotel name,'" continued the manager. "Lawyers were engaged. Letters were written and law suits were threatened by Hilton. It got pretty nasty, but the hotel held firm."

"Wow that was pretty ballsy," I said.

"Finally, an agreement was reached whereby Hilton would pay a financial sum to the owner who, in turn, would change the name. Once payment was received, the owner did change the name," explained the manager. "But, not quite in the spirit of the agreement... it was changed to 'Formerly, The Blackball Hilton.'"

"Cheeky!" I laughed.

"That's not the end of it. The payment was used to install toilets and upgrade the sewage system for the hotel," he continued with a conspiratorial twinkle in his eye. "In other words, he continued to shit on the Hilton."

Still chuckling, I moved on to the campground and proceeded to get soaking wet setting up the tent in the rain. It bucketed down all night long and into the late morning, sending sheets of water across the lawn. Luckily the campground had a hot shower. And a dryer.

I wasn't exactly sure which setting to use for the dryer. There were whites, colors, leathers, tennis shoes, hats and delicates, all lumped together. Everything seemed to come out more or less the same color and size it was before I put them in, so I considered the exercise a success. Even though it was still raining, I was able to start the next leg warm and dry.

Seventeen minutes after I left, I felt that cold trickle again. And for the remainder of the day, I carried on northwards with my crotch wet.

Arriving back in Picton, at the top end of the South Island, I headed over to the ferry terminal and scheduled a space for the next day. Then mounting back up, I rode the narrow coastal road ten miles out to Whatamango Bay and pitched my tent on the beach. Only seven feet from the water's edge. The lovely breeze dried the tent out in no time and I slumbered off to the sound of a gentle surf lapping the shore.

North Island – Home

MD 144.03.30.09:10
March 30, 2017

Bright eyed and bushy tailed, I broke camp and got ready to head for the ferry at 8:45 am. The campground had a spigot with non-potable water. I figured if you can't drink it, it must be for washing things. So first I gave myself a quick bath and then the bike, to wash off the road grime from all the previous rain. Funny how the bike stays clean with the sun and dust but gets dirty when it rains.

At the ferry I ran into a couple of HOG members I'd met at the rally and again at the Formerly, The Blackball Hilton. They were planning to ride Route 66. We started talking, and even though the weather was really nice, we stayed inside for the first part of the ferry journey. Once we hit the high seas of the strait though, I went out on deck and forward to the bow. There I stood with arms outstretched, legs spread apart, feeling the swells beneath me and the salt spray on my face.

Turns out, you're not allowed to get up on the bow railings and do the *Titanic* pose. So, I had to stay inside after that. But it was still a lovely crossing and before I knew it, we had arrived in Wellington.

My accumulation of points for the ABC competition had been going pretty well. I'd collected all the big things and regions needed, plus a couple of spares. There are no cities beginning with X, V or Z in New Zealand. There are only three J's – and they're all within about a 50-kilometer radius of Wellington. I figured it shouldn't be too hard to find a sign in Johnsonville. Right?

Let me just say that parking a Harley illegally on the footpath on a busy street with "No Parking Anytime" signs in abundance, while wearing black leathers and taking photographs of a police station, requires diligence, speed and huevos. If I don't say so myself.

Castle Point had been my intended destination when I'd made my slightly ill-fated trip around the east coast the previous year, and I still wanted to visit. I'd sailed close by with Tristin back in 2008 but the weather had been so foggy we couldn't see it. It's one of those places where the wind usually howls. But we were under motor in calm seas when we passed.

It's a long ride out on a dead-end road to get there, but what a spot. A lighthouse sits atop a short, jagged peninsula. The hike from the campground to the lighthouse crosses mostly barren rock because the waves have wiped out almost all living plant life, but in the process, have also created some delightful rock sculptures. Closer to the lighthouse, I read an information board and discovered there is a daisy and a moth that live there, and this is the only place in the whole world they are found. The moth is unique in that it comes out only in the daytime. Uniqueness in the midst of desolation. Who would have thought?

When I went to take a shower later that day, there were sniggers from the other guys in the men's facilities at the campground. I couldn't figure out what was so funny until I looked in the mirror. Sitting in the waterlogged saddle so long over the last couple of rainy days had left my bottom all moisture laden and wrinkly. Because my leather pants were wet, some of the black tanning agents had leached out and stained my skin a very dark purplish black. That left my bottom end looking like a couple of raisins. I actually had to smile. But you have to be careful because bikers give other bikers their riding name based on these kinds of incidents. I hadn't received mine yet and I surely didn't want to end up being known as ol' Raisin Butt.

With tent pitched firmly about 160 ft from the high tide surf line, I went to sleep enveloped by the music of crashing waves. Sometime during the night, the waves became much larger and the crashing much, much louder. Enough to wake me up for a few minutes. But that was all. What a wonderful world we occupy.

The good weather was forecast to deteriorate the next morning, and unfortunately the forecast was correct. I thought I'd try a new water ingress prevention technique for the next leg of the journey. I wore everything I had. I figured that by the time everything was soaked through, I'd be at the end of the trip for the day.

At first the rain was sporadic and I decided to try some exploring. I've learned some interesting things about New Zealand roads. If they have white lines on the edges and down the middle, you're OK. If the white lines disappear from the edges, but the road still looks good, you've got a 90 percent chance things will work out. If the road continues narrowing with no center line but is still paved, you've got about a 60 percent probability of winding up in a paddock. If the pavement then suddenly ends and turns to gravel, you have a 90 percent chance it will dead end into a paddock somewhere. And soon.

Backtracking two or three times after ending up in a couple of sheep paddocks, I finally found Palmerston North. By then I thought I had a pretty good handle on figuring out the roads. Feeling confident, I tried a shortcut to Taihape. Suddenly the paved road had no white lines. Oops!

I soon found myself traveling up the aptly named Scenic Pohangina River Valley along the base of the Ruahine Ranges on a gravel road. The rain became quite heavy at times obscuring any long-distance observations. I spotted a shepherd sitting on his quad bike wearing a green raincoat.

"Excuse me but I seem to be kinda lost," I confessed swallowing my pride. "The road curls around on itself several times and I'm not sure if there is more than one way in and out."

"Don't care for our country roads eh?" he said looking at my once shiny road bike.

"It's a spectacular part of the country," I allowed. "But it would be more enjoyable riding a dirt bike on a sunny day."

"It's easy," he said after considering my response. "At the junctions just go right, left, right, right and left. That'll take you right back to the sealed road to Taihape. Then it's a few kilometers into town."

"Right! Thanks." *Right, left, right, right and left. Right, left, right, right and left.* I repeated silently to myself as I rode away. *Right, left, right, right and left.*

And after about 12 kilometers of riding on intermittent gravel roads, I finally found myself on State Highway 1 just short of Taihape as promised. I arrived with less than half a liter of fuel remaining.

That's when the rain decided to quit messing around and got serious. A deluge ensued as I joined the Desert Road. Mount Ruapehu poked his head out a couple of times and kept me inspired, as I tried to find the unmarked turnoff to a campground.

A hot latte bowl sat in front of me the next day as I gazed across Lake Taupō. The water was calm but the clouds were still so low you couldn't see very far. Grey sky reflected on the gray surface. On the ride in from the campground, I'd caught up to a bike I recognized and followed him into the coffee shop parking lot.

"Did you enjoy the rally?" inquired Hitman as he blew on his flat white.

"Always," I stated. "It's been a challenging trip though. Also, it seems a bit wetter than normal this year."

"My thoughts exactly."

"This was the first time I've had to set up and strike the tent in a downpour. With no time to dry out, last night was indeed a damp one."

And as to my experiment, while wearing everything hadn't really slowed the water ingress, it did mean that I had nothing left to wear that was dry. It had still been raining lightly in the morning when I took a long walk in the Kaimanawa Forest in the only dry article of clothing I had left. My togs!

"Well, one thing's for sure," speculated Hitman, "with the excessive rain the Huka Falls should be more impressive than ever."

The Māori name "huka" translates to "foamy" or "frothy," and in the flow towards the falls, the water churns so violently that it turns a pale cerulean blue. Along its 200 m (650 ft course), a nearly straight gorge has been carved vertically down into the rock, before the torrent plummets over the edge into a wide expanse of a much slower flowing river.

"So much power in that water," I reflected. "If you ever fell in it would be impossible to stop yourself, let alone scale the 15- to 20-foot-high vertical walls and avoid going over the falls."

"And yet I've seen kayakers deliberately shoot through there and then into space as they drop over the edge," said Hitman.

"No thanks. Think I'll stick to the bike."

"Where you headed next?" he inquired.

"I thought I'd ride back through Matamata and Hobbiton on my way back to Auckland. I want to ride out to the Shire again to collect more information about the tour. Hoping to entice my daughter to come down for a visit with me."

"Ride safe," he yelled in response to my wave as we parted ways on the main road.

Although their big footprints were evident in the mud all around, the shy little hobbits were nowhere to be found that day, so I only hung around long enough to collect the information I wanted. The day was running out, pressing me onwards towards the big smoke.

And after 27 days on the road, I arrived home. I pulled into the carpark at the marina and killed the engine. Sitting in the saddle with the tick, tick, tick of the engine as it cooled down, I considered the 6,760 new kilometers (4,225 miles) on my trip meter and the 105,600 kilometers (65,600 miles) on the odometer. Such a beautiful country. So many wonderful sights and experiences. A grand adventure indeed. Once again, the Lord has blessed me with a safe and exciting trip.

And once again I had rediscovered that my body actually likes sleeping on the ground. I felt healthier. My needs were much less than my wants. All I really seemed to require was water, food and petrol. And one thing became increasingly clear. My desire to see and explore appeared to be insatiable.

But for now it was time to rest and get ready for another trip to the US.

2017 Layover

MD 144.04.02.12:10
April 2, 2017

Having arrived back safely from my South Island adventure, I decided to take stock of the situation and all the things that needed to be done before I left for my next Stateside bike trip, a mere six weeks away.

Seemed there were heaps of things I'd left unattended. And, like savings bonds, the longer you take to address them, the greater they mature. I started a "to do" list.

Bontekoe had so far remained unsold, and she still needed to be hauled out, scrubbed and antifouled for the winter months. Not to mention lubricating the through hulls, installing zincs, and a host of other minor tasks. Organize paperwork for taxes. Fill out taxes and post. Tristin's engagement party celebration planning. And so on.

Armed with a comprehensive list of tasks and a reasonable program for accomplishing said tasks, I determined I would need just over five weeks of eight-hour days. Which, if I was diligent, left about three days of free time. Like I said, a reasonable and comfortable plan.

So, I bought another boat.

I realize my purchase might sound out of the blue and perhaps a bit over the top. However, I'm a goal-oriented person, and as much as I'd received enjoyment from my motorcycle adventures, I knew I'd need a new adventure to focus on once I returned from the US. I just jumped the gun a little bit, that's all.

With Tristin's support, I'd been threatening to buy a bigger boat for a while. Tristin and Jordan wanted their own stateroom for when they came to visit. Hopefully, an upgrade would inspire more frequent visits. One of the boats I had on my "ideal list" was a Valiant 40. Turns out, there was one sitting two docks down from me in the same marina.

Her Latin name, *Vela Dare*, translated as "Dare to Sail." Or "Let's Go Sailing" or "To Navigate." For the benefit of the sailors out there, she was a Robert Perry designed double ender with a cutter rig (40 feet long; 12 feet, four inches in beam; drawing about six feet at the fin keel, with a skeg rudder). She had two staterooms and all up she could comfortably sleep six. There were lots of frilly bits, but many hadn't been used for 20 years, implying they would require repair or replacement.

To add insult to injury, she had been let go for a long time and had suffered dearly. Not having been hauled out for seven years had left a thriving community of marine life, complete with associated marine plants three feet long extending from the sides of the hull, and I suspected, down from the keel to the ocean floor. Similarly, growths of mold and fungi covered the top sides. All her canvas work was shot, not to mention the lines and halyards that had chafed through, and a couple of broken shrouds. While her internal brightwork looked reasonable, all the cushions were beyond their use-by date.

Nothing like a challenge.

After 36 trips dragging a dock cart back and forth between the two vessels to transfer my belongings, *Bontekoe*, no longer weighed down, was floating back at her normal waterline. A phenomenon that hadn't been seen for some 28 years.

I then set off to haul her out, tidy her up and drop the price on Trade Me for a quick sale. This plan worked beautifully. Until I began to run my hands over her ever-so familiar curves and caress her bottom as I sanded and prepped her underside for painting. With the weight off and sporting new paint, she had again become the fast and lively boat she used to be. I was going to miss her.

When a serious buyer showed up with all the right skills, the desire to take care of her and cash in hand, something happened inside me. And although I still cannot quite comprehend or explain it, I turned him down.

That's how I became a man with two boats and two motorcycles. Fully aware that I can only use one of them at a time. No to mention the fact that sailboats and Harley-Davidson motorcycles are very demanding. Both on my wallet and my time.

But, since I didn't have a woman in my life, I figured it all works out about the same.

I rattled around in the vast spaciousness of the new vessel, cleaning and tentatively stowing my belongings until each had found their new spot. I learned early on to place my glasses, hearing aids, wallet and a flashlight on the top corner of the navigation station, permitting me easy access to the vitals and the necessary equipment for searching for items that had become momentarily lost. The amount of work staring me in the face became overwhelming. I began worrying that I'd bitten off more than I could chew.

The morning of my departure for the US found me frantically scrubbing the last of the major growth of mold and fungus off *Vela Dare*'s topsides. That at least gave the appearance of a clean boat when Tristin collected me for our drive to the airport.

A few months previously, I'd been looking forward to the upcoming motorcycle trip, but my mind had become so occupied with boats that I'd already begun looking ahead to my next sailing adventure as well. *How will I ever be able to transition back to motorcycles again?* I wondered.

Settling in on the airplane gave me time to unwind. Forget all the boat ownership pressures. And focus instead on motorbikes, riding on the other side of the road and the adventure ahead.

Turns out, the transition from boats to motorcycles was complete by the time we passed over Hawaii.

Book 5

USA 2017

Washington – Idaho – Montana

MD 144.05.17.09:29
May 17, 2017

"Welcome back," said my sister Judy, greeting me with a warm hug.

"Great to finally be here," I respond as we walked to her car. "Darkness was coming earlier every evening in New Zealand. I'm looking forward to the longer days."

"How was the flight?"

"All up, from Auckland to LAX, to Seattle, to Spokane, used up the better part of 24 hours," I told her as we were driving out of the airport. "I was able to watch three good movies though."

"Did you hear author Robert Pirsig died a couple months ago?" she asked cautiously, as we pulled off the highway.

"Yeah, I heard." *Zen and the Art of Motorcycle Maintenance* is a veritable biker's bible of wisdom for self-happiness and the elusive definition of quality. "His motorcycle adventure and observations have provided hours of contemplative subject matter for me. Filling the voids on many a long passage. I'm sad he's gone."

"I didn't mean to cast a pall over the start of your trip," she apologized. "But it is a reminder our time is short and we need to make the best of every adventure."

She was right.

Two days later, I collected the Black Pearl from her winter storage environment. It felt grand to be riding her again. And it only took 15 minutes, two shocked cars stampeding for the ditch, and one terrified bicyclist scrambling off the sidewalk, for me to remember which side of the road to ride on.

After a couple of days of dodgy weather, adjusting to the time zone difference, and catching up with Judy, I headed east to Kalispell in northwest

Montana. Primarily to seek out more free food and lodging under the guise of visiting with my brother Allen and his wife Becky.

Unfortunately, he is well aware of my cunning ploy and immediately put me to work trimming the hedge. Which was actually a lot of fun. The end result was perhaps a little less than what he expected.

"It's not very level," he noted with some concern in his voice.

"It's like the difference between a good haircut and a bad one," I explained. "Two weeks and you can't tell the difference."

"Hedges don't grow as fast a hair," he countered.

True, it might be more like six to nine weeks, but I'd be a long way down the road by then.

Afterwards, we took a tiki tour around town in his car, then out to a park high up on the plateau overlooking the city – a magnificent view out over the valley to the nearby mountains. Off in the distance, we observed a small herd of buffalo at the city limits. Coincidentally, when we were out that night, I ate my first Buffalo Burger.

"Where to from here?" asked Allen as I began loading my gear onto the Pearl next morning.

"Through Glacier Park, Browning and then to Valier to collect a V for the ABC competition," I replied, stretching bungy cords over my sleeping bag.

"I suggest you include Hungry Horse Dam and Essex in your stops."

"Okay. What's in Essex?"

"The Izaak Walton Inn. It was originally built to house workers on the railroad during the turn of the century. They've been developing that topic further by taking old cabooses and even an engine and outfitting them as cabins for lodging. You'll appreciate the railroad themes," he added. "A very creative environment to have a retreat or romantic weekend."

"OK, I'll stop," I said climbing into the saddle. "But I doubt there'll be much romance."

"The forecast is for very strong winds," he reminded me as I loosened the clutch. "Ride safe."

My first stop was Hungry Horse Dam, which was the second highest and third largest dam in the world when it was finished in 1953. I took a short spin along the shoreline to look at the beautiful mountains reflecting off the lake in the Bob Marshall Wilderness Area. It appeared the weatherman had been correct – strong winds began to buffet me on the exposed road.

On the way back across the dam, a huge gust hit, lifting me and the bike completely off the ground. Twice. Then sent us sideways into the other lane. The force of the wind continued to push us towards the edge. Even though I was leaning into it at a 30 deg angle. When it finally released me, I was going five miles an hour and was one foot from going over the steep embankment on the wrong side of the road!

I carried on skirting the southern boundary of Glacier Park for a brilliant, but still breezy, ride through the snow-capped mountains, climbing steadily until I was above the snow line. Simply beautiful. The temperature continued to drop and soon there were scattered snow flakes flying about. *Uh oh! I've been here before*, I fretted. But the appearance of snow was brief and ended soon after. Even if the cold remained.

I stopped for a lunch break at the Izaak Walton Inn. In addition to the railroad themed lodging that my brother had described, the inn itself had been restored with railroad memorabilia. I could easily imagine myself there in the middle of winter, snowed in with a pair of cross county skis leaning against the entry, a crackling fire in the hearth, reading a good book while sipping a hot drink. Yes, I'd say romantic.

Once out onto the prairie, the wind came at me again with a real vengeance. The upside was that by riding at a 30 deg angle in order to maintain a straight trajectory, I should get much better mileage out of the tires. Most people only wear out the bottoms and not the sides. Strong winds indeed!

I'd forgotten how tight my US helmet was and the way it contorted my forehead, until I pulled into a service station on the Blackfoot Indian Reservation. There I overheard the teller saying something about a Klingon in the back. I just smiled to myself and tried to act natural. "Live long and prosper," I said flashing the split finger V to him as I pushed the glass door open on my way out.

By the time I arrived at Valier, Montana, I had already racked up points for four forests and one national park in a single day. The only cities still missing from my list were ones beginning with X and Z.

Following Route 66 the previous year had afforded me with a purpose and direction for my trip. The ABCs had added extra value. It was always easy to just ride and live life for the day. And I was all set to follow the same approach again.

However, the discussion with my sister about Robert Pirsig's death and making the most of our adventures had been weighing on my mind. I was keenly aware that places and things are only part of the equation of life. There are also people. And family.

Now, I'm not the most socially adept person around. I do sort of OK with one or two at a time, or small groups if I know everyone. But it has always been a struggle with more than four or five people at a time. At dinner parties I'm known for sticking my foot in my mouth at some point, but the other guests wait patiently for the real excitement that inevitably ensues when I insert the other one right in beside it. One of the reasons I frequently ride alone. But, even though personal growth is often difficult, it was time to make an effort.

Therefore, I decided the other thing I would be collecting during this trip would be time with friends and relatives. While not quite sure how to assign points to this activity, or if that's even important, my goal was to see as many cousins, classmates, friends, cuzzie bros and rellies as possible.

I also began to consider this trip my Farewell Tour of the States, since I knew it would be some time, if ever, before I'd be able to return. And we're all getting older... well, some of us are. Despite the years, I recognize the distinctive mannerisms of my friends, and they talk and act just the same as they always have. Our age hasn't been a barrier to friendships that have survived the years.

I was hoping that it would be the same with my relatives. I no longer have living parents, grandparents, aunts or uncles. That only left the remaining 19 cousins. Luckily they were strategically scattered all across the States, which meant time to visit and recuperate between long rides. And perhaps some free room and board to boot.

I let people know (via Facebook and emails) that I would be traveling around and wanted to see as many as possible, and if they were interested, to let me know. Some, especially my cousins, didn't have a choice; I just showed up on their doorsteps. As they say, "You can pick your friends, but you can't pick your relatives."

I did my first practice run in Helena by visiting three classmates, Patty, Don and Bill. I discovered that bringing beer helps. Stories and recollections abounded till late into the night. Laughter is so good for you. And boy, did we laugh a lot.

Bolstered with success, I tried another classmate Mary the next day in Boulder and friend Slim in Laurel the day after that. I was on a roll!

Actually, it wasn't nearly as hard as I had envisioned. More importantly, I seemed to be filling a void I wasn't aware even existed.

Central Montana

MD 144.05.26.20:35
May 26, 2017

I stopped in Columbus and spent the night at a lovely free campground, Itch-Kep-Pe Park. The name reminded me of the song "Itchycoo Park" by the Small Faces. Camping in Montana is certainly different than New Zealand. And to be fair, probably different than the rest of the US. It's simple secluded campsites with long drop toilets, a water tap and a rubbish bin. None of that glamping stuff. People are super friendly and laid back, creating a relaxed atmosphere.

The next morning, Todd, a friend from my early days in Miles City, preached a wonderful sermon at a church in town. Afterwards he drove us around the surrounding countryside to see some of his favorite views of the mountains. Amazing panoramas indeed. We eventually wound up in Fishtail for lunch.

From a bench in the city park, we saw a red-headed woodpecker, yellow finch, green finch, red robin, sparrow and a couple of others. The only one we missed was Montana's state bird, the meadowlark.

"Step in the Fishtail General Store and you step back in time," he said as we left the park for the old time establishment.

I noticed the centrally located potbellied stove that provided heat in the winter but also defined a gathering place. Surrounding it were rows of shelves containing all manner of items from sewing supplies to books, hardware to foodstuffs.

"They've recently added a coffee shop and a kitchen," he noted. "You can purchase good food at a very reasonable price here." Like the huge hamburger he ordered for $3.75.

"You should try the taco in a bag," he suggested.

"Taco in a bag?"

"They take a bag of taco chips, cut it open along the side, throw in guacamole, salsa, cheese, mince or chicken, and sour cream, then shake," he explained. "A real novelty."

"Very creative," I said, and ordered one.

Everyone was sitting around a big table where a checkerboard sat ready for action. We found a couple of empty seats and began to eat as I continued to take in my surroundings.

"You can buy just about anything you might need when coming in off the range. Even make your own peanut butter by throwing in some raw peanuts and turning the crank on that machine," he said pointing out the old grinder.

The wine shelf displayed interesting labels like Bull Rider, American West and, my personal favorite, Miles City Bucking Horse. Which I purchased. Actually, it tasted pretty good, with a slight kick, even if it was a bit expensive.

The bike had been running well and I decided to keep it that way by staying ahead of the game. It would soon be due for new cam tensioners. So I grabbed the bull by the horns and planned to do it while I was in Montana, where there's no sales tax.

Turns out Memorial Day weekend was coming up. Every man, woman, child and dog was getting their bike ready for the summer, meaning a couple days' delay before the service shop could fit me in. Best laid plans. I decided to use the delay time judiciously.

Billings was a good place to stop for servicing since there were a potential five classmates and three relatives to visit in the area. When my classmate Valerie suggested there was room for me in her basement until the bike was repaired, I jumped at the offer. She had expressed an interest in an extended ride last year at the All-70s reunion. Unfortunately, her mother had taken ill, putting the kibosh on anything more than a day-trip.

The radio announced that Beartooth Pass had just been opened. This was the same pass where I'd been caught in a snow blizzard the previous year. Black Pearl was still waiting her turn at the shop, so I coerced Valerie into a ride by promising we would be back by three that afternoon. With Valerie riding pillion, we headed out on a crisp cloudless morning from Billings towards Red Lodge. Even though the sun was ascending and the day was warming up, we were climbing in altitude, meaning the actual temperature didn't increase. Then, once we started up towards the pass, the temperature began to drop quickly. At the top, even under sun-drenched blue skies, the mercury hovered just above freezing.

But man-o-man was it beautiful. A veritable winter wonderland. The snow drifts ranged from a couple of feet to 16 feet (5 m) high, where huge snow blowers and plows had cut through. The longer expanses felt like riding through a tunnel, only without the top. At one point I thought I saw the end of some handlebars in the snowbank. Maybe a biker who had got caught up in the storm last year?

Traffic moved slowly since the vertical snow walls reduced visibility around the curves. And really, the road was all curves. People wanted to relish the experience anyway, so going slow was fine. We stopped at a pullout and had a snowball fight while herds of people were skiing, snowmobiling or just frolicking around.

I was thinking we would get a cuppa hot chocolate at the Top of the World, a café and trading post, then return down the pass. But, with snow still four feet deep on the front porch, the place was closed, so we carried on to Cook City. Once there, while devouring a bowl of thick, hot soup, we watched a buffalo wander down Main Street. What a country!

Traveling a mere four miles further would get me an ABC point for the Yellowstone Park entry sign. Next thing you know, we'd continued on into the park and out the other end at Gardner, heading towards Livingston and taking the long way back to Billings. By the time we reached the Interstate, the last of the late afternoon sun was shining on the Crazy Mountains, igniting even more visual stimulus. For fear of hitting deer on the highway, we hurried along to avoid riding in the dark – a very real and present danger in Montana.

Over the course of the excursion, we saw pelicans, geese, bald eagles, pheasants, crows, golden eagles, elk and deer in velvet, buffalo, raccoons, antelope, and other critters I'm probably forgetting. The number of buffalo in the park was more than I'd ever seen before. A taste of what this country must have looked like 200 years ago.

Instead of arriving back around three, as planned, it was closer to 10:00 pm when we completed the 400-mile ride. Backing the Pearl into the garage for the night, we both had an opportunity to stand up, stretch our legs and agree on what a glorious day it had been. So much so, I was forgiven for the late return.

Still on a high the next day, I went to visit another classmate Vicki and her husband Lionel. The conversation was fairly sedate and gentle until Lionel began to pour the gin and tonics. Lionel is an accomplished musician and soon two guitars appeared, closely followed by a stack of sheet music. It was mostly bluegrass, with the likes of John Prine, who I adore. When Vicki appeared from the study with a video camera, I knew I was in big trouble. I don't remember much after that, but evidently, we played and sang until the wee hours. Ever since, I've lived in fear of monetary demands to prevent Vicki's recordings from reaching the internet.

After collecting my bike from the shop and significantly lightening my wallet in the process, Valerie and I headed off to meet another classmate, Libby, for a drink. I had tried several times to get hold of Larry to come and join us as well. He was always a shy kind of guy at school and waffled on with several excuses until I finally told him I would catch up with him in a couple of days.

We made the best of it without him. It was a grand afternoon of sharing, reminiscing and laughter with friends. How fortunate for me to have grown up where I did. And amongst the people I did.

A couple of days later I made a run to Roundup, Montana, to visit Roberta, Dana and Kelly, some cousins I hadn't seen for nearly 40 years. How had that happened?

Dana had played an instrumental role in me becoming a biker, even before Bronson came along. She'd taken me for my first ever ride, at a very young and impressionable age, on the back of her Vespa. I'd crawled up onto the back of the seat all excited about the opportunity.

"Hold on," she laughed and opened up the throttle. Hang on I did! And for dear life, as we skidded down the drive and out onto the country road. Our speed continued to build as we fishtailed around the curves in the loose gravel. I was nearly thrown off when we hit the washboards on the outside wheel track, so I clung on even tighter. My eyes were watering. Her hair whipped back and forth as she turned her head to the side and asked, "How you doing?"

My answer, "OK," was snatched away by the wind as soon as it left my lips.

She scared the ever-living daylights out of me. It was awesome! And the seed of my addiction was sown there and then.

My cousin Roberta and I sat out on the back-deck reminiscing about these and other things – older and maybe a little wiser – while I demolished an elk steak that simply melted in my mouth. A small flock of turkey buzzards occupied a tree next door. These are big ugly birds with a wing span of some ten feet. Several more arrived and circled before descending to land on a branch. And then a few more. Soon the entire tree was cloaked in turkey buzzards. It seems this flock, varying from 50 to 100, spends its days flying around the surrounding countryside looking for road-kill, and comes home to roost every evening in one of several trees about town. Then, in a couple of months, they'll move on to another part of the country. Nature's road cleaning crew in action.

After dinner, I took Roberta on a short ride around town, then out past the city limits where people had built houses into the sides of the rocks during the Depression. Although a bit more advanced, with glass windows and better building materials, they were essentially the same as the Chinese gold miners' shacks back in Arrowtown, and similar to the Hopi cliff dwellings I'd visited the previous year. The more things change, the more they stay the same.

Even though my cousin Kelly had been suffering from cancer for some time, she graciously agreed to spend some time with me at the hospital. While the illness had ravaged her body, it hadn't diminished the light of her spirit shining through her eyes. I could also discern vestiges of her mother – one of my favorite aunts – in her face. The visit was short as she tired quickly, but I was so happy to have seen her. A few short weeks later, she passed away. Life is so tentative and fragile, but it made me even more determined to see the rest of my cousins.

Montana's hot, blue-sky days often lead to huge thunderheads and heavy downpours in the late afternoon. One of these deluges ensued as I was donning my rain pants under a tree at the edge of town. In less than 15 minutes, almost an inch of rain had fallen. I felt pretty dry and cocky, having been smart enough to stand under the tree, until I had to wade out to the curb through four inches of water to where the bike sat. That wasn't the only thing that dampened my spirits.

While I was standing under the tree, I received a phone call that my shy friend Larry had died of a heart attack. It was yet another reminder of how delicate the thread of life is and the importance to celebrate it often and with gusto.

And live with gusto I would I promised myself, as I departed for Eastern Montana.

Eastern Montana

MD 144.06.03.14:12

June 3, 2017

Heading north out of Billings once again, under the immense blue sky, I began to pay closer attention to the landscape. First, rolling plains led into several badlands, followed by grass-covered rolling hills, with the Snowy Mountains off in the distance to the left. Then back to open plains. The rich green hills were slowly shifting to light green with scatterings of brown.

Ingomar is famous for Jersey Lil's bar and restaurant, and a stop to have a squiz was in order. In days gone by, this part of Montana had been the largest sheep shearing area in the world. I wondered if Ingomar was one of the places where the sheep shearer I'd met in Oamaru had practiced his trade. The town had grown and shrunk over the years as the economy changed. Less than ten structures now remain. But Jersey Lil's had been there throughout the majority of these transitions.

I parked the Pearl out front, next to the hitching posts and was tempted to tie a leather rein from the rail to the bike, like the horses further down, but thought better of it in the end. Then I walked up the wagon-wheel-lined timber boardwalk and through the swinging front doors. Out of the heat and into the cool. While sitting at the ornately carved timber bar eating a bowl of Lil's famous chili, I soaked up the western ambiance. The heads of buffalo, elk, mule deer, whitetail deer, moose and pronghorn antelope were mounted on the walls; along with a trophy-sized four-point jackalope. Also included amongst the taxidermist's art were birds such as grouse, pheasant and turkey.

A point of interest sign at the edge of town proclaimed this to be the most sparsely populated area of the US of A. When you look at the world from outer space at night, it's easy to make out New York, LA, Chicago and other major metropolitan areas. The east and west coasts of the United States are nearly continuous lights. In contrast, a big dark area towards the central northwest is nearly black. That's Eastern Montana. And the blackest part was where I was standing just then.

I was on my way to visit a classmate Dan and his lovely wife Nancy. They live out in this desolate country. Which of course creates great confusion for people used to living in crowded metropolitan cities. Dan told me of a long-distance phone conversation he'd had just the day before.

"Sure, we can mail that item for you, sir. What is your address please?" asked the lady with the southern east coast accent.

"East of Ingomar, Montana," Dan responded.

She paused before she asked, "And the street address?"

"There isn't one."

"That's it? East of Ingomar, Montana?!" she asked incredulously.

"Yup. It's out in the country."

"And it will get there if I just put 'East of Ingomar' on the package?" she asked dubiously.

"East of Ingomar, Montana. Yup."

"How will they know where to go?" she persisted.

"There's only two houses out here until you get to Forsyth," he patiently explained.

"Don't you, like, miss people... get lonely?"

"Not one little bit," Dan replied.

She paused again, "OK then – East of Ingomar."

"East of Ingomar, *Montana*," he corrected.

It was easy to find his mailbox, as it was the only one I saw on the 15-mile ride to the turnoff. From there, it was another ten miles on gravel to the homestead. The other house is a further five miles down the highway and on the other side of the road... no confusion.

Word must have gotten out about me leaching off friends, because Dan told me right off that we were helping brand at the neighbor's ranch the next day.

Towards evening, after a catch-up and a superb fiery taco dinner, we meandered over to Dan's hangar, where he pulled out a Piper Super Cub and we climbed aboard. He'd been flying since just after the Wright brothers

220

launched their plane at Kitty Hawk, and I think he bought the first Cub right off the assembly line.

"It's the most realistic way to cover these 10,000 to 40,000 acre ranches," he pointed out.

Besides counting cattle, we saw lots of deer, antelope, prairie dogs and coyotes. I'm relatively confident that at no time during the flight did we exceed 300 feet above the ground. But it was great sport strafing the prairie dogs. Afterwards, we proceeded back to the house to bend elbows and tell tall tales of the old days till late, in preparation for the morrow.

We got up so early I think it was still yesterday. After four cups of coffee and a hearty breakfast, we were halfway along the 42-mile drive to the branding area when the sun rose. My eyelids still took another 12 miles to fully open.

After a round of introductions, the neighbor assessed my skills as a seasoned cowboy. When assigning tasks for the day he said, "You stand right over there and be a fence post." Which, considering the hour and the previous night's limited sleep, I did with as much enthusiasm and precision as possible.

In truth, I had spent some time as a cowboy in my younger years, and how exciting it was to take part in a branding once again. The bawling cattle, whinnying horses, the animal smells and dust in the air all enhanced the round-up festivity. Several times people commented on my fence-post abilities as we separated calves from cows. The crew placed branding irons by a propane torch fed into one end of a large half pipe, and soon the irons were glowing a dull red.

Five mounted cowboys entered the corral, roped the calves by the hind legs and dragged them out the gate to a waiting pair of wrestlers. Wrestlers, one forward and one aft, held the critter while it was branded, castrated, dehorned, tagged, inoculated in three different locations, marked with chalk and finally released. The bewildered calves quickly ran off to their calling mothers in the adjacent pasture.

Everyone had a job – even the younger kids, who were assigned the task of marking the calves with chalk. The best roper was the daughter of the neighbor. She couldn't have been more than 15, but I only saw her miss once.

The five crews worked quickly and efficiently as horses continuously dragged new calves in between those being addressed. These seasoned horses knew their stuff and guided by their riders, weren't distracted by the smell of burning flesh or the cacophony of noise.

After concluding my fence-post duties, I remembered my promise to live life to the fullest. I threw caution to the wind and joined in a crew as the rear wrestler. It was a task I had often performed in my youth. Grab the top leg with one hand, free the leg from the rope with the other hand, while simultaneously placing your right foot against the hind quarters of the other leg. Thus stretching the calf out in readiness for the hot iron. The technique came back pretty fast after the second calf. However, getting up and down was hard on my old knees.

It was all very exciting. Every now and then a calf would break loose and raise havoc until it was recaptured and wrestled to the ground.

One such time, I was holding the rear legs of a good-sized animal when the forward wrestler lost his grip and the calf was suddenly afoot. The brander dropped the hot iron and tried to hold him but failed. To avoid getting kicked to death, I let go too.

I'd only just got to my feet when the calf, still tied at one foot, went behind me to the left, while the horse was to the right. The lariat snapped tight, catching me just above the ankles, propelling me high into the air for a three-quarter gainer. I landed on my elbows with my SKs well over my head, which must have hurt immensely, because I injured my left shoulder.

I say "must have," because my attention was focused on the hot branding iron under my butt. I yelped as I rose horizontally three feet into the air. Once I regained my feet, I began running in circles looking for the water trough.

In my haste, I failed to see the woman with the inoculator until I collided with her and took a full dose in the left arm. Feeling a bit lightheaded, I decided to sit out, or rather stand out, the rest of the afternoon. At the least, there was some comfort in the notion that I wouldn't ever have to worry about worms.

When it was time to leave, there was a bit of commotion about ownership since I'd been branded. But I was having no part of that argument.

Although only 70 miles (115 k) away, the trip onwards to Miles City riding the Pearl was a long one, as I had to stand most of the way.

South Dakota

MD 144.06.09.08:08
June 9, 2017

Seeing as it was my hometown, I had plenty of friends and classmates in Miles City. I took advantage of the sympathy of my classmate Maureen and sort of moved in to convalesce. The trip to the clinic for x-rays revealed that my left shoulder was indeed separated and I felt justified in acting like a wimp each time I tried to raise my arm. Although, it turned out the diagnosis was only partially correct, creating all kinds of issues later. In any event, it was obvious I was going to need more than chicken noodle soup. Much to Maureen's surprise, I decided to take six days to regroup before I felt like I could handle the bike safely.

I spent my time wisely and industriously. Sleeping in, lounging in front of Netflix, going for walks and swimming at the local lakeside pool to exercise my shoulder. But more importantly, visiting friends and rellies.

"While cleaning out my belongings last year," I told my friend Scott as we lounged on his back deck, "I discovered a plastic bag full of old receipts, beer coasters, maps and other paraphernalia from our trip. I thought we should go through them once more before I toss them out." The year after we'd graduated from high school, Scott and I had set out on an adventure. We'd hitchhiked across the US to New York, flown to Europe, and hitchhiked across Europe for four months before returning home.

"I can't believe you kept all this stuff," he said in astonishment as I emptied the bag on the table. "Can you believe we only paid $268 per person for the round-trip ticket from New York City to Luxemburg?" he laughed, holding up the ticket.

"Here's the song we made up that day we waited forever for a ride outside of Trier," I said and read off the verses that at one time must have made sense. We spent most of the afternoon going through it all and reminiscing, each reminding the other of important facts or stories we'd forgotten over the years.

"I'm into competitive barbecuing now," Scott informed me later.

"I never knew such a thing existed," I said as he showed me his recently purchased pellet-fueled BBQ. He explained the whole competition process and I was surprised and happy to hear that after the food was judged, it was given to those in need.

"What are you doing with your days?" he asked as we sipped another beer.

"Swimming mostly," I laughed. "Can you believe my entry is free because I'm from out of town and therefore a guest? What a city!"

"Blocking off the serpentines of the Tongue River and turning one into a swimming pool and another into a boat lake was a stroke of genius," he said. "How many towns in Montana can boast a swimming pool with a sandy beach between the changing room and the water's edge?"

The pool also sported a swimming platform, diving boards and a water polo area. As a kid, I used to spend nearly every day of summer in this pool. It was, without a doubt, one of the key reasons our species was able to survive in this country before the advent of air-conditioning.

"Do they still use the boat lake?" I asked. When I was a kid, the adjacent oblong boat lake was surrounded by a cattail marsh and had a ski jump in the middle. On busy weekends, there would be two or three boats circling around trailing skiers.

"No. They've made it into a duck pond now. In fact," he continued, "it's hard to believe even one boat could do anything more than go in a tight circle. It doesn't look much bigger than a football field."

"It seemed bigger back then," I said. "How fortunate we were to live and grow up here."

At church that Sunday, I was able to catch up with six more classmates, two friends with whom I used to work, and my cousin Brian. Well, actually it was my cousin's wife, since he was out of town for a couple of weeks working up north. I had seen him two years earlier, but still hoped to catch him on the way back.

It was time for a test run to see how my body would handle the bike. Off to the small town of Terry I went, where I visited my cousin Evelina. Visiting with relatives was proving a very enjoyable experience. Each one was able to provide me with the current addresses or phone numbers of their siblings or other cousins to add to my contact list. Besides filling me in on history or anecdotal stories about my parents and grandparents, I began to learn about them as individuals. And of course, to know them is to love them.

Finally, Maureen said, "Enough! How are you going to see anything if you don't leave?"

Thanking her profusely, I loaded the Black Pearl like a packhorse, and headed south of town the next day. A whole 50 miles later, I reached Mike's ranch for another grand visit with a classmate. I'd called ahead to confirm he'd already finished branding. Just in case. We drove around the countryside checking on his cattle and investigating the quality of the grass he would soon be cutting for hay. Mike's ranch was similar to Dan's. "South of Miles City" would be an appropriate address. Lots of open space.

Then onwards into the Black Hills of South Dakota. The area was a reservation for the Sioux until gold was discovered and then, of course, the land was taken away.

The Harley-Davidson National Rally is held in Sturgis every year. Since I was planning on coming back for the rally and I sort of knew the area, I didn't spend nearly enough time for a proper visit. But it afforded me a chance to check out campgrounds for when I came back to the rally. Then I stopped and walked around the streets of Deadwood, an old gold mining town. Wild Bill Hickok had been killed there while playing poker. Many other old cowboy names kept coming up as I looked around.

As is so often the case, I had dawdled along until nearly dark without arrangements for the night, enjoying seeing several mountain goats and lots of deer as they ventured out towards dusk. But then it started to rain as I approached the last chance for a campground.

"Sorry. We're full up," apologized the campground host.

"Tents don't really take up much room," I countered. "I don't actually need a whole campsite. Just a flat spot."

"Well," he considered as the rain began in earnest, "take that spot over there by the tree."

"Thanks heaps," I said, quickly withdrawing from the doorstep to begin setting up camp. I think he just wanted me to leave so he could get out of the rain.

The next morning, he ambled over as I was striking the tent and admired the Black Pearl. "Nice ride."

"Thanks. And thanks again for letting me stay last night. I wasn't keen on riding in the rain."

"I figured. I used to be a biker myself. They called me Skids," he smiled, with a distant look in his eyes. "You just come from the Needles?"

"Yeah. Actually, the whole of Custer State Park was an incredible ride. I just love how the narrow road winds its way through the maze of rock formations. And the one that looks like it has a needle eye in it is brilliant," I replied animatedly. "Spectacular scenery. Grand vistas across the valley. And the tunnel at the top is magic."

"I know. I try to explore as much of the area on my days off as I can," he stated.

"How does that work as a host?"

"I get two days off a week to travel. Otherwise, I have to stay around the campground."

"Tough life."

"Someone's got to do it," he smiled. "If you're heading south you'll want to take in the Wind Cave National Park."

"Sounds interesting."

"It is," he continued. "There's a huge cave network, but even if you're not up for going underground, the visitors' center is an entertaining visit."

"Why's that?"

"The funny thing is, there were two people fighting over who actually owned the property, and unwilling to compromise, they eventually took each other to court. After the judge heard their arguments, he decided everyone would be best served if it were a National Park instead. So, both parties lost out."

"One for the people!" I said as I finished stowing the tent on the bike and brought the big V twin to life.

"Ride safe," he yelled as I negotiated the Pearl onto the dry pavement and brought the rpms up to a satisfying purr.

After miles of tree-covered mountains, it was an eye-opener to cross the Oglala National Grassland. Nary a tree in sight. Just miles and miles of rolling grasslands waving in the gentle wind like waves on the sea. It was easy to let my mind wander. And while reflecting on the situation at Wind Cave, I thought to myself, *How often have I fought with someone, where both of us were unwilling to give any ground until suddenly realizing we'd both completely lost out?*

Shortly afterwards I reached the end of the park and rolled on into Scottsbluff, Nebraska.

Nebraska – Kansas

MD 144.06.12.18:45
June 12, 2017

Scotts Bluff holds a historically significant position. For the early settlers, it marked the end of the vast flat and vacant plains as the wagon trains tracked their way across the land. An unfortunate traveler named Scott was left for dead by his friends after being involved in a skirmish with the local Native Americans. The following year his friends returned, only to find his skeleton some distance from the fighting area, where he had apparently crawled and attempted to climb the bluff. I think they felt a bit guilty, so they named it after him.

The bluff itself sits prominently above the plains, and with a quick ride to the top, I was rewarded with a comprehensive view both directions. From there I could see another prominent point to the east, Chimney Rock – or Elk Penis as it was originally called by the Lakota Sioux. It was another landmark for the wagon trains, marking the beginning of the Great Plains. I was looking forward to passing by it on my departure.

The wagon trains that passed through here bragged a pretty determined group of people. Traveling just 10 to 15 miles a day, you have to give them high marks for determination and patience. And, the reality of it was, according to the stories in the nice museum at the base of the bluff, many of them had to walk the whole distance on foot.

Part of the reason for being in Nebraska was to see my cousin Tennis who lived in Scottsbluff. He was another relative I hadn't seen for over 40 years – let alone meet his lovely wife, kids or grandkids. They agreed to put me up for the night.

After dinner and a fantastic catch-up of the missing years, they informed me about the following afternoon's drastic weather forecast. Hail, tornadoes, heavy rains and the like. At first, I shrugged it off. However, the next morning they showed me the weather channel radar imagery and my courage waned somewhat.

I spent the early part of the day looking at touristy things. Then I accepted an invitation to head out and see the feedlot Tennis manages. I figured he was going to ask me to help him throw some hay over the fence to a couple of cows.

Turns out, the feedlot was a complex and intricate conglomeration of computers, software, haystacks, silage towers, truck circulation roads, scales and cattle pens, capable of handling thousands of cattle. "We raise and cut our own hay and corn for much of their feed from properties in the surrounding countryside," he informed me. It took us a couple of hours to drive around all the enormous fields. Then it was time for the afternoon feeding.

"The feed is a delicate computer-controlled mixture of ingredients," began Tennis. "Hay, silage, corn, molasses and vitamins are all mixed based on the desired growth rate or the specific needs of the cattle in each pen." As he input the recipe on the computer, a hopper was filled with the correct mixture.

"This is remarkable," I said. Then he began demonstrating how the whole mechanical process worked. A truck pulled in under the hopper.

"Now we just dump the hopper into the delivery truck. Why don't you climb aboard and go with the driver?" he suggested.

So I did.

"The feed trucks are monitored by the base computer via GPS," said the driver as we proceeded down the corridor between pens, auguring out the feed. "That ensures each truck deposits the correct amount of feed at the appropriate pen. Fool-proof really."

"What if you were in the wrong corridor?" I asked playing devil's advocate.

"The augers wouldn't work and an alarm would show up here on this panel," he pointed, "and back at the base station."

Sitting in that truck, I fed a lot of cattle and never threw a single bale of hay over a fence.

As predicted, it rained heavily that afternoon. Hail stones as big as four inches (100 mm) in diameter fell at the outskirts of the city. Three or four tornadoes touched down in the near vicinity and moved eastwards out of town to outlying communities. Suddenly all the cell phones in the house went off as each received a text message alert: "Tornado imminent in your area. Seek shelter below ground immediately!" Wow, what wonderful technology!

Of course, we immediately ran out into the back yard to see if we could see the twister.

I confess I had mixed emotions. While not wanting to see the destruction of people's homes, I would like to have seen a funnel from a reasonably close distance, and at least some of the golf-ball-sized hail that was being reported all around the city. However, the main thrust of the storm seemed to split around both sides of our suburb. The hail was only pea-sized, but the rain was so dense I was unable to see the funnel when it dropped down only blocks away.

The next morning the sky was blue, the sun was out, and all was beautiful again. I headed roughly northeast to investigate the damage from the storm.

The area just before and after Alliance seemed to have borne the brunt of it. Several miles of power poles were down, hundreds of trees were broken or overturned, and debris was scattered here and there. One field was covered with deformed sheets of corrugated metal, ripped from the sides and roof of a barn that had been completely destroyed. Later, I saw 26 railroad cars that were overturned. When I worked on the railroad, we figured an empty boxcar weighed 32 tons and loaded ones upwards of 110 tons. That was a mighty powerful wind to tip over all those cars.

Staying the extra day in Scottsbluff had been a smart move.

People are usually proud of their area and there are often local attractions unknown to the wider world. I frequently met people along the way who would say such things as, "You have to stop at..." or, "You must visit..." Well, this time it was, "Go see Carhenge."

So I did.

I pulled into the carpark and stared in awe. Old cars had been half-buried and placed on top of each other to replicate the more famous Stonehenge in England. The wrecks had been painted gray, and from a distance looked remarkably similar to the original. The city boundaries had had to be redefined to bypass building regulations and allow it to remain. Although, apparently some of the locals didn't appreciate the humor of the place. But I certainly did. It's now a popular visitor attraction, with other car-part artworks displayed on a walking trail around the site.

Build it, and they will come.

I'd been making the most of American delicacies, and as I approached Thedford for the night, I felt the crown on one of my teeth start to wiggle. Uh-oh, too many sticky Hot Tamales. North Platte was the first town of any size close by and I went in search of a dentist the next morning. After checking out six practitioners who would only see me if I made an appointment for the following week, I finally found one who could see me that same afternoon.

"Please complete these forms," said the smiling receptionist as she handed me a clipboard bearing a wad of paper.

"That's a lot of pages," I observed.

"That's because you're a new client and we need the information for our files and the insurance companies." Then handing me another sheet of paper, "Here are the prices for tooth repairs, painkillers, anesthetics, new client fee and insurance claim form fees."

She seemed shocked when I said, "Look, I don't need to be in your files. After today you'll never see me again. I don't have insurance. I'll pay cash right now for the service. All I want is my crown reattached."

"But it may take several visits," she stammered.

"Then I'll have to pitch my tent out front because I have no place else to stay," I threatened.

She looked like a deer in the headlights.

"Look," I said, "I'm confident that all the dentist has to do is take off the existing cap, clean it and re-cement it back in place. I'll pay you cash. And I'm out of here in an hour."

Which was in fact the case, and I succeeded in only paying for the work done – a reasonable fee at about a third of the cost of what would have been charged if protocol had been followed to the letter. So much of what we pay for nowadays is the result of overcautious bureaucracy. I truly believe that if there were no insurance companies, the cost of medical services would actually be affordable for the average person.

At Gothenburg, I found a local park where there had once been a Pony Express Station. These guys were incredible. They were known to have ridden up to 300 miles a day. At 20 miles an hour, that would be 15 hours. Even traveling 300 miles a day on paved roads on my bike is a long time in the saddle. Buffalo Bill Cody was only 15 years old when he rode for them. He was fortunate the Pony Express only lasted a couple of years. Otherwise, I think he might have died early of kidney failure due to the strain of always riding at full gallop.

The land began changing from the previous flat grassy plains. Now there were sand hills covered in grass, and hundreds of windmills. One little town offered up a sign stating something about "Windmill Capital."

Crossing the border into Kansas, the land-forms changed again – still very flat, but now the land was workable. More trees appeared, as well as fields of wheat. The valley along the Platte River was lush and green, although it appeared to have flooded a bit.

I passed a small development that included a petrol station in the shape of a four-story tepee, and surrounding it were a number of smaller tepees used as motel rooms. Someone had painted high water marks on the big tepee recording previous severe flooding. There was one in 1935, which reached to the top of the entry door. And one in 1951, which reached clear up to the window sill on the second floor! This is relatively flat country, meaning any flooding would have been spread out over a considerable distance. It boggles my mind to consider water that deep from a flood.

Cawker City borders the cool and picturesque waters of Waconda Lake, and also lays claim to the largest ball of twine in the world. I suppose someone had to have it, so good on them. Eight million feet long and 43 feet (13 m) in circumference is pretty impressive.

Harley-Davidson had a factory in Kansas City where they built bikes like the Heritage I was sitting on. I intended to take a tour and collect an ABC point. Unfortunately, they were revamping their operation for 2018 production and not receiving visitors, but I managed to take a photo outside to prove I'd been there.

I continued on to find a lovely little campground located in Leavenworth, alongside the Missouri River, where I pitched my tent for the night. Leavenworth is home to a medium security United States Federal Penitentiary – a fairly desolate looking prison from the outside. Now I can say I did time in Leavenworth. Ha ha. When it suits of course.

Several of my fellow campers were fishing along the river. One caught a huge catfish about 30 inches long. He set up an old ironing board, which he used as a bench, and proceeded to clean and skin the fish with a pair of pliers. Pretty clever. These fish make it pretty tough to get at their meat.

That night a storm came through. I became concerned about the stability of the surrounding trees as the wind began to blow in earnest and rattled them something fierce. I was afraid one might blow over on top of me, and considered moving closer to the river. Good thing I didn't. A four-inch diameter branch fell through the roof of one of the RVs parked there. The end of the branch stopped about a foot above the bed where the owner was asleep. With rain entering the hole, a soaked bed, the branch swinging just inches from his nose, and copious amounts of adrenaline coursing through his body, there wasn't much sleep for him that night.

Missouri – Arkansas – Louisiana

MD 144.06.15.15:15
June 15, 2017

I have always felt a bit naked in big cities, until I get to know them, or have a guide and a secure place to leave the bike while I explore. So I only took a quick tiki tour up and down several of the main streets in the central business district of Kansas City before heading east. Both the Kauffman Performing Arts Center, facing out over the valley, and the Convention Center, which straddled several blocks and streets, looked pretty interesting architecturally and structurally. But I didn't take the time to investigate either of them internally.

As soon as I escaped the city, I took to the rural roads again.

My destination for the day was to be Jefferson City. Having visited my cousin Kim and her husband Troy on my previous trip, I was keen to see them again. I'd covered the lower half of Missouri last year, so I decided to stay to the north half this year. While looking at obscure routes to get to Jefferson, you can imagine my surprise to discover the small city of Slater! How could I not go there?

The ride was sensational, with good roads all the way. But of course, the real thrill was seeing my surname plastered all over the place. Starting with the "Slater City Limits" sign, to the Slater Police Station, Slater Newspaper, Slater City Department of Public Works, Slater Veterans Memorial Park, Slater Library, Slater General Store and, my personal favorite, the water tower. I've gotta say, there's just something really magical about seeing your name on a water tower.

Several men were loitering near the Public Works entry, and I expected them to be just as excited as I was. Y'know, something like, "Well, I'll be danged. You mean to say your name is the same as our little town here? Can I shake your hand?"

Or, "Amazing! Maybe it was named after one of your forefathers. Isn't that something?"

Or, "Let me buy you a beer!"

Unfortunately, none of these things happened.

While I was sitting in front of Slater First Bank, a guy pulled up and walked towards me.

"Good afternoon," he said.

"Hi," I said, "I'm Rod Slater," sticking out my hand.

He looked at the bank and then at me. I puffed up a bit.

"OK. Can you tell me how to get out to the main highway from here?"

"Uhmm. Actually, this is my first time in town and I have no idea," I confessed.

But that still wasn't enough to take the shine off the afternoon.

Kim and Troy are enthusiastic bikers, but the previous year they'd been without a bike when I'd arrived. This year they were determined to make up for the lost opportunity by taking me on some of their favorite rides. The next day had already been organized – a charity ride involving three motorcycle clubs. Troy belonged to the Saddle Bastards MC club, and we rode with them a hundred miles north to where the official ride began. Then it was 120 miles around country roads, with a short break along the way, arriving back at the start an hour and a half later.

Black skies threatened in the near distance on the 100 mile ride home, sending bolts of lightning to accompany us. Some serious rain chased our tails the whole way. Lightning frequently lit the highway in front, well beyond the reach of our headlights. As luck would have it, the first drops of rain hit us just as we pulled into Kim and Troy's driveway.

The next day they took me on another ride to Lake of the Ozarks, then on to a state park. We looked at the intriguing ruins of an old mansion perched on a hill overlooking 5,000 acres of brilliant lush native old growth forest. It must be a sight to see in the fall, when the leaves explode into vibrant color in the throes of death, before relinquishing their hold and falling silently to the ground.

Before I left, Troy presented me with a proper silver bell for the Black Pearl. The skull and crossbones emblazoned on it was the perfect choice, matching the nautical theme of the bike. A generous and much appreciated gift.

For those uninitiated in the mysteries of motorcycle travel, there are many dangers lurking and ready to strike the unsuspecting biker. Trolls being one of them. These malicious creatures hide under bridges or in deep potholes waiting to pounce and wreak as much havoc as possible. The silver bell provides protection when given as a gift. Hung as close to the ground as possible, it sends out a pure ringing resonance, terrifying the trolls and causing them to scamper into hiding.

Or so the theory goes.

Monday morning, safeguarded by the protective qualities of my shiny new silver bell, I hit the road again in search of more ABC points. I crossed Route 66 and recalled having seen a Harley-Davidson dealership off the main road the previous year.

The ABC competition allowed a maximum of 20 points for Harley-Davidson dealerships, and I already had well over that figure. But it's interesting to visit different stores and experience each one's unique character. There's always a space set aside for HOG members, and more importantly, a free cup of hot coffee and a chat with like-minded people. This dealership was no exception and I was glad to have stopped. Then it was back on the road, down through Arkansas.

I'd picked up a map ahead of time with the best scenic routes already marked out. But first I headed towards an old mining town called Zinc, to get my second to last missing letter. A lady at a petrol station along the way assured me they had a post office there which would suffice for the photo.

Turns out, the town was more or less gone. Unaware of this fact, I carried on as the road diminished from two-lane asphalt to a one-lane gravel track. When I finally arrived, I found about 10 to 15 scattered dwellings in various stages of dilapidation. I knocked on the door of one, which looked to be inhabited, to ask where the post office was. No one answered, but a couple of guys and a dog soon appeared out of the forest.

"Could you tell me where the post office is?" I asked.

"Nah. Gone."

"It's the building I'm interested in. I don't care if it's closed."

"Nah. Gone." He paused. "Burned," was his response as he pointed to the adjacent vacant lot. Bits of charred timber were strewn about the site.

I would have asked him more, but I think he'd used up his vocabulary and wasn't taking too kindly to my presence. I did find a building down the road that indicated I was in the right location. It had a small hand-painted sign designating it as the "Zinc Volunteer Fire Department." Not sure that it would pass inspection for a point, I took a photo nonetheless.

Arkansas is such a beautiful, tree-covered state.

While winding along the scenic route through the forest, I would often come across clearings where artists had installed sculptures or artworks of various kinds. One was a metal structure composed of various machinery parts depicting a biker doing a wheelie. Later I passed a letterbox along the side of the road that said "MAIL" on it. And immediately after was another box mounted on top of a barber pole, 20 feet in the air. It had "AIR MAIL" written on it. While it might be conceivable that a drone could drop off a letter, I couldn't envisage a person shinnying up the pole to retrieve it.

Fireflies started showing up again as I erected my tent just before sunset. They always catch me unawares at twilight. Little flashes of light and a "What's that?" Then, almost before you can see them, the pretty little creatures are gone.

Tucked away in a valley, a short distance off the road, was a place called Boone's Lick. It had been a salt lick once run by Nathan Boone – Daniel Boone's son. I'd heard of salt licks for animals before, but this one was a salt water spring. For some reason, I'd never considered springs to be anything other than fresh or artesian water. And here was a salt water spring, hundreds of miles from the ocean.

The Ozark Mountains provided another enjoyable riding experience. Vacant roads, with intermittent pullouts to observation points, offered grand views across tree-enveloped hills and lake-speckled valleys. I experienced a feeling of solitude in this sparsely populated area. Just me and nature. Consequently, the hustle and bustle of the city of Hot Springs caught me a bit off guard.

I'd been looking forward to arriving, and had a mental image of sitting in a small secluded hot pool. But, as near as I could tell, instead of a main spring with a series of pools where people soaked, then retired elsewhere to a hotel, it appeared that each hotel sported their own hot pool. The busy town projected the feel of a high-end resort community. Not that I really checked, but I suspected the price of hotels was beyond my reach.

The call to soak in hot water was strong, but I was already yearning for a return to the solitude and peace of the forests by the time I'd reached the city center. I cruised on out of town and over the lengthy bridge across Lake Hamilton, then set up camp along the water's edge, rationalizing that since it was summer, a swim in the cool lake was just as rewarding as a soak in the hot springs.

And it was.

I spent the next night in the campground at Candy Lakes just over the border in Louisiana – a beautiful forest setting that bordered yet another lake. Evening brought a glorious red sunset that reflected across the water. Followed by a red sunrise the following morning. Being a sailor, I took to heart the old adage of delight at night and warning in the morning. Sure enough, a check of the internet on my phone indicated a hurricane was approaching.

I figured it best to stay inland, where the storm would lose its power, rationalizing that if I continued across the top left corner of Louisiana, then traveled on into Texas, the brunt of it would miss me.

Right?

Texas to Mexico

MD 144.06.21.19:36
June 21, 2017

Hurricane Cindy was all over the news. Intensifying and forecast to cross right over the top of me. I figured that, since everything was bigger in Texas, this one would have to be a doozy before anyone took notice. At least the tempest was still a day away and, therefore, still not quite real. I pushed on.

Arriving at Carthage, I noticed a shrine and statue on the edge of town dedicated to Jim Reeves, the famous country western singer, followed soon after by signs for the Country Music Hall of Fame. Having grown up on country western music, I was obliged to stop and take the tour. Plus, it would be nice and cool inside.

"Welcome to the Country Music Hall of Fame," said the diminutive woman behind the desk as she stood up. Decked out in a fringed western shirt, tight jeans, boots and a silver belt buckle, she sure fit the part. "You can select any music you want on the jukebox while you look around."

"Thanks," I said, looking through the selections and pushing the buttons for Willy Nelson, Kris Kristofferson and Jim Reeves.

"Did you know Jim Reeves actually got his start as a radio announcer and sang songs between his radio shows to fill in time?" she asked as his voice came to life over the speakers.

"At least that way you could guarantee yourself air time," I laughed.

I began wandering along, reading about the origins of Roy Rodgers and Dale Evans, Red Sovine, Rodger Miller, Waylon Jennings, Sons of the Pioneers and the like. All music I'm familiar with. Each artist had a booth dedicated to them that included their history and a personal item – such as a guitar or a costume they once wore.

"Tex Ritter was one of the original singing cowboys," the lady informed me while I was studying his display.

"Yeah I knew that," I responded. "But I never made the connection that actor John Ritter, of *Three's Company* fame, was his son."

Before long it was time to get on the road again. Go places that I'd never been and see more new.

"Well, thank you, this has been enjoyable. But now it's back to the heat," I lamented as I finished the exhibits.

"You must get really hot wearing your helmet, boots, gloves, jeans, leather chaps, leather jacket and leather vest," she observed.

"It's been hot, but not unbearable so far. But it does provide good protection."

"In case you fall off?" she smirked.

"Falling off is considered bad form. But better safe than sorry," I admitted.

Once outside, I dug out my hydro vest, in the hope that it would provide for a cooler ride. I soon discovered that humidity has a big part to play in the cooling process. For instance, once humidity reaches 75 percent, and the air is laden with moisture, water doesn't evaporate as quickly and so it doesn't have the same cooling effect. Truth is, I'm perspiring so much in that environment, I sort of generate my own natural coolant for evaporation anyway.

Back to drinking plenty of fluids.

At the city of Nacogdoches I stopped to put some air in my tires. It was about 98 deg F (37 C) and my soaked pants and chaps were plastered to my legs as I bent over. This must have put a strange torque on certain muscles because suddenly there was a loud POP in my left leg and I went down like a ton of bricks. Near as I could figure out, I'd pulled a hamstring.

Walking hurt like the devil but sitting on the bike proved OK, so I decided to carry on a bit. However, I knew something serious had happened. After passing through Davy Crockett National Forest, I decided it would be wise to stop and pitch the tent. But first I bought a bag of ice, two cans of soup and a candy bar to tide me over for a couple of days while I mended – and waited out Hurricane Cindy.

Riding to the campground in this high temperature, combined with the heat from the engine directly below, meant the bag of ice on my lap was melting at the rate of a cup per minute. For once, the cold trickle down to my crotch wasn't completely unpleasant. But my biggest concern was that there wouldn't be any ice left by the time I arrived.

At the campground another cause for concern became apparent. Even though it was a weekend, there was only me and one other couple in a campervan. That sort of put the fear into me. Maybe this storm was more serious than I had assumed? Despite all this, I sat on the picnic table with the ice under my thigh until 10:00 pm, reading by flashlight. Just me and the fireflies. Then I retired with a very tender, cold, blue leg.

It turned out to be an exceptionally long night with heavy winds. But still no torrential downpours. With both cans of soup and the candy bar gone by 10:00 am, and only able to walk with a painful limp, I decided to bite the bullet and move into a motel room in Crockett. At least there would be better food and I could get some proper rest; and hopefully the motel would have an ice machine.

By now I was beginning to feel like the walking wounded, with the left side of my body having borne the brunt of the injuries. Shoulder, tooth and thigh. Safely ensconced at a motel, every couple of hours I alternated between ice and walking around the town whose namesake was another of my childhood heroes. I even saw a sign painted on the side of a building that read, "Davy Crockett slept here 1836." There was a small park at the edge of town with a log cabin and a ceramic tile mural depicting the man himself. It wasn't clear if the cabin had belonged to him or was just representational of the era. In either event, it was a fitting tribute to the King of the Wild Frontier.

The storm didn't really amount to much in this part of Texas, except for lots of thunder and a couple of small showers. Late the next morning, I headed west once again – just hoping I didn't drop the bike or need to do any other corrective action in a hurry, because my body, in its current state, would definitely not be able to lift the Pearl.

Remember the Alamo? During the Spanish American War in the 1800s, legends such as Davy Crockett, Jim Bowie, William B. Travis and the like, to a total of about 200 men, were holed up at the Alamo Spanish Mission. They held off a much larger Spanish Mexican contingent of about 6,000 men, led by General Antonio Lopez de Santa Anna, for 13 days. They vowed not to surrender. Consequently, every last man died. This inspired the remaining part of the country to rise up in indignation and defeat Santa Anna a few months later to the battle cry: "Remember the Alamo!" The end result of which was independence for Texas.

Of course, if you read the small print, the Alamo held no military significance. General Sam Houston had ordered the men to leave and not engage Santa Anna there, as it conflicted with Houston's future battle plans and he couldn't provide backup. These famous guys all more or less decided no one was going to push them around and they would go out in a blaze of glory.

Which they did.

The Alamo is located right smack-bang in the middle of San Antonio, since the city has grown up around it. Luckily, a couple of prominent ladies noted that the site had historical significance and stopped the course of progress from totally eradicating the old mission. It does look a bit puny stuck there amongst the modern skyscrapers, but it contains a pleasant exhibition and was a great place to be in the afternoon. Especially when the clouds opened up for a torrential downpour later on.

After purchasing a cheap plastic poncho, I walked along the San Antonio River, where I found a cowboy art museum. It contained a large collection of saddles, both in American and Mexican styles, and some impressive bronze sculptures. But the paintings were the real drawcard for me. Several delightful works depicting cowboys herding cattle and portraits of young Spanish women caught my eye.

The Riverwalk is an outstanding example of good urban design, as it cuts its own magical swath right through the heart of the city. Bridges of various designs span the river at random intervals. Numerous restaurants are tucked under walkways and bridges in the shade. It was a vibrant, charming and pleasant place to be in the heat of the day. Or equally, as in my case, to once more duck out of the rain.

Later, I went to the San Antonio Mission on the edge of town. This mission has been restored to much of its original condition and is maintained quite well. Walking around the grounds helped me gain a level of understanding of what the Alamo was probably like before the war. These missions were ambitious and yet selfless works established by dedicated missionaries. They provided education, food, safety, work, medical care and religious instruction to the indigenous population, and were generally well regarded.

Two potential ABC points waited further south – the country of Mexico, and the city of Zapata along the Texas border. By now, daily temperatures were running at 105 to 110 deg F (40 to 43 C), and it seemed Hurricane Cindy was a thing of the past. The landscape was pretty much flat, with heavy trees to each side of the road. The further south I went, the more the trees turned into shrubs and became sparse. It was only when I rose up on an overpass that I could see off into the distance. And then, it was just more of the same.

In Laredo, I rode the number two bridge across the river into Mexico and took my photo in front of the "Welcome to Mexico – Immigrations" sign. Then I rode six blocks down the street, turned left and took the number one bridge back to the United States... where I was forced to sacrifice my apple (which had just come along for the ride into Mexico) to a customs agent.

Most of my two-hour visit to Mexico was spent in a queue getting back onto US soil. The traffic moved at a snail's pace across the shadeless bridge. The Pearl got so hot while idling that I shut her off, taking a risk with my injured body and pushing her ahead one car length every five minutes until I reached the gate.

Thirst had been calling for some time. But now it was shouting loudly. I set off in search of refreshments while I sang to the tune of the old cowboy song, "Streets of Laredo,"

As I rode onto the streets of Laredo

As I rode into Laredo that day.

I spied a young biker sitting at Starbucks

Drinking his coffee in the heat of the day.

I see by your flat white that you are a Kiwi

These words he said as I boldly rode by

Come sit by my side and tell me your story
About this bike trip and the reason why.

Well… you know… maybe the heat had affected me more than I thought.

Mexico – Texas

MD 144.06.25.11:58
June 25, 2017

Every day there was a race between humidity and temperature to see which would hit 100 first. At sunrise, humidity's in the lead at around 91 percent. By 10:00 am it's neck and neck at 95. If humidity wins, the rain holds the temp just below 100 deg F, creating a veritable steam bath for the remainder of the day. If there are no clouds, temperature wins, then really revs it up – usually about 105 with 110 deg F the warmest I'd experienced so far. (That's 45 C my friend!)

After an iced coffee in Laredo, I continued on towards Zapata to nail that elusive Z. I believe there are only two or three towns in the US beginning with that letter of the alphabet, making it a tough one to find. But not as hard as X. I was afraid Zapata may have suffered the same fate as Zinc (Arkansas), Zero (Montana) or Zap (North Dakota) and idled into non-existence. But since it was a mere 100 miles away, I thought I'd go and find out. Success! The town was still there, and I located the post office with its all-important sign. Zapata translates as "shoe." I have no idea why that's an appropriate name for a place.

Leaving Zapata, I saw huge rain clouds approaching. Looking across the open landscape, it was obvious where the rain was falling and the direction it was headed. I felt pretty cocky as I took several deviations on local roads to dodge the downpours, until I finally ran out of options. The torrent that caught me would have to rate amongst the most severe deluges I've ever faced – on land or sea. Visibility was cut to about a hundred feet maximum, so I pulled over and got off the bike to reduce the amount of water accumulating around my crotch. When the rain lightened, I noticed every vehicle on the highway had pulled over as well. It was later pointed out to me that walking away from the bike was a smart move, because people often pull over while still moving quite quickly and can end up colliding with parked vehicles.

It was a long day riding from San Antonio to Laredo to Corpus Christi. The heat really wore me out. But I was looking forward to a beach campground I'd found on the free camping app I had on my phone. Arriving right at sundown was a thrill. I seem to have this "just in time" mentality when selecting campgrounds, and often arrive at sunset. The margins are pretty small, the variables many and my knack not infallible, so I guess one of these days it's going to be "just missed it."

As I was riding down the beach in the encroaching darkness, my phone dropped out of its holder. I wasn't aware of this until I started to set up the tent and saw the naked charging cable hanging down. Bugger!

Boats out in the Gulf of Mexico were treated to the sight of a frantic headlight sweeping back and forth as I raced up and down the beach several times. Finally, while standing on the footboards, with a torch in my mouth and moving at five miles an hour, I spotted a familiar black shape half buried in the sand.

Whew! It's scary how much I depend on that contraption. I use it as a timepiece, alarm clock, phone book, notepad and GPS map, to name a few. Not to mention all my precious ABC pictures which would have been lost.

The campground was at Padre Island National Seashore. The sand didn't prove to be as comfortable to sleep on as I'd hoped, but listening to the surf all night and feeling the breeze more than made up for it. When I awoke, it was high tide. Even though I'd put the bike and tent as close to the dunes as I could, the top of the surf line had risen to about five feet away.

And at first light, for the first time in 35 years, I took a dip in the warm water that washed in from the Caribbean. Perfect.

As I headed over the bridge from Corpus Christi, I noticed the aircraft carrier USS *Lexington* tied up to the shore. Not only was it possible to go up close for a look, but the vessel had been turned into a museum of sorts, with period aircraft on the flight and hangar decks. The officers' quarters had been set up with displays and information on where she had served, from Pearl Harbor and Vietnam through to her retirement. Continuous footage of the attack and aftermath of Pearl Harbor was shown on a big screen. After visiting the F14 Tomcat fighter jet, the F4U Corsair with fold-up wings (my favorite aircraft) and the Cobra attack helicopter on the flight deck, I moved on up to the bridge. From there I took command of the ship, shouting orders, launching planes, and taking evasive maneuvers, until I realized I was no longer alone.

Right about dusk, I found another campground just short of the Louisiana border and proceeded to make camp. A large cloud of mosquitoes had been gathering around my head while I finished setting up the tent. And when I reached down to unzip the entry, they saw their opportunity to position themselves for a night of feasting as I slept. Two squadrons broke free from the cloud and dove for the zippered opening.

Unbeknownst to the mosquitoes and myself, a rather large contingent of sand flies, with the same feeding intent, had entered the tent earlier in the day while I had been taking my morning swim at the beach. But their plan had been foiled when I'd struck camp and rolled up the tent soon afterwards.

Since then, they'd been compressed, steam heated until the morning dew on the rain fly finished evaporating, vibrated, blasted with 110 db exhaust and finally barbecued in 110 deg F heat as I rode across the desert.

By now, they were motivated to leave!

As I unzipped the flap, the two squadrons of hungry mosquitoes entering the tent encountered the departing four battalions of desperate sand flies fleeing for their very lives.

What followed next was one of the most savage insect battle encounters ever witnessed by a human being. The upshot was, after I'd flicked out the dead and maimed, the few survivors were too exhausted to pester me and I slept rather peacefully.

Have I mentioned that everything is big in Texas?

As I was nearing the Louisiana border, I thought I ought to stop and take a photo of a Buc-ee's Gas Station – the largest petrol station I'd ever seen. The main building was like a miniature mall and food court, combined with all the usual things you can buy at petrol stations nowadays. On the way in, I believe I counted 24 bays with four pumps per bay. I shouldn't have parked at the last one. It took me nearly 15 minutes to walk to the cashiers' station to pay. It was so far, I could see the curvature of the earth. Pumps disappeared over the horizon.

"What pump are you paying for?" inquired the cashier. I hate it when that happens.

It felt like at least a mile hike back to the pump to check the number, then back again. Forty-five minutes later, gas paid for, exercise for the day completed, windscreen cleaned, oil checked, and back in the saddle, I headed off towards Louisiana and New Orleans.

And gators!

Louisiana

MD 144.06.28.13:06
June 28, 2017

I pulled into New Orleans towards the end of the day, in search of the Airbnb room I'd booked two days earlier. Turns out, it was in a pretty good location – one block off the Canal Street cable car route. First thing in the morning, I set off on my daily walk. Which took in the cemeteries.

Morbid as it may seem, these cemeteries are a sight to see. I suspect that putting coffins in the ground in a Delta area is a bit like trying to bury a balloon in the bathtub. As the water table rises, so would the coffins. Which might explain all the above ground monuments and mausoleums. Since they are visible, people have taken the opportunity to create some extraordinary designs. Intricate little buildings sit side by side and are arranged along streets that form miniature cities. A necropolis of monuments.

The first time I'd ever seen these was in the movie *Easy Rider,* when the two protagonists dropped acid and wandered around the cemetery with some chicks all night long. Apart from the fact that it was daylight, I wasn't a young man, no drugs were involved and I was alone, my experience was remarkably similar to the movie.

I explored for a couple of hours, always drawn deeper and deeper into the cemetery. Some families had had continuity in the same plot from the early 1800s right through to the present. Along with the various designs of the mausoleums, epitaphs, descriptions and dates etched into stone gave hints about the people entombed there. Imagining the missing details of their lives extended my exploratory morning walk to nearly lunchtime.

Riding the cable cars was a cheap way to get a feel for the city. I bought an all-day pass, traveling out to the end of a couple of different routes, then back again. After that, I got some real exercise, walking along the waterfront and through the French quarter, before heading back for a nap to ensure longevity for the approaching night life.

Bourbon Street lived up to its reputation for wild musical entertainment after dark. You had your pick of jazz, rock, country and more – and every band was very good. The bands competed with one another for attention. Doors and windows were thrown open in the heat, creating a clashing cacophony of musical melodies for anyone standing in the middle of the street.

I later found a group of musicians playing traditional New Orleans jazz in the middle of an intersection. Although I think the set-up was staged, it still maintained an impromptu feel, and it was easy to get caught up and carried away in the music.

It seemed to me that everyone was tolerant of everyone else. Rich, poor, sober or drunk. Such a laid-back city.

Ohhhh, how I like the Big Easy.

There's something about the Bayou that has always captivated me. It's totally alien to anywhere else I've ever visited. Now it was time to jump right into the thick of it. I found a tour package that promised alligator encounters and travel through some real back country Bayou.

"If I wake up in the morning, open my tent flap and there's an alligator there, what do I do?" I asked the guide. This was one of the big questions that had been plaguing me the last couple of days. "Running isn't an option as they can reach speeds of 30 miles an hour, and nowadays I'd be lucky to get past a trot on a smooth downhill stretch."

"No one in the Sportsman's Paradise State of Louisiana has been killed by ah gator, so don you worry none," came the response.

"That's not the case in Florida," responded one of the other punters. "Three dead last year."

"How do alligators know when they have left Florida and are now in Louisiana?" I asked. "What if they're on holiday? Or maybe just feeling a little peckish and, after a visit from a cousin down south, decide to give it a try?"

"Don be silly," scolded the guide.

Leaving me still unsure of the answer to my question.

Seventeen of us boarded a slender rectangular aluminum boat, with a canopy overhead and seating down the middle facing outward to each side. In no time, we were propelling along at a decent speed into the Bayou. We turned right. We turned left. We went down straightaways that branched out one way or another. All the while surrounded by trees that, to the untrained eye, looked exactly alike. On and on, with nary a street sign in sight. How in the world they knew where we were, beats me. Suddenly the boat stopped at a wide spot in the waterway.

"All right. Keep yer appendages well and truly inside the boat," advised the guide as he began putting a hot dog on a long stick. Soon several heads could be seen swimming our way. The guide held the stick about five feet out of the water, waving it gently back and forth. Abruptly, a gator shot into the air and snatch the hot dog. "Some gators can get 75 percent of their body outta of the water to get that titbit!"

I took a photo where all four legs and two feet of its tail were out of the water, and his head was above the boat canopy!

"Females grow to about six to seven feet," continued the guide. "Males never stop growing, so depending on the food source, they can reach well beyond ten feet."

We moved out of the channel and in between the trees, until we reached a place where a sow was feeding with her piglets. They came to the boat to munch on small corn cobs we threw into the water.

Several alligators competed for the corn and the mama pig was quick to ensure they kept their distance from her young. Though the guide said there seemed to be fewer piglets now than several weeks ago.

Amongst intermittent torrential downpours, we saw ample numbers of alligators, swamp pigs, raccoons and bird life. And I got a nice feel for the Bayou. I like the moss hanging down from the trees, and the clear water out of the channels. But I still think I'd feel more comfortable walking through the mountains with bears and rattlesnakes than wading through the Bayou with alligators and water moccasins.

Mississippi – Alabama – Florida

MD 144.06.30.07:43
June 30, 2017

Towns in this area are difficult to see, let alone find your way around in. I could never discern a main street structure in the smaller communities. And the trees were so thick I couldn't see any landmarks. Like a water tower. I'm glad Slater was in Missouri.

When I arrived in Slidell, I just rode around a while until I found a place serving tacos and beer – generally a great combination, and judging by the good-sized crowd, it appeared the food there wouldn't disappoint. I ordered the Big Ass Burrito. When it arrived, it hung over both ends of the 12-inch platter, well and truly living up to its name, and was accompanied by a half Cajun and half Mexican salsa that was very spicy and hot. Just the way I like it. The music blared away as I sat enjoying the food and beer.

All too soon, the shadows began to grow long, and I climbed back aboard the Pearl and moseyed out of town in search of a place to pitch the tent for the night. Nearby, I found another semi-primitive campground that was supposed to have a porta-potty toilet and potable water. It didn't. But by then it was too late to go anywhere else.

Next morning, the burrito's hot sauce kicked in early, giving me cause for concern. Searching for privacy, I set off down towards the edge of the swamp and then along the fringe of the bayou.

Remembering the mountain camping experiences of my earlier years, I came equipped with three tissues and sought out a tree with a nice low-level branch – the likes of which I could hold onto, while leaning out and away to protect my pants piled neatly at my ankles.

I should point out that with recent memories of gators jumping for hot dogs, I thoroughly scouted out the area around the tree first – carefully poking a stick into the water and underbrush to disturb any snakes or alligators lurking thereabouts. Satisfied I was alone, I continued with the task at hand.

I was just about to make use of the final tissue when the branch parted company with the trunk.

Just out of Biloxi in the Magnolia State of Mississippi, I spotted a biker, obviously in trouble, off to the side of the road. I pulled over, killed the Pearl's engine, put down the kickstand, dismounted, removed my helmet and walked over.

"I think it's an electrical problem of some kind," he said by way of greeting. "I was able to get hold of my roommate by cell phone shortly before you arrived but it'll be a while until he gets here."

After considering my limited abilities in electrical trouble-shooting and my feeble attempt at finding a loose battery terminal bolt on my trip around the East Cape in New Zealand the previous year, I offered to help. "How about we check the battery terminal connections first?" I prompted with a knowing air.

"I don' have any tools," he apologized.

"No worries. I'll just grab my tool kit," I said heading back to my bike. "And some water. You look a little warm."

"Thanks. I've been here over an hour and this heat is a killer."

The terminals were tight and secure, which pretty much depleted the extent of my expertise. But together, using reason and logic, we went through everything we could think of.

"Well, it's not the fuses, or the spark plugs, and there are no bare wires that I can see," I said.

"I guess we just give up," he said sounding quite depressed.

We sat on the edge of the road, and handing him the bottle of water, I told him how my day had started with a misadventure.

"Wow," he said.

"It's funny how there's always someone worse off than ourselves," I began. "Suppose you put ten people in a room and each one took a turn telling the group how bad things were for them. By the time the last person finished, each person would feel that someone else was having a harder time than they were and find some reason to be thankful. Your friends are coming

254

to collect you and your bike," I continued. "I'm thankful that I haven't broken down in this state, because if I did, it could potentially become a major catastrophe."

"How so?" he asked.

"I have no friends living locally who could come to collect me, I'm unfamiliar with the area, requiring a real effort to find a tow truck or repair shop. The likelihood of a campground next door to the repair shop would be practically nil, meaning I would probably have to stay at a hotel and take taxis back and forth. That would be expensive. Not to mention the cost of repairs and the loss of valuable adventure time," I concluded.

"I think I understand now," he said as he seemed to sit up a little straighter. "And I'm thankful I didn't start the day sitting in my own feces!"

Houses along the Mississippi Delta and coastline are all raised up on stilts, to deal with the huge surges brought on by hurricanes. Perched some 18 feet (5.5 m) up in the air on columns, they resemble giant spiders. Some of them have been enclosed below, but these additions will inevitably end up being sacrificial. As an architect, I couldn't help thinking about the challenges of disabled access. Ramps would have to circle the building twice to gain enough elevation.

While chatting to the ladies in the information kiosk at the Florida border, I asked, "Is this forested area shown on the map very hilly?"

"The highest elevation in the whole state is only 381 feet!" they laughed.

Turns out, Florida isn't much more than a huge sandspit.

I was surprised at how dense the forests were though – and, in fact, how much of the surrounding countryside was tree-covered. There were very few open areas along the highways and trees lined both sides of the road. Crossroad intersections gave the impression of walled highways heading off in four directions. With no hills allowing for overviews or outlooks, I felt like a rat in a maze much of the time.

It was onwards to the Tampa area, where I had another two cousins I hadn't seen for 40 years. Loren and Ron, with their lovely wives, each put me up for a couple of days, fed me, let me lounge in their pools and showed me the sights. It was the rest and relaxation I desperately needed. When I left Tampa after the Fourth of July celebrations, I felt refreshed and invigorated. There's something intangible about family which really binds you together. I'd also learned several new things about my family history, which had piqued my curiosity. I was headed for New York, and when I got there, I intended to investigate the Ellis Island Immigrant Log Books to see if I could find my grandparents' arrival dates and signatures.

I had planned to visit to Disneyworld but opted out in favor of Cape Canaveral instead. Ron had mentioned something about an upcoming rocket launch. An organized person would have checked the launch schedules, but I just set out, on a leisurely route that took me through the Indian River orange plantations.

I stopped at the Indian River Citrus Museum and Heritage Center to take a break and escape the heat. I was astounded to learn that all the orange trees in Florida have their origin from one orchard located in this area. There was a big freeze one year, killing all the other trees in the state, and so branches from the surviving orchard were grafted onto the remaining root stocks of the others, until all the orchards were restored. Nature and humanity working together.

When I reached the coast, I took Highway A1A. Jimmy Buffett had titled one of his albums in honor of this stretch of road. I sang "A Pirate Looks at Forty" as a soundtrack to my ride, playing peek-a-boo with the ocean through the trees and buildings. The highway seemed deserted much of the time, but would swell with traffic and houses on both sides whenever I passed through a city. When I reached Daytona, it did a bit more than swell. It blossomed!

As well as being famous for the race track and spring break shenanigans, Daytona hosts a big bike rally every year. From the posters and all, I got the impression it was more or less the Sturgis of the east. As such, there were several clothing stores and shops that catered to bikers. I stopped for a squiz and an ice-cream cone.

Afterwards, I headed north out of town and camped on the beach about 30 miles south of Cape Canaveral. After setting up the tent, I set out for a walk along the water's edge. Before I took ten steps, a loud crackling roar stopped me dead in my tracks. Even though I was some distance away from the launch site, it was obviously the sound of a rocket lifting off. Bugger! Oh well, I'd nearly timed it right.

Cape Canaveral and the Kennedy Space Museum were a pleasant surprise and were much more than just a bunch of launching pads. I touched a moonstone, rode in a lift-off simulator and looked at all the exhibits. What was most awe-inspiring was an actual space shuttle, which had been suspended from the ceiling. The top was covered in a material that looked like cloth – all fuzzy and completely different to the sleek smooth skin that I would have expected for something designed to fly through space and land back on earth. But I suppose with no air friction in outer space, smooth is not a requirement.

Later that afternoon, continuing up Highway A1A, I found another beachfront campground. Since it was still early, after I'd pitched the tent, I set out to explore. Walking the beaches, at intervals I saw little fences with flags, indicating that turtles would be coming ashore to lay their eggs at night. I sat up in the dunes with a half full moon until late, but I gave up on seeing one. After all, the chances are pretty small with miles and miles of beach.

Following a refreshing morning swim in the Atlantic (my first ever), I headed up to St. Augustine to look at the Castillo de San Marcos – the oldest masonry fort in the continental United States, built over 300 years ago to defend Spain's claims in the New World. On the way, I stopped at the early warning lookout for the fort. The quarried stones used for both were made up of compressed seashells – making them soft and spongy, as stones go. The end result was that when cannon balls hit the fort and outlook (courtesy of the British in 1702, 1728 and 1740), they just sort of bounced off. While the fort and outlook changed hands several times over the years, it was never captured.

The best part of my visit was watching one of the old cannons being fired, which was done with tremendous pomp and circumstance. There was a good deal of explanation about the number of men on the gunnery team and their roles. With all the talking, it took 15 minutes to load and fire the cannon, compared to the real crack teams of the past, who could have loaded and fired the cannon every two to three minutes. I suppose when people are shooting at you, there's significant motivation to return as many shots as you can.

The rest of the city looked like it might be fun to explore, but parking was a nightmare. Instead, I simply rode around and observed from the street, before moving on from the Sunshine State.

Georgia

MD 144.07.07.18:22

July 7, 2017

Florida's top half is covered in signs Ponce de León this and Ponce de León that: alluding to the famous Spanish explorer. Which piques the imagination and begs the question, "What if?" I went to the Fountain of Youth Archaeological Park, which was tucked away in the foliage near the edge of St. Augustine, then set off to find someplace cool to quell my thirst.

Inside a dimly lit pub, I struck up a conversation with a gentleman who looked about my age. He was dressed in smart casual but I could tell he was a man of means. We talked a bit about everything. He was in a very positive, if not jovial, mood.

"You seem to be in a very upbeat mood. What's the source of your happiness?" I inquired.

"It's my birthday today," he beamed.

Naturally, I shouted him a round, and we continued talking for several more rounds. He seemed knowledgeable. "I'm enjoying our talk," I said. "It's so hard to find people who are straightforward and who you feel you can trust. So many people fail to look beyond the surface of their expectations to see the opportunities right in front of them."

"Well said," he responded. "I too have been enjoying our conversation." He contemplated for a moment, then, "And I'll let you in on a little secret." Leaning towards me in a confiding manner, he continued, "I'm 500 years old!"

I was pretty much speechless at that. The fountain being the reason for his youthful appearance, I supposed.

He carried on, "I was a porter for Juan Ponce de León and the sole survivor when the party was attacked by natives. I managed to hide in the underbrush and they never found me. Later, while trying to navigate my way back, I stumbled onto the fountain we were looking for and, well, here I am!"

Oookaay

"To celebrate, I decided to give five people a gift," he continued. "One for each 100 years of my life. And you, my good man, are the fifth one."

Yeah, right!

Turns out, the gift was a "map" to the Fountain of Youth, drawn on the back of a bar napkin.

I thought I was about to be conned. Something like, "If you could see your way to giving me $50 or $100 for this priceless information, I would be eternally grateful." But there were no strings attached. I accepted the sketch and thanked the man profusely, before heading out into the harsh light of day.

The destination on the "map" was indicated with a large X. It appeared to be on my way, so I thought, *What the heck!*

GPS coordinates would have been helpful. But as I deciphered the accompanying handwriting, the directions presented themselves as a series of short commands. Such as: go three miles, turn right, turn left at large oak tree, look for rock with red scratch. And so on. Off I went.

Four hours later, I was totally lost. At first, the markers on the "map" and the directions held true, but soon the roads dwindled to trails and the trails to paths. Finally, the only option was to park the bike and go by foot through twists and turns, up a series of steep inclines. I walked 400 yards as instructed, then the directions said something like, "At the top of the hill, turn 90 degrees to the right and walk 50 yards. There will be a tree with three trunks." But there was no tree with three trunks.

While holding the map open to reread the instructions and figure out where on earth I'd gone wrong, a deluge of warm rain suddenly struck, and despite my best efforts to keep it dry, dissolved the napkin into a blueish pulp. I was just about ready to quit when I heard a disturbance nearby. Looking through the dense foliage, I could make out a small clearing lined with big leafy plants. The heavy rain had left water dripping from all the leaves. However, off to one end of the clearing there was a small trickle of water leaking out of some rocks and running into a mud puddle.

I could make out four youths, two girls and two guys, splattered with mud and stripped down to their underwear. Which, I noted, seemed oddly old-fashioned. Old clothes were strewn on branches around the perimeter. One girl was sitting in the puddle gleefully rubbing mud all over her body. The other three were running around the clearing whooping and hollering. One guy was laughing and swinging a walking cane at the other woman, as she shrieked in mock terror before collapsing in laughter. They were totally oblivious to my presence. Two young couples on a double date, tearing the place apart, and most likely on some kind of drug.

I was soaking wet and disillusioned at the amount of time I had invested in this misadventure. And frankly quite disgusted by the youths' antics, I turned around and left the mud hole without talking to them.

I found my way back to the Pearl after half a dozen attempts and false trails. Then the trail widened into a road, the road to pavement, and I could pick up speed. Once I was back on the highway, I began drying out. Oh well, it was still an adventure.

But crossing into Georgia, I couldn't shake a strange nagging feeling that perhaps I'd missed something and passed up on some kind of opportunity.

Georgia provided a change of pace, as I hummed the gentle song, "Georgia on My Mind." Floridians treated the speed limit as a suggestion, usually traveling at about 20 miles an hour over whatever was posted. Here the highway speed limit dropped from 70 to 55. And motorist stuck to the law.

The ride on up towards Macon was again hot and humid, as the country road weaved between fields and forests. By late afternoon, I arrived at my destination – the home of another cousin, Monte, and his lovely wife Gail, whom I'd never met. Again, somehow 45 years had passed. They took me in for the night and Monte showed me around the countryside the next day on his quad bike.

"I'm continually amazed at how forested this part of the country has remained. Riding along, you really have no idea what lies 50 yards off either side of the road," I observed.

"During the Civil War, armies passed by less than a mile away from each other without either knowing the other was there," said Monte.

That night we went out on the town to catch some of the famous local music talent.

The Slater half of my relatives have always seemed to carry musical genes. During my visit, Monte and I spent considerable time catching up on our family history and reliving fond memories of my dad, uncles, aunts and their cousins gathered at Monte's parents' house. Memories of guitars, fiddles and mandolins, and songs like, "You Are My Sunshine" and "Red River Valley." Filling the night with melody, laughter and cigarette smoke until long after us kids had fallen asleep wherever we lay. Seems the musical genes have continued to filter down to Monte's kids too. He showed me a YouTube video of Slater House Band playing their original song, "How Handsome Dan Became a Zombie." I'm so proud of my cousin and his musical family.

"Make sure you take in the Macon Aviation Museum before you head out," reminded Gail as I saddled up the following morning.

The museum boasted a large number of vintage fighter aircraft – including Snoopy flying in his Sopwith Camel. The collection also included a P38 Nighthawk (the fastest plane in the world), F15 and F111 fighter jets, a World War 2 era P51, an A-10 Warthog, and numerous other displays both indoors and out. Magic!

The slow-flying Warthog is basically a 30 mm Gatling gun with wings. Known as the "tank killer," it fires armor-piercing bullets so fast, it must be like a continuous wire of metal from the cannon to the target. Not much need for cross-hairs. Moving the ribbon of bullets up and down or right and left would simply cut the target in pieces. Sort of like waving around a garden hose of destruction.

One of the real treats was the B-17 Flying Fortress bomber that was undergoing restoration. After talking to a staff member, I was taken behind the rope cordon to get a real good look inside. The underbelly ball turret was sitting off to one side where I could almost crawl inside. Imagine sitting exposed in a position like that, hanging down, shooting at planes that are shooting back at you.

Aircraft have become so refined over the years that they are now the preferred method of military defense and aggression. Distances mean less as speeds have increased. Weapons are more specific, accurate and lethal. Lives can be saved by the ability to act remotely, while a huge effort has been put into more efficient and advanced ways of killing people. I fully understand and appreciate the need for defending our country. However, I think it would be so much better if the government didn't sell *any* military technology to other countries. Allies or not. I don't see the need to keep the world on a level playing field in this area. After each deal is done, another plane, faster and better, has to be developed to take its place. Which, of course, is paid for by you and me. I understand how all of this gets tangled up in corporate interests, but there are other ways of stimulating the economy.

I felt bad, as I only took in the corner of South Carolina, then shot through North Carolina almost as quickly. It would have been nice to go a bit closer to the coast and look at the old southern mansions. But I confess the heat was wearing me down, and there's only so much time to explore. I was feeling the pressure to keep a move on.

Shadows frequently fell across the woodland roads, keeping the direct sunlight off my black leathers as I wound my way through the countryside. That helped take some of the edge off the heat. And it was nice to finally see some bumps and small hills appearing in the landscape.

Near the border between North Carolina and Virginia, I found a really nice Army Corps of Engineers campground on the edge of High Rock Lake.

"One person with a tent," I said.

"You're paying for the site," came the reply. "Same price for one person, four people, RV or a tent. Water and electricity included."

I've always felt somewhat cheated having to pay for electricity and water at campsites. I thought that was a luxury for RVs and not much use for people in tents. But the setting was splendid and the view superb. Plus, the lake called invitingly for me to come in and cool down.

So I did.

I arose early to take my morning walk, followed by another short swim, before the heat of the day began in earnest. You can imagine my surprise to see that local campers had brought air-conditioners for their tents to deal with the heat. These units were typically sitting on a tub, with a tarp draped between the tent and the air-conditioner to help duct the cool air under the rain fly and inside. Extension cords snaked across the ground to the power pole by the carpark. And thus, the reason for the fixed fee. What extravagance! What decadence!

Next, I headed off to Walmart to see what size air-conditioner would fit on a motorbike.

🏍️ 🏍️

Virginia – DC – Delaware – New Jersey

MD 144.07.13.09:14
July 13, 2017

I rolled on through the central part of Virginia along tree-lined rural roads, until the trees began thinning, revealing more and more open space. Off in the distance to the west were the mountains – a welcome sight, even if I wasn't heading in that direction for a while.

I was astonished that the open spaces were just grass – all trimmed and manicured like lawns. I'm not positive, but I suspect these areas were once tobacco fields. Off to the sides of the road, I saw a number of very old two-story log cabins, and timber buildings that I took to be drying sheds.

Passing through Richmond on old Highway 1, I could see the remains of tobacco manufacturing plants on the edge of town. Pretty dilapidated and run down – hopefully due to lack of sales. I scooted quickly through the city.

Further north I came to a shrine for the Confederate general Stonewall Jackson, set in the location where he died of pneumonia, subsequent to being mistakenly shot by one of his own men after the Battle of Chancellorsville, during the Civil War. A little further along I came to Fredericksburg, where a series of battles had been fought – Fredericksburg, Spotsylvania, Chancellorsville and the Battle of the Wilderness. I visited the information building and took a walk along the old battle lines.

Fredericksburg was one of those unbelievably terrible battles where foot soldiers were ordered to run uphill across a huge expanse, with nothing for protection, towards an enemy that was well ensconced behind a rock wall. Out-and-out slaughter ensued. Having witnessed the mosquito and sand fly conflict back in Texas, I shuddered as I envisioned the human death and carnage that must have taken place here.

I must confess I'd been looking forward to the current leg of the trip with mixed emotions. I'm curious about the East Coast and all its history, but traveling through involves spending time in big cities. Mountains, deserts and oceans don't worry me much. Cities do. I guess I'm more afraid of people than of sharks, bears, alligators and snakes. Not knowing what's socially acceptable and safe, compounds this fear. The sheer number of people intimidates me. I do believe that most people are good. It's just the fact that some aren't – and they're camouflaged in amongst the good ones.

At least in the ocean, the sharks stand out amongst the fish, and if you see a bear in the woods, you pay attention. But to me, walking around in New York City feels a bit like walking around in a herd of bears, or swimming in a very large school of sharks. There are most likely two or three in there that are dangerous, but since they all look alike, you don't know which ones to worry about. As such, stress levels remain elevated, making it hard to enjoy the surrounding scenery.

Through skill, experience and diligence, I'd managed to make my city exploration even more intrepid by timing my arrival at every metropolis precisely at the beginning of rush hour traffic.

The breeze generated by moving along at 40 to 60 miles an hour makes being hot and sweaty all day more tolerable. But speed is the first casualty in a traffic jam. Since my motorbike engine isn't water-cooled, without sufficient airflow it runs even hotter. And of course, I'm sitting directly on top of the motor as we creep along in stop-start traffic. Heat radiates outwards from the cylinders striking my leather-clad legs from the ankles to the thighs. Then it continues to waft upwards and towards my chest and head. Sometimes it's like looking at a desert mirage through the distorted hot air.

There have been times when I've had to pull over onto the shoulder and read a book while everything cools down. Much to the intrigue of other commuters. However, the number of other bikers who have stopped to see if everything's OK has been inspiring and comforting. We watch each other's backs.

To literally add salt to the wound, my pants and underwear had been completely saturated by sweat for so long during this journey that I'd developed salt water sores on my bottom! And I thought it was bad when it was fresh rain water coming in through the seams. In the future, I may have to investigate a seating solution that allows air flow between me and the seat. Maybe one of those beaded seat cushions that taxi drivers use.

Washington DC was my second attempt at using an Airbnb. Nervous about vandalism and theft if I left my bike on the street, I asked the landlady, "Is there off-street parking?" when I made the reservation.

"How big's the motorcycle?" she asked.

"It's a Harley-Davidson cruising motorcycle. Pretty big," I answered.

"Yes, you can leave it in the back yard."

Hot dog! The price was OK so I entered the dates on my iPhone. The price came back even cheaper than than the one listed. Better yet! However, after locating the house, it became obvious that there had been a failure in communication. I made another call to the landlady.

"Your yard is big enough," I said, "but the gate to the yard is not. I had a hard enough time squeezing through it myself, let alone the bike."

"OK. Well, can't you just carry it up the stairs and leave it on the front porch?" she asked. I then realized the source of the misunderstanding.

"This bike weighs in excess of 700 pounds," I explained, "I'm not going to carry it anywhere. Also, your porch is shorter than the bike is long."

"Oh my! I had no idea," she exclaimed. "Well let me see what I can do. I'll call you back."

I headed on inside to discover the reason for the reduced price. The bedroom I'd viewed on the internet had been taken by someone else whilst I had been on the phone reserving it. I'd been demoted to sleeping on the couch. Not ordinarily an issue. But this one was shorter than I am tall. By quite a bit.

I went for a walk to think things through, get my bearings and plan my method of attack for the morrow. Even after dark it was hot and humid, but the neighborhood was full of people out dining, drinking and having a good time. The average building was four to five stories high, offering a comfortable human scale as I explored the local streets. By the time I'd returned, the landlady had found a willing neighbor a couple of doors down with a bigger gate, so I stowed the Pearl in their backyard.

In my accommodation, the AC was turned down so cold, I slept in my sleeping bag with the zipper all the way up. If it isn't one thing, it's another.

The DC Mall is quite a large place to explore, but I gave it my best shot. After a 45-minute walk from my lodging, I arrived at the White House. Unfortunately, President Trump was in Paris for Bastille Day so I wasn't able to give him any advice. Actually, no one was allowed closer than the opposite side of Pennsylvania Avenue, and even that was closed off to vehicles. The Washington Monument was also closed, so I couldn't go inside and make the climb to the top. Most of the monuments in this area have been photographed from every conceivable angle, so even though this was my first visit I knew what to expect visually. But to walk around them and actually stand at the base of or inside them is another experience altogether. A marvelous one.

With the heat of the day approaching and rain forecast for the afternoon, I sought shelter at the Smithsonian Art Museum and Museum of Flight. Having recently been to Cape Canaveral for my fill of space travel, I elected to spend more time examining the early flying machines – including the Wright Brothers' original plane. It looked brand new, since the canvas had recently been replaced. One thing's for sure, with the tour of the USS *Lexington* (navel aircraft), Kennedy Space Museum (rockets to the moon), the Macon Museum of Aviation (modern military aircraft and fighter jets), and now the Smithsonian Museum of Flight (first and developing aircraft), I had certainly broadened my education regarding machines that fly. I doubted there was much left to see and therefore no need to stop at any further museums of that kind for the remainder of my travels.

It was fascinating to discover that the aircraft engines developed by Glenn Curtiss had often been tested on motorcycles. I was particularly drawn to the V8-cylinder Curtiss motorcycle. That must have scooted right along!

The Smithsonian Art Museum comes in two parts: the National Gallery of Art, and American Art. Figuring I had time for both, I went to the National Gallery first. I spent way too much time studying and admiring a particular Italian marble sculpture. It has to rank as the single most intriguingly realistic sculpture I've ever seen. It's a bust of a woman with a veil over her head. There are many folds in the veil with smooth areas partly clinging to her face. The overall effect is transparency. Stone made to look transparent. A remarkable achievement.

Since my interests primarily lie in maritime art, it was also a real novelty to see some Turner and Homer paintings with my own eyes. Very inspirational. Come closing time, I had nearly finished exploring the first gallery.

I felt a strong sense of disappointment at missing out on the American Art museum as I motored past the Jefferson and Martin Luther King monuments the next morning. I would have to be more efficient with my time in Philadelphia.

The next Airbnb was located in a pleasant, quiet area in the countryside, about a 20-minute train ride from the heart of Philadelphia. Leaving on the train at daybreak, I pretty much covered all the primary attractions before arriving back at my lodgings just as it got dark.

I still find it amazing that our forefathers included so many insightful components in the Constitution. Of course, the big surprises to me were the fact that the vote for independence was taken on the Second of July and the actual signing was in August. The Fourth of July was only the day the document was formally written – but it's too hard to change it all now. Anyway, it's hard to imagine any day other than the Fourth as Independence Day.

Independence Hall is a simple and humble building – as it should be, in my opinion. In fact, I think politicians should meet in First Grade classrooms. It's hard to be a pompous ass full of self-importance when sitting in a little chair with your knees up to your ears. It's also difficult to sit there very long, encouraging faster resolutions and fewer filibusters. But most importantly, it would be a constant reminder of why they are there in the first place – for the future of the country.

The Second Bank of America building had an art gallery filled with life-like portraits of famous men painted by C.W. Peale. Completed before the days of photography, Peale's incredibly detailed artworks captured the character of his subjects to a degree that often escapes the lens of a camera, and are similar to the famous works of New Zealand artists C.F. Goldie and G. Lindauer. Peale left a great legacy behind. That is, in addition to his 17 children, most of whom were named after famous painters, such as Raphaelle and Rembrandt. No pressure there. But it comes as no surprise that a number of them became well-known painters in their own right.

I spent hours studying the way C.W. Peale had layered his colors to achieve realistic results. I decided to deviate from my usual maritime scenes to apply what I'd gleaned and try painting at least one portrait once I finished the trip.

There was quite a queue waiting to look at the Liberty Bell. Similar to the disruption of my understanding about the Fourth of July, I was again disappointed to learn the bell hadn't cracked while ringing to announce the winning of our independence. I suppose now someone's going to tell me there's no Easter Bunny. But it's intriguing that a faultily constructed bell became such an important icon to America.

Every creation of man, when investigated closely or broken down to primary elements, will expose imperfections. Yet the potential of the whole can become greater than the sum of the parts, overshadowing the faults and defects. Pealing out a pure tone to rally a nation. I wondered what the bell sounded like.

Turns out, it's considered bad form to try and ring the bell.

I found it curious that so much of this trip had passed by historic attractions that focused on war. During a walk along the Delaware River waterfront, I discovered tours for the WWII submarine USS *Becuno*, and an old steam warship USS *Olympia*, used in the war of 1812. They didn't seem to mind me crawling around and investigating every nook and cranny of each vessel. It didn't take long to figure out that living on a submarine wouldn't be for me. I much prefer being able to see more of my surroundings than the myopic tunnel vision available in a periscope. Mind you, mooring fees would be non-existent and dragging anchor a thing of the past. Simply set her down on the bottom at night or when you reach port.

Now that I'd seen where the nation was formed and her seat of government, it was time to visit her most famous city.

New York

MD 144.07.18.14:10
July 18, 2017

I was singing "Margarita" by the Traveling Wilburys – "went to the Big Apple, took a bite" – as I arrived in New York. My first stop was the Statue of Liberty, where I strutted right up to the ticket counter.

"I'd like a ticket for the Statue of Liberty, please," I asked with confidence and determination.

"For what date?" asked the ticket lady.

"This morning," I replied. "And I want the ticket that allows access to the crown and then up the arm to the top of the torch for that iconic view across the harbor."

"None available," she said with a look that hovered somewhere between incredulity and irritation.

"OK. Well, this afternoon then."

She shook her head no.

"Tomorrow?," I pleaded.

"People are no longer allowed up the arm. And tickets to the crown must be purchased two to three months in advance," she informed me, taking away the last of my steam.

A boat ride to Ellis Island and another to the lower base of the statue itself was the best I could do on short notice. Up-close, the statue is a wonder, and it's hard to believe the exterior copper sheeting is only the thickness of two US pennies. Equally hard to believe were the logistics of construction and the methodology used to get her to where she is. Hammered out of copper sheets, riveted together, disassembled, shipped to the United States, then reassembled around an inner support structure. The artist, F.A. Bartholdi, certainly earned his fame. The interior cast iron structure is also fascinating because of its designer, A.G. Eiffel, of Eiffel Tower fame. Thank you, France! What a lovely gift.

I was trying hard to think of any recent gifts from one country to another. Other than weapons, nothing came to mind. Perhaps the world could do with a bit more of that Statue of Liberty kind of spirit.

So far the day had been a thoroughly enjoyable, but there was another reason for my visit to New York.

"Hello," I said to the cute young woman at the Ellis Island info desk. "I would like to look through the book of arriving immigrants to see if I can find my grandparents' arrival date and their signatures, please."

"Unfortunately, the actual books are not available for public inspection," she replied.

"Oh," I said as my face fell.

"Everything's digitally available nowadays," she added helpfully. "You can use those computers over there or log on to our site via the internet."

"What a country!"

Since the day was too nice to spend in front of a computer, I decided to delay my research for another time. It was a grand morning to be riding the ferry and walking around through the displays. Also, I needed to kill some time to ensure arrival in the heart of the city at rush hour.

My grandparents had spent months at sea on their way to America from Prussia. Seeing the grand old lady with her torch held high, with the city spread out in the background, must have been exhilarating. But then came hours of paperwork, waiting in quarantine, and finally crossing into a densely-packed metropolis of crammed-together apartment buildings occupied by numerous nationalities. It must have been a traumatizing experience. All that effort just to get a proper bagel!

My iPhone had done a pretty good job of navigating me around the country. Only twice had it totally failed me. On one occasion, it sent me to some obscure hayfield in the middle of nowhere. Those hiccups aside, I'd naturally become somewhat dependent on the device. However, it would seem that the code writers and toll road operators were in cahoots. It just loved to reroute me onto toll roads – all under the guise of saving me valuable time.

I suppose people going to work might appreciate one minute knocked off their commute. But I'd already purposefully selected a route that was 15 minutes longer for better scenery. And the toll roads were not marked as such on the iPhone maps. Often the first notice I had was a toll booth in front of me. There were times when the device took me five miles off course just to find a toll road that ran six miles long!

I envisage a range of actions taking place inside the navigation app...

MD 144.7.18.14:10

Location: Bridge of the USS *Surprise* Navigational App

Smock: Captain is on the bridge.

Molotov: Captain. Am I glad to see you!

Quirk: What is it Molotov?

Molotov: He keeps missing the turns, Captain. I re-route but he keeps ignoring the turn onto the Toll Road at the last minute. He's only ten miles to destination and has yet to take a toll road. I can't take it anymore.

Quirk: Easy, Molotov. Spotty, I want you to lock on to him and steer him back to the last on-ramp he passed.

Spotty: I'ma doin' the best I can Cap'n. But I donna nu how long I can hold 'im.

Quirk: Cartledge, what do you make of his mental state?

Cartledge: Dammit Quirk, how should I know? I'm a programmer not a doctor!

Spotty: Cap'n I kina hold 'im. He's breakin' off. He's breakin' off!

Quirk: X-ray, turn off all alternate streets displayed on the monitor and force him to exit at 176th on my mark.

X-ray: Aye aye, sir.

Quirk: Three. Two. One. Mark!

Smock: Well done, Captain! He's on a no exit entry to the Holland Toll Tunnel.

Which explains why I arrived in Manhattan Island in a frenzied state with my wallet $20 lighter.

I traveled right through the heart of Manhattan Island, and continued out the other side to a northern suburb where Melanie, the daughter of my cousin Ron, generously allowed me to stay. What a boon it was to have that accommodation. Close proximity to Manhattan. Safe parking for the Pearl, and a nice bed to boot. I was introduced to Melanie's husband and their charming little girl – all three for the first time. We spent the evening getting to know each other, and they educated me on the best ways to get to and move about the city, then filled me in on places of interest for my northbound trip. My extended family rocks!

I was able to realize the full New York City experience. Taking the train into Grand Central Station, walking to the Chrysler Building, riding up to the top of the Empire State Building, seeing Madison Square Garden, Times Square, Fifth Avenue, Broadway and Central Park, and visiting the Guggenheim Museum, Rockefeller Square and several other places along the way.

I also sampled the famous New York bagel and consumed authentic New York pizza by the slice. All I needed now was an I♡NY t-shirt. But there was no point going overboard. Besides it would have exceeded my three t-shirt limit.

Seeing these sights on foot was about a ten mile walk all up, so I was once again dripping with sweat in the heat. The Guggenheim Museum was about halfway along my route and was the perfect place to cool down while looking at art – and more of Frank Lloyd Wright's architecture.

The building is really a work of art in its own right. Knowing that it had been designed to house the Guggenheim's extensive art collection, I had imagined a much larger structure. But it looked small compared to the surrounding buildings. What it lacked in size, it made up for in character. I took the lift to the top floor, then followed the circular ramp all the way back to the ground level. A giant Pollock painting near the top started the visit off on a positive note.

Most museums I've been to have no progressive lineal route through them, so it's often easy to ramble from one space to another and get lost. Not so here. In addition to the spiral display nodes around the open atrium, there are more conventional rectangular off-shoot galleries on a couple of the floors.

The space is so much larger than it looks.

The credo of John D. Rockefeller Jr. is set in stone at the base of the Rockefeller Tower – quite a moving collection of ten beliefs, and a great inspirational guide for someone wanting to succeed in life. Statements like: "I believe that whether by head or hand, the world owes no man a living, but that it owes every man the *opportunity* to make a living." Or consider this: "I believe that the law was made for man and not man for the law. That government is the *servant* of the people and not their master." Wow, pretty good stuff I reckon.

It might be a good thing for school children to recite some of these occasionally. Somehow, young people today seem to follow a new credo: "I believe only in myself, and what I *want* is the most important thing; everyone else should agree with me and it should be given to me *immediately* without needing to expend any effort on my part."

It transpired that my anxiety about big city crowds was a waste of mental effort. While their brashness takes a bit to get used to, the New Yorkers I met were just people on the move with no time for nonsense. Underneath, they were actually polite, friendly and pretty dog-gone nice. Not a shark to be seen.

Whilst waiting in the queue for the elevator at the Empire State Building, we were continually encouraged to move along by various staff. An elderly woman with a cane was just ahead of me, making her way as best she could. The lift staff person was a big, burly, tough-looking woman who was running a continuous monologue.

"All right. All right. Keep it moving." "Come on people, let's get into the lift." "Squeeze up. Make room. People are waiting." "Hold it up there for a minute. All right, come ahead. Keep it moving," she droned on as she herded us like cattle towards the lift doors.

Then suddenly her voice got softer when she noticed the old lady in front of me. "Hi dear, are you OK there? Let me help you. Next stop is the top of the Empire State Building. Mind the gap when alighting onto the lift platform. That's it. There you go, dear," she said, helping the lady inside.

And then just as quickly reverted back to her no-nonsense voice. "All right. Keep it moving, keep it moving. Everybody makes it to the top."

I had really been enjoying my time in the city that never sleeps, but all to soon it was time to say goodbye to the Empire State.

Connecticut – Rhode Island – Massachusetts

Mystic Connecticut, just as the state motto suggests, was certainly "Full of Surprises." In the old days it had a reputation for building whaling ships, and they've set up an entire village as a working museum, including a shipyard, chandlery, sail loft, blacksmith, cooper and clock and sextant shop. Most places had someone on hand demonstrating the relevant trade and answering questions.

The masts of a couple of square riggers tied up at the docks were visible over the tops of the New-England-style houses from almost everywhere in the village. On board, there were demonstrations of raising the anchors, freight or tenders onto the deck via the capstan. Replica skiffs were sailing in the light winds on the bay. This must have been a town full of hustle and bustle in its heyday. Such a romantic setting.

While the whole village was educational and enjoyable, my personal favorite had to be the long, skinny hemp rope-making building.

"The winder walked backwards," said a man in period costume. "Slowly feeding hemp into a long, low structure, like this one, where the rough hemp was wound into strands," he demonstrated. "And then the strands were fed into a machine twisting them into rope."

"That looks like a bit of walking," I said.

"They say the winder walked backwards about 11 miles a day," he informed me.

"Hard work no doubt," I said.

"For which he probably got paid a dollar a week," added the costumed man.

"And, all he could smoke," finished the glassy-eyed dude next to me.

"I know people who would jump at that opportunity," giggled his friend.

On the advice I'd been given by Melanie in New York, when I reached Rhode Island, the "Ocean State," I took a side tour. My intention was to see the extravagant mansions of the rich and famous, of course. The Great Gatsby must have lived in a cushy neighborhood like the one I visited. I asked around but no one seemed to know which house was his.

Just to be posh, I rode down America's Cup Avenue. My celebratory mood as a Kiwi-American cup winner was not mirrored by the local sailors. Since I'm a citizen of both countries, it's not really important to me which nation won. Only that one of us did.

And we did!

I had a near miss with another vehicle that apparently hadn't seen me coming. Perhaps for some reason I'd become a little too relaxed, and the incident caught me off guard. Remember, the number one rule of motorcycling is: You Are Invisible.

A motorcycle cop had pulled me over a while back. Dressed up in his orange and yellow jacket and reflective tape, he looked like Priscilla, Queen of the Desert, on the way to a day-glo party.

"You need to get a high-vis vest," he informed me.

"No thanks," I said. "If I wore one of those, I might start thinking people could actually see me and then I might lose some of my vigilant edge. Don't want to become complacent."

It's not clear exactly when – perhaps about 1930 or so – but at some point, I believe a Romulan Bird of Prey warship with a cloaking device landed on earth. The crew realized earthlings might pose a threat in future. Therefore, they came up with a clever plan to specifically eliminate the kind of adventurous earthlings most likely to venture into space.

Using their technology, they engineered a way to attach a cloaking device to some innocuous part required on every motorcycle. Not sure exactly what part it is, but it may resemble something as simple as a nut or washer. Ever since then, motorcycles have been invisible to the average driver once they are moving. And sometimes even while parked.

There's a scene in the Harry Potter movie *Deathly Hallows*, where Harry is hidden under his Cloak of Invisibility to avoid detection by Professor Snape. He could have just as easily accomplished his task while riding a motorcycle, because Snape wouldn't have seen him.

If Harry had been on a Harley, Snape sure as hell would have heard him.

But he wouldn't have seen him.

When I got to Boston, I had one thing on my mind: seeing *Old Ironsides* – the famous American battleship of the War of 1812. Her official name is USS *Constitution*, but she gained her nickname because, with her double-planked hull of oak, the British cannon balls just bounced off.

There were a couple of reasons, beyond the general attraction I have to old sailing vessels, for wanting to see the *Constitution*. The first was that I was building a scale model of her back in New Zealand and, when I'm doing that, I always enjoy seeing the real thing. The second reason was that a friend of mine had taken the tour, and subsequently presented me with a flag that had flown from her. Because it was a gift, that flag had special meaning and would have even more after I boarded the *Constitution* myself.

Turns out, after having been in dry-dock for several years, they were finally ready to launch in a couple of days, which meant the scaffolding had been removed and all tours were halted. But I did get to wander around and look at her masts, yardarms, cannons and whatnot, and took a squiz at her copper-plated bottom before she went back in.

The "Spirit of America State," Massachusetts, has a lovely coastline and is now on my "Must Come and Sail" list. I have a lot of lists. Quite specific lists. Anyway, the coast of Massachusetts is lined with quaint little anchorages and picturesque seascapes. It's easy to see why so many New Yorkers escape here by land and sea.

But there were still too many people for my liking, so I decided to make my own escape, further north.

Maine – New Hampshire – Vermont

MD 144.07.21.08:55

July 21, 2017

The immediate plan was to go as far north and east as Portland, Maine, then head across state back westward, before turning south along the Appalachian Mountains.

I felt guilty that I'd been missing so much of what each state had to offer. If someone told me they had two days and wanted my recommendations on what to see and do in Montana or New Zealand, what would I advise? My first advice would be, "Find more time." Just riding from one end to the other takes more than two days, let alone stopping to see things. How can anyone expect to really see or understand anything about an area's countryside and its people in just a couple of days?

But there were practical implications to consider. If I managed to visit 43 states, spending just two days in each, that would take three months. So I'd made the choice to see a little bit of everything rather than a whole lot of something – all the while making mental notes of particularly intriguing places for a potential return trip in the future. Hopefully, the things I saw were special or unique for each area, and I continued to meet interesting people along the way.

The state motto for Maine is "The Way Life Should Be." I could accept that. Arriving in Portland, I dutifully explored the heart of the old city, enjoying the feel of the place. They still had cobblestone streets in some areas. Mind you, cobblestone streets are hell on a bike. My eyeballs bounced around in their sockets like lottery balls during a draw, and my teeth chattered like it was 40 degrees below. After I bit my tongue, I said, "That's it," concluded the tour and headed out of town.

The temperature had finally cooled down enough to make riding enjoyable again. This was just as well, because the salt water blisters on my bottom side really needed a chance to heal.

Speaking of healing, my shoulder still wasn't quite right from the branding session in Montana. (I'd hotly dispute anyone saying that riding a motorbike for 12 hours a day had anything to do with it not healing.) Spying a Walmart's Pharmacy, I pulled over and ambled inside.

"Can I help?" asked the attendant staring at the vertical ridge on my forehead.

"Yeah, I've injured my shoulder and someone said you had some type of special tape here. Suppose to be as good as duct tape."

"Oh. Sure," she said leading me down the aisle. Handing me a small box, she said, "This elastic sports tape is just what you want. Much better than duct tape."

"Yeah?" I said dubiously. "Application looks complicated," I said, looking at the photo on the box.

"Instructions are on the inside. It's pretty straight forward." And then, the dreaded phrase: "Even a four-year-old could do it."

I hate it when they say that! It means I must have reached my intellectual peak at age four and it's been downhill ever since.

That evening I did my best and applied the tape in my tent at the campground. Of course, I got it in the wrong place the first time, forcing me to pull it off, along with copious amounts of body hair and small pieces of skin.

"Are you OK in there?" inquired a Canadian biker couple camped next to me.

"Yeah, I'm fine," I answered.

"With all the gyrations, growling and cursing from your tent, we feared you were being attacked by a wild animal."

"Just trying to get this blasted tape on my shoulder. But it won't stick now because there's so much blood," I explained.

I think they felt sorry for me and, as they helped tape the shoulder correctly, said, "We're riding into the village for a proper Maine lobster meal. Would you like to come along?"

They rode two up on one of their BMWs and I followed along behind on the Pearl, cruising in the warm evening breeze.

"Apparently the restaurant was once a fishing tool and net shed," said the Canadian woman as I noted the rough walls adorned with tools of the trade. "We love the rustic atmosphere and the lobster here is the best."

"Bibs and everything for my first Maine lobster. What a treat!" I exclaimed.

"We're on a two-week trip down from Montreal," said the man as drinks were served.

I told them of my trip, feeling quite proud of myself. Then, realizing I'd been bragging and dominating the conversation, I asked, "Ever do a long trip?"

"A few years back I rode from Montreal to Buenos Aries, then down to Terra Del Fuego on a 250 cc dirt bike," he said in a matter-of-fact voice.

That sort of put my little adventure in perspective.

We stopped off for ice-cream on the way back to the campground. Choosing between the 15 original flavors was difficult. But the two scoop cones were huge and delicious. The warm evening kept me licking as fast as I could to prevent ice-cream running down my hands and dripping off my elbows.

The only thing tarnishing the evening was my inability to fully lower my left arm. I only used the sports tape twice after that because it pulled downwards on my left cheek and I kept drooling. Perhaps I had applied it a bit too tight. Man, I detest four-year-olds!

For some reason, I expected everyone to live along the shoreline in this part of the country, with nothing but forests inland. Instead, I continuously came across little villages as I rode westward – all quaint and of similar architecture to the 1700s design vernacular. Red brick. White trim. Cupola on top. I kept expecting to see Paul Revere riding along the back streets swinging a lamp.

Better still, I was moving up into the Appalachian Mountains. The air began to cool even more and the mountain panoramas were good for the soul.

Cruising through the White Mountain National Forrest and into New Hampshire was very picturesque. The "Live Free or Die State" revealed a number of ski hills as I continued upwards. They appeared to be challenging hills too. Having passed through the big-name places of the Rockies, Aspen, Vail, Steamboat and the like, I was expecting to see puny little mountains with beginner runs. Prejudiced thoughts are terrible in all aspects of life, aren't they? New Hampshire's ski areas appeared to be quite competitive and accessible. I'd love to give them a go sometime.

I wasn't quite ready to stop for the day, but how could I not when I saw a sign proclaiming "Zealand Campground?"

My neighbor came over as I was pitching the tent.

After a few pleasantries, he inquired, "Have you been to the Mount Washington Hotel?"

"I just passed it but didn't stop."

"Pity," he said. "It's a beautiful old resort built in the 1900s. During its heyday, it bragged 57 trains a day full of tourists traveling to and from the city."

"Really!" I said surprised. Fifty-seven trains a day is significant no matter how many people were on board. "You come here a lot?"

"Fairly often for the hiking," he answered. "Tomorrow I'm going to attempt the Presidents Trail."

"What's the Presidents Trail?"

"There are several local mountains named after presidents and it's called the Presidential Range. Washington, Madison and Adams all rise up along the 23-mile hike. If I leave before dawn, I should be able to make it back just about dark," he said.

Once the tent was set up and the Pearl free of my gear, I took the man's advice and rode back to the Mount Washington Hotel. Magic. And true to his word, he was gone by daybreak. "Good on ya, mate."

I moved on to the Laconia Harley dealership to get a 35,000-mile tune-up on my bike. The beautiful lake views throughout this area added to the gorgeous morning ride. I rolled the bike over from left to right to left and so on, as the road snaked along the shoreline. What a day.

With the Pearl checked over and tuned up, I was all set for the miles ahead. Which is a good thing, since I've discovered why Harley-Davidson can afford all their fancy new dealerships. With my wallet lightened once again, I carried on with the journey. If my wallet got much lighter, I'd be riding two feet off the ground.

Crossing the border into Vermont was another eye-opener. The "Green Mountain State" it surely was. But there was a noticeable change in the level of wealth. Houses were not as well maintained. Towns seemed more run-down.

I was enjoying cruising the countryside and running through the gears, when I saw a sign for Augustus Saint-Gaudens' residence and studio. The word "studio" always conjures up an artist hard at work, bent over his or her latest creation, and the name seemed important, so I made a detour to see what it was all about.

Turns out, Augustus Saint-Gaudens was indeed a famous artist. His bronze sculptures, such as "The Pilgrim" and a whole series of Abraham Lincolns, were what I'd been seeing on my travels through the eastern states. It's always remarkable to see works of art, and then review the preliminary studies made in the development of the final piece.

After dawdling too long in the studio, late afternoon was upon me and there were limited camping options available. Two attempts were obstructed by "Campground Full" signs. I was ready to give up and look for a nice quiet field a short way off the main road, when a small unmarked campground appeared just outside the little town of Peru. Perched on the edge of an attractive and petite lake, it was perfect. In the morning, the lake beckoned me for an early swim. The water was warm and refreshing.

It was a Sunday, and on the day of rest, I typically start out by riding around the first town I come across to find a church with a service starting within the next half hour. If there are none, I move on to the next town and look there. Usually there's something that works out perfectly. Peru was no exception. When I arrived, there was a church service starting in five minutes. I parked the bike out front and walked in.

When showing up at these smaller community churches, where everyone knows everyone else, it's difficult to pretend you're not a visitor. Especially when you're the only one dressed in black leathers and everyone in the congregation turns to look at you. Boy, was I glad I'd had that morning swim to clean up.

As always, they were lovely people. Afterwards, over coffee and cookies, I spoke with several of the congregants who were curious about my trip. Then I was invited to lunch with the minister and a few others. Followed by a swim at another nearby lake that afternoon. And then a BBQ.

Ultimately, I ended up staying another day.

And, greeted with heavy rain the next morning, I was highly tempted to stay even longer. But, with the forecast promising rain for the next several days, I was concerned that if I lingered, I'd eventually take up residency and never leave. I bit the bullet and moved on.

Wrapped in the plastic poncho I'd obtained in Texas, rain pants and rubber gloves, I was dry enough. But the beautiful Green Mountain and Finger Lakes National Forests were lost to a misty haze, a rain splattered windscreen and a foggy face shield.

On a positive note, at least I passed through the wet weather system in only three hours. If I'd stayed in Peru, it would have taken two more days for the rain to pass. Still, I would have liked to have seen more of the countryside that had been hidden by the clouds.

There was one highlight. I spotted a covered bridge off one of the side roads and turned around immediately. There's something especially romantic about crossing a bridge with a roof overhead. This one had the sides filled in as well, amplifying the Pearl's pleasant, deep, reverberating rumble as I made a pass through. Then again, on the way back. And again, over the next couple of passes.

Just to be sure, you understand.

Massachusetts – Connecticut – New York –New Jersey – Pennsylvania

MD 144.07.24.16:05
July 24, 2017

The smaller states really make you feel like you're traveling great distances. By nipping through the corners where they all adjoin, I could say I covered five states in one day!

I relished being in the Appalachian Mountains. Traversing up the switchbacks awarded views across the valleys. I passed through a small town with a lake along the edge of a park, which had a quadrant roped off for swimming. It looked remarkably like the swimming pool from my home town. Perhaps it was the flood of memories, I'm not sure, but for some reason that made me feel really good.

As the day wore on, the rain came back and took the shine off my mood. I camped next to the Delaware River which, at that location, was quite a large body of water. The recreation area also boasted waterfalls and several hikes. *Right! That's tomorrow's activities lined up right there*, I thought. The campground office had closed at 4:00 pm, so I found a space for myself amongst the 25 or so empty slots.

First thing next morning, I decided I'd hike up to the falls I'd passed a few miles back. No such luck. The hiking trail was only open between 10:00 am and 4:00 pm. I was too early. As I traveled on, I passed a visitors' center, also only open between the hours of 10:00 am and 4:00 pm. Who only works between 10:00 am and 4:00 pm? Seems they either really don't want people to see things around here, or they want to regulate visitors like cattle so as to comply with the leisurely lifestyle of the state employees. I fear that the "Who serves whom?" question has been muddied beyond reconciliation.

It definitely falls into the "In Order to Serve You Better" category. This sneaky little phrase is a catch-all employed by banks, power companies, and the like. It often appears in letters and emails, and usually translates as, "We are reducing our services and increasing our fees." Communications such as, "In order to serve you better, we are no longer mailing you invoices. You will now have to print your invoices which are only accessible online," translate to, "We have found a way to reduce our costs, make you do the leg work and will also charge you more in the process." Funny how the reduction in *their* costs always costs *me* more.

Being a cynic, it's possible my translations sometimes go over the top. "In order to serve you better, we are reducing the opening hours for trails, visitor centers and campgrounds. Working between the hours of 10:00 am and 4:00 pm ensures our employees will not be stressed from driving in traffic and will remain happy at work. Please take note of these hours and schedule your life accordingly, to better suit our needs."

The weather, and my mood, had definitely improved by the time I entered Pennsylvania. I dropped down to the lower end of the state and skirted along the edges of the mountains. My goal for the day was the city of York, where Harley-Davidson offers a tour of their facility. I'd also collect another point for my ABCs.

I was a bit surprised to only see one horse-drawn buggy along the rural roads. I thought I had entered Quaker country in the "State of Independence" and hoped to see many more. *Perhaps they're at the other end of the state*, I reasoned.

About 50 miles short of York I found a road sign for Hershey. *Great. It'll be fun to see what a town named after a candy bar looks like.* The place didn't disappoint. The main street featured street lights in the shape of Hershey Kisses. There was a huge amusement park with at least three giant roller coasters. And the smell...

I was running late to make the tour at the Harley plant, but the smell of chocolate had eroded my resolve and I decided that candy was more important than motorcycles. That ended up being a good decision, since the York plant tours had already ended for the week. I really must look up some of these details ahead of time.

Turns out, the town of Hershey had been built by Mr Milton Snavely Hershey himself, and the whole town was pretty much dedicated to the manufacture of various confections – including my personal favorite, Reese's Peanut Butter Cups.

The Hershey Museum covered everything – from the life of Hershey, to the behavioral characteristics of cocoa beans during the manufacture of chocolate. There were even hands-on laboratories where you could make your own creation. Interestingly, Hershey failed at about 20 occupations, and went bankrupt a couple of times, before he succeeded at making caramel, using fresh milk. Later, as you are no doubt aware, he excelled at making chocolate. How's that for tenacity? There's hope for me yet! I know I've certainly failed enough times. In any event, learning about Hershey's life and business methods left me feeling motivated by the time I left. That delicious-smelling town had been the big surprise of the day. And I'm glad I saw it.

It was half an hour before dark when I found the Gettysburg campground – sufficient time to ride around the area and familiarize myself with the battlefield for explorations the next day.

The campground itself was right on the edge of the battlefield. But that's not such a big feat, since the battlefield is huge. They've done a tremendous job of keeping the city and battlefield undeveloped and looking like it did back in the day. It's easy to get a proper understanding of how things really went down.

Which is to say, terribly. At the time, the population of the town and surrounding district was less than 8,000. That number swelled beyond 180,000 over four days during the battle.

When I thought of 180,000 men lined in one area, the battlefield suddenly became much smaller. To put this in perspective, 180,000 people on 500 football fields would mean about 360 people per field.

Markers show where different regiments from both sides were located during the fighting. The combatants were pretty much shoulder to shoulder. Row upon row. In fact, it would have been pretty hard to shoot and not hit something. What a nightmare. Not to mention logistics. That's a lot of porta potties!

Inside the visitors' museum is a cyclorama painting of the battle by a French artist, Paul Philippoteaux. Standing in the middle of this incredible 42 ft x 377 ft (12 x 115 m) artwork, you're completely surrounded by a view of the entire battlefield. I could almost hear the pipes playing "Gary Owen" amidst the thunderous volleys of guns and cannons. And the screams of the wounded.

They give statistics of how many shots were fired and how many cannon balls fell. But when you look at the number of lives lost – roughly 50,000 – it all becomes meaningless. What difference does it make if you kill 50,000 people with 100,000 rounds of ammunition or 200,000 rounds? They're still dead. The maimed and wounded suffered terribly and many more died in the days following the battle.

When Texas and California make noises about seceding from the US, and others riot around the country complaining about how hard things are for them, they should come here and see the consequences of those kinds of comments and actions. Division is not what made or will make America strong. Tolerance, coming together and embracing our differences, respecting each other and building on our strengths will keep us strong. From this perspective, Lincoln's address becomes all the more powerful due to its brevity, simplicity and content.

My heart went out for this country as I headed back out on the highway. And for the first time on this trip, I wasn't singing inside my helmet.

Pennsylvania – Maryland – West Virginia

MD 144.07.24.16:05
July 24, 2017

After all the battle stuff, I felt the need for something a little more light-hearted, creative and fun. I set my course westwards towards the other end of Pennsylvania. Most of the roads run north-south due to the mountains. With the mountain ranges now running perpendicular to me, the westward routes were determined by various mountain passes. Taking this into account, I dropped down into Maryland, where the map showed a greater abundance of rural roads running east-west.

Riding through the Appalachian Mountains continued to impress me more and more every day. And I had a sneaky feeling I was just catching the tip of the iceberg.

I'll never figure out how they came up with the dividing lines between Maryland and West Virginia. The panhandle must only be about 50 miles wide in some places as it stretches westward. Maybe that's why their slogan is "America in Miniature." But the scenery was pretty, and since I was enjoying the ride, I guess it didn't really matter which side of the state lines I rode.

I found a campground alongside a lovely lake at Rocky Bay State Park just before dark. And in the morning, I took a refreshing swim. My daughter often says, "You never regret a good swim." Indeed! It does set the tune for the remainder of the day.

The roads leading to the day's destination were narrow, rural and windy – perfect for the bike. And then, there it was – Fallingwater. For those of you not well acquainted with architecture, Fallingwater is a quintessential master-work by Frank Lloyd Wright. The place is open to visitors, and I have to admit, as a significant destination objective for this year's trip, it did not disappoint.

Mr and Mrs Kaufmann were the parents of one of Wright's students. Following their son's advice, they engaged Wright to design them a new house. He visited the proposed site and they showed him their favorite location, which overlooked the falls and provided the best vantage point.

The story goes that Mr Kaufmann later called Wright to see how the design was proceeding. Even though he hadn't yet started, Wright said it was coming along nicely. So Mr Kaufmann said, "Fine, I'll be there in three hours." Legend has it that Wright immediately sat down with tracing paper and pencils and, with his students watching, produced a design in time for the meeting. The final build was 90 percent unchanged from those first drawings.

Wright ignored the clients' suggested site and instead built the house cantilevered out over the waterfalls. The view from their favorite vantage point now included a sculptural building that appears to be the source of the waterfall, and Wright's finished design complements the natural surroundings beautifully.

Many books have been written about the house, so I'll not cover all the details, but during my visit several things stood out. Firstly, it's easy to forget that this house was designed in 1935. Even today, it's pretty futuristic in appearance.

Secondly, Wright was a short man and designed for his own stature. I'm taller, and therefore had to duck a lot. At knee height to me, the balcony walls were short. It would be easy to fall over, and they wouldn't pass code nowadays. But they did allow for great views while seated in the house.

Thirdly, there's always something about seeing such a work in person versus seeing pictures or videos. Walking through the house conveyed a wonderful feeling of spaciousness and direct connection with the outdoors. It's nearly impossible not to feel connected to nature when in the house. Every room has a vista to the surrounding forest.

Magic!

I spent some time riding around Fallingwater's locality, which is still heavily wooded and undeveloped, with views of rivers, rapids and waterfalls. A great place to escape. Then I leaned into the turns and headed southward, out on the country roads again.

Many barns had quilt-like patterns painted on them. I assumed these were occupied by members of one of the religious sects, such as the Quakers or Amish. Notably, these farms were generally in much better condition than those without the markings. The grounds were tidier, the buildings better maintained, and the edges of the fields were crisply defined – all signs of someone who cares and has taken the time to show it.

Riding off the beaten track continued to offer so many opportunities for unexpected discoveries and local history. Small towns suffer from a lack of business and often look run down, meaning you'll also find plenty of old gas stations boarded up. But every now and then you find a real gem.

One such gem was Sharp's County Store. What caught my attention was the adjacent barn. A man was hanging by his hands from the hay loft opening, with his ladder leaning off to one side and just out of reach of his foot. Turns out, the man was a manikin. But by then I'd slowed down enough to notice all the relics strategically placed around the ancient Esso gas pumps – all part of a cunning plan to lead me into the establishment. It's more or less an antiques store now, alongside being a proper general store. Run by three generations of the same family, seems half the stuff inside never sold and has sat there so long it's become valuable again.

Sort of like the paisley shirts in my closet.

The clouds settled in overhead and I could see from the weather forecast we were heading for several more days of heavy rain. My light plastic poncho had shredded from windage over time. Having learned from experience in Vermont that beautiful mountain scenery is completely lost when riding in rain storms, I decided to hole up in Petersburg, "Wild and Wonderful West Virginia," for a couple of days. In a hotel. And rest.

It was a semi-good decision. The rain was very heavy, with lots of flooding all the way to DC. But Petersburg had a very limited number of attractions. And the wi-fi coverage was poor. With little to do for distraction, I spent most of my time reading in the hotel room and taking twice daily walks around town in the rain.

Oh well, the rain wouldn't last forever. And I was thoroughly rested for the next leg.

West Virginia – Virginia – Tennessee

The sky eventually began to clear as I powered through the Blue Ridge area of the Appalachian Mountains towards the Great Smoky Mountains.

Bikers I'd met along the way had told me about various "must do" rides, and an extraordinary number of these were centered in and around the Blue Ridge Mountains. To top it off, the weather was looking good for the next few days.

I got hold of a map called "Wild Rides.info" that showed the best motorcycle routes for Tennessee, Virginia and the Carolinas. Different rides were marked out in different colors with distances and times noted for each. There must have been at least 50 different routes indicated.

I have to say, if you live near Knoxville, Tennessee, you are as close to biker heaven as any place I've ever been. In fact, I believe you could ride a different route every weekend for an entire year.

Right near the top of the list was the Blue Ridge Parkway. Built in 1936, the year after Fallingwater, it's been around a while. It starts in Virginia and ends up 469 miles (755 k) later in North Carolina. But the real beauty of this ride, other than the outstanding scenery, is that while peacefully traveling along at the 45 mph (75 kph) speed limit, you're not distracted by towns, billboards, gas stations or stores. Instead, there are on- and off-ramps every 40 to 50 miles, allowing you to exit for towns and cities, or whatever other services you might need. So romantic. No wonder they say "Virginia is for Lovers."

But I'm getting ahead of myself.

Leaving Petersburg, West Virginia, the day's ride had started out in the Monongahela National Forest and wound along through gorgeous scenery to the Tennessee border, where I inadvertently discovered Highway 421 – The Snake. After a fabulous narrow, curvaceous, uphill, then downhill run, I arrived at a general store, where hundreds of bikers were resting and telling tall tales of their adventures. Then onwards for part two – an equally long but steeper and snakier run. Wow! The scariest part was the sports bikes racing by in both directions at speeds too fierce to mention.

I tapped into the Blue Ridge Parkway near Linville Falls, North Carolina, and stayed with it until I reached the Smokey Mountain National Park. On the way, I came across Mount Mitchell. At 6,684 ft (2,037 m), this is the highest mountain east of the Mississippi, with great views from the top. Luckily, I could ride almost to the summit. Tree-covered mountains as far as I could see in every direction regaled me as I stood in the chilly wind. I was continually astounded at the vast areas of unsettled and forested country around this neck of the woods.

Other loops, such as The Rattler, Copperhead Road, Aces and Eights, and Moonshiner 28, would have to rest in my imagination for some other time, because I was heading to the famous Tail of the Dragon.

The heavily wooded area receded near the beginning of the ride to accommodate a few buildings. I pulled under one of several dragon sculptures at a pub where people were gathered to share stories and take photos.

"Want me to take your picture?" asked a blonde woman in black leathers as I was attempting a selfie.

"Cheers," I said handing her my phone, leaning against the Pearl and holding up the latest edition of the HOG magazine as proof of the date for my ABC points. "Please make sure you include the Cherokee National Forest sign in the photo."

"I'm Blackbird," she said with a sultry smile, once the photo was taken, handing the phone back. "Your first time on the Dragon?"

"Thanks. Yeah, a friend told me to make sure I did it. There's supposed to be a lot of turns."

"Three hundred and eighteen curves over 11 miles," she smiled again. "At the other end, it spits you out in the 'Volunteer State' of Tennessee."

"That's pretty short," I observed. "I should be able to ride it up and down several times."

"Sure, many people do. The speed limit is 35 miles an hour," she advised. "You'll see markers along the way for those who were not so successful trying to double it."

"I'm all for the ride, not the record," I declared, as I fired up the engine and waved goodbye.

What followed was a fantastic ride with enough turns to take the excess tread off the sides of the tires to match the bottoms.

With twilight swiftly approaching, I began my latest last-minute online search for a place to spend the night. I located a campground that looked promising near Ocoee and put the coordinates into the navigation app... naively trusting the device.

The road turned from two paved lanes to one, then became gravel. I could make out switchbacks carved into the mountainside rising up in front of me as I climbed from the valley floor. Then the road deteriorated with wash-boarding and potholes, bigger than my front wheel, appearing at the limit of the headlight beam ahead.

MD 144.7.31.19:27

Location: Bridge of the USS *Surprise* Navigational App

Quirk: Quirk to bridge.

Smock: Bridge.

Quirk: What is the cause of this heavy turbulence?

Smock: Molotov determined a time-economy of 1.6 minutes by taking a gravel switchback shortcut rather than the new paved road two miles further south.

Snotty: Aye Cap'n, it's a wee bit bumpy, but she'll hold together.

Quirk: Good job all of you. Your hard work is exemplary and I intend to put you up for a citation at the end of this voyage. Our client must be very happy.

Smock: Thank you, Captain. However our facial scans currently indicate client displeasure.

Molotov: He never seems to appreciate what we've done for him.

Quirk: It's OK, Molotov. We know our efforts have saved him valuable time.

Molotov: Stupid Klingon.

Quirk: Now, now, Molotov.

Molotov: But Captain, doesn't he realize riding with his cloaking device on all the time could get us all killed? I don't think he even knows how to turn it off!

I finally reached the top to discover the nice paved road to the campground. Which I took when I left the next day on the way to Chattanooga for a much smoother ride.

There was no "Bugle Boy from Company B" that I could see in Chattanooga, a much larger city than I'd anticipated. But I did follow the Chattanooga Railway line for a while. I switched from the Andrews Sisters Boogie Woogie to singing The Lovin' Spoonful's "Nashville Cats" as I turned northwest towards the famous city of Nashville. My plan was to see a few of those 1,300 guitar pickers, and take in the Grand Ole Opry – another big item on this year's bucket list. Since 1925, the Grand Ole Opry has been broadcasting its weekly country and western shows live on the radio.

I tried to take the back roads, but as time wore on, I realized if I wanted to make it in time for the show that night, I needed to make tracks. Consequently, against my usual modus operandi of waiting for the peak of rush hour, I arrived early by taking the Interstate for the second half of the ride.

And things worked out wonderfully. I arrived in Nashville at 5:00 pm, pulled up to the Opry ticket counter and bought a ticket for the 7:00 pm performance that night. I landed a seat only six rows back, and I was front and center! One of the advantages of traveling solo, I suppose.

I'm not up to speed on today's music stars, but listening to live music is always enjoyable. Each performer in the line-up sang three songs and then moved off for the next group. All were very good if not exceptional. It was easy to applaud – even if they hadn't used a sign to instruct us for the sake of the broadcast.

The biggest mistake I made that night was not going out on the town afterwards. The next morning, I rode around and saw a lot of the famous bars and venues that are still the cradle of musicians trying to make the big time. Seeing all these places so close together along the strip, I suspect the night life is a lot like New Orleans. Oh well, the campground had an entry curfew and I would never have made it back in time.

That's my excuse, and I'm sticking to it.

On the way out of town, I passed by a park and noticed a familiar-looking building. Turns out, it was the Parthenon! Usually located in Greece, and in a state of ruin, this one was in Nashville and in fine shape. I had to stop and find out the story.

"This Parthenon is an exact replica built for the 1897 Tennessee Centennial Exposition," proclaimed the guide. "The primary differences from the original include: This one is intact. It is made of concrete instead of marble, and the statue of Athena Parthenos still resides within. The modified basement houses an art gallery and artifacts."

And, of equal importance, it had air conditioning.

"Weren't much of the original Greek Parthenon and its friezes lost when it was used as a munitions warehouse during the 1600s?" I asked.

"Correct. Plaster molds were made of the original freeze sculptures in Greece. And approximations filled in where the originals had been demolished or destroyed to present the completed friezes you see on our facades."

"Athena really has a sense of presence here," I said looking up in admiration at the huge, seated gold-colored statue.

"That's because she's plated in real gold," he beamed.

It continued to amaze and fascinate me what can be found in this country, even when you're not looking. No matter the size of the town, someone comes up with a unique project to make the place stand out – and most of these ideas are successful. In their own way. Each one creates a sense of identity for that area and becomes an attraction, reinforcing that sense of identity and making the area even more special. Which, in turn, makes it fun to go and see. Little gems like this were just waiting to be gathered up and filed away in my memory and the memories of thousands of other adventurers.

Eventually I tore myself loose and got back on the road. I was still on the hunt for my X!

Tennessee – Kentucky – Ohio

MD 144.08.04.22:11
August 4, 2017

I'd heard about Kentucky so often that I thought I knew a bit about the place and had developed a host of preconceived ideas – most of which were somewhere between "close, but no cigar" and "flat out wrong."

For one thing, it's a state that struggles with poverty, and the reality of this hit me as soon as I crossed over from Tennessee, still heading north. I was expecting to see picturesque pastures surrounded by white timber fences with thoroughbred horses frolicking about. But afterwards I recalled songs like "Coal Miner's Daughter" and other things about being poor.

I had a vague recollection that there were some caves here too and for once I actually checked the internet before I arrived. Lo and behold, the Mammoth Cave was just over the border past Bowling Green. The GPS tried to send me the wrong way to the cave entrance. After 20 minutes of riding up a road, I discovered it dead-ended onto a horse trail. The scenery was pretty, but I was very concerned the cave would be closed before I got there.

Another 40 minutes passed before I finally reached the parking lot. Parking the Pearl near the information kiosk, I got off, marched up to the window, and boldly asked for a ticket to see the whole cave.

Turns out, it's a big cave – the largest known cave system in the world in fact. Approximately 480 miles (772 k) of the network has been explored, with an estimated 200 miles remaining to be documented. Phew! Mammoth indeed. That's more than I could walk in one go, so I bought a two-hour ticket that just skimmed the surface, so to speak.

Similar to the Merrimack Caves, Mammoth was mined mostly by slave labor to make gunpowder. In addition to the more recent artifacts from the miners, plenty of relics have been discovered that identify previous human occupancy. There were a number of items on display dating back 2,000 to 5,000 years, including moccasins, digging implements, and burnt reeds used for torches. Most were quite well preserved.

Coming back up to the surface, I was surprised to discover there had been a heavy downpour while I'd been below ground. It would have been a horrible life working underground all day and not knowing what was happening in the world above. Sort of like working in an office without windows.

Come to think of it, I *have* done that and it *is* horrible. The only difference, I suppose, is being whipped if you're working too slow. Although, I have endured the odd verbal lashing over the years too. I guess some things never change.

The discoveries and unexpected gifts of staying off the main highways continued. This time it was a Shaker village. I idled into the carpark and found a shady space under a tree. Removing my gear, I noticed a tour was just starting.

"The Shakers were a religious sect that set up a commune and prospered in the New World away from the religious persecution they'd faced in England," began the female guide dressed in authentic garb, including a large white bonnet. "This village held up to 500 people for a while in the 1800s and was, more or less, self-sufficient. They also began to sell their goods to outsiders and gained a reputation for top-notch products."

"Where are the Shakers now?" I wondered aloud.

"The original Shakers eventually died off in the early 1900s. Because they failed to excite newcomers into joining to carry on the sect, there are none left now," she answered.

Most of the buildings in the village were attended by someone in period costume, on hand to explain the nuances of Shaker life in general and each building's specific usage. Several also had artists in residence who were creating artwork sympathetic to the village's objectives.

"Just look at that spiral staircase," I said in wonder when I entered the converted gift shop/cafeteria building. "Even with the aid of computers, these things are tricky enough to design today. Let alone envisioning and constructing the final product with the hand-tools of the 1800s."

"Yes, they were highly creative," replied a burly guide wearing big suspenders. "You'll enjoy the meeting hall too."

At the meeting hall, another guide, sporting a full beard, explained, "They were called 'Shakers' because of the dancing they did during worship."

"I see there are no columns in the structure, so they had a lot of open space for that," I observed.

"Exactly," he responded. "They incorporated an ingenious double truss system, built without nails, allowing a second floor to be built over the large open space. Something quite advanced for that era."

When I began exploring the dormitories, I discovered that all the rooms had pegs attached to the walls at 12-inch centers about six feet above the floor. I asked why.

"They were used for storage and to keep the floor clear for cleaning," the guide explained. "You can hang just about anything you could imagine on them." The next room displayed that fact: chairs, lamps, clothes, hats, bags, pictures and shelving were hung from pegs.

There's still a sense of peace and tranquility about the place. I could have spent the whole afternoon lying in the shade of the trees – even though that type of sloth would probably have flown in the face of the original inhabitants.

As I journeyed northwards, the forests receded, creating open pastureland. And here I found the timber rail fences and frolicking horses I had envisaged.

Nonetheless, I still had the sense that it was, generally-speaking, not a wealthy state. But riding through the rolling hills was invigorating. As I crossed into Ohio, I passed through the town of Ripley. Believe it or not. (Sorry about that. Sometimes I get a tailwind that pushes carbon dioxide forward and my mind takes off on tangents.)

Now, I'm sure Cincinnati and Columbus and other places in Ohio are pretty nice, but I was on a mission and a sense of tension and urgency was building as I left the "Unbridled Spirit State" and began to close in on the only letter missing from my ABCs. The elusive X.

And X marked the spot at Xenia, Ohio.

The town of Xenia turned out to be a tidy little place. I found the courthouse and took my highly coveted photo. Then, leaving the Pearl where it was with the engine making that lovely tic tic tic sound as it cooled down, I made for an adjacent diner. I felt a grand sense of accomplishment as I ordered my sandwich. Looking at the map, I discovered there is a Zanesville just down the road... meaning I could have skipped my trip along the Mexican border to Zapata. In fact, with the exception of Q, I realized I could have achieved the whole alphabet in Ohio alone!

But then I would have had no excuse for this marvelous road trip. Mounting the bike, I observed some dark clouds off on the western horizon.

As usual, it was getting quite late and I still hadn't decided where to spend the night, and those ominous purple-blue clouds continued to threaten rain. Since the land had flattened out, the farms I rode past had become quite consistent in size and shape. Roads in this neck of the woods are laid out pretty much on a grid. And all are paved – even though they're just farm roads and probably not used very often. It was a blast riding three miles and turning 90 degrees right, then another five miles and turning 90 degrees left, and so on, as I zigzagged cross country through corn fields towards Indiana. It felt like being in *Tron!* Except the Harley performed less than instantaneous 90 degree turns.

Jackson Center is a smallish town where they build Airstream campers. My smartphone app identified a campground there called Terra Port. Just after dark, I negotiated the bike around the closed entry barrier gate and pitched the tent in lush grass under the canopy of a tree. As I threw the sleeping bag into the tent, the rain started in earnest. Lightning filled the air, with thunder claps so close I jumped every time. At first, violent wind gusts from all directions accompanied the downpour, but eventually they departed and left the rain to drum a relaxing tattoo on my tent for the remainder of the night.

Turns out, Terra Port campgrounds are for the sole use of Airstream trailers... which are top-of-the-line camping domiciles, and which are purchased by people of a certain mindset and economic standing.

You can imagine my surprise the next morning when I found myself, my motorcycle and my blue tent in a sea of shiny aluminum cylinders. Not to mention the puzzled look on the faces of the office staff when I came to pay and check out.

I think mingling with people out of your comfort zone is a good thing.

Even if they don't.

Indiana – Michigan – Wisconsin

MD 144.08.06.13:38
August 6, 2017

As I left the "Buckeye State" of Ohio, I could see the rains were going to continue for the duration. There was nothing to do but dig in and hang on. I wouldn't have minded going to Detroit and taking a tour of one of the auto manufacturer's plants. Or even touring one of the cereal factories. But with the rain pummeling down, I needed to focus very hard on just keeping the bike on the road and dodging cars. My mind had little time to consider other things. As such, I just ploughed along, sending a small wave towards the edge of the road and leaving a mist floating in the air behind.

Kalamazoo! How could you not stop in a town with a name like that? I mean, at some point it's going to come up in conversation. "So, you ever been to Kalamazoo?" Or, "What's the most unique town name you've ever come across?" Or, "One time I was over by Kalamazoo, when..." I enjoyed visiting this splendid place and cruising up and down the main streets several times in the rain, before peeling off onto an obscure road leading out of town.

Now, I've got a bone to pick here. I know I mentioned them earlier in regard to the habits of navigational apps, but I've got more to say about toll roads. I understand the principle. A road is needed and it suits a certain select group of motorists. So, you build a road. It makes their life easier and you charge them to use it. Everyone is happy.

However, the Interstate Highway System was funded by the federal government. Everyone in the country contributes to the cost of these roads and reaps the benefits accordingly. And individual states are required to assist in their maintenance.

But a problem arises when some states elect to put a toll on their Interstates. This, in essence, means they're making people from outside their state pay for the maintenance. That means people from states that maintain their own roads, without an extra charge, are forced to pay for maintenance twice – once through their state taxes and once via tolls of other states. Which, in my mind, is double-dipping by the lazy culprit states who are shirking their responsibilities. Not to mention the fact that it's taxation without representation for all the out of state travelers using the highway.

Taking it a step further, state sales tax is actually the same thing. Travelers are paying tax as they pass through but have no say in how it's spent. It seems to me that we fought a revolution over that very same principle back in the mid to late 1700s.

So much for the term "Freeway."

I was hoping to reach my elusive cousin, Tom. When I was in Georgia, he was in Tennessee. When I was close to Tennessee, he went to North Carolina. When I got to North Carolina, he was back in Tennessee. And when I returned to Tennessee, he was in Michigan. "Pure Michigan," they call it. It's almost like he was avoiding me. But now I had him cornered. And I wanted to get there before he found out that I was on my way and before he had a chance to flee yet again.

You can imagine his surprise when he opened his RV bus door to a thoroughly soaked biker squishing up the steps. But his lovely wife Debbie took pity on me. After I was forced to strip naked and wrap myself in a towel, I was allowed inside to spend the night, while my clothes continued their rinse cycle outside on the clothesline.

Tom and Debbie spend most of the summer touring around the country. Seems like wanderlust must be in the DNA of the Slater side of the family. It was really good to see them, but given that it was a surprise visit, I decided to keep it short. We made the best of the time available. Tom was a wealth of information, providing details for cousins I was yet to visit. And, in return, I filled him in on what I had learned about our wider family. The next morning, he made some of the finest blueberry pancakes I've ever eaten, while I washed the bike.

As mentioned earlier, one of the curious facts about riding is that the bike often becomes dirtiest when it's raining. Grime from the road splashes up and leaves a thin, opaque film over everything. And riding a dirty bike is akin to showing up at an executive bankers' meeting in cut-offs and flip flops. Really bad form.

Over the years I'd often taken advantage of Tom and Debbie's hospitality when they were living in California, and I reminded them the door was always open for them at my house in New Zealand. It wasn't until later the next day that I remembered I'd sold my house and now lived on a boat. But, you know, the principle still applies.

The Mackinac Bridge spans nearly five miles to connect northern Michigan with the southern "Mitt." The rain had cleared, and I rode across the Straits of Mackinac under lovely blue skies. The winds that whistle across the Great Lakes can get pretty ferocious, and I wouldn't want to cross on a bike in a big blow. Even in the gentle 20-knot breeze that day, I was leaning hard to port most of the way across.

The whole of upper Michigan and northern Wisconsin are heavily forested and sparsely settled. Instead of finding huge cities and wall to wall people, I was taken aback to discover long stretches of land covered in trees, with an abundance of bicycle trails, magnificent scenery and a pristine shoreline.

History plaques along the route described the trapping and fur trade that once took place in the area. Seemed to me it could still be a thriving business, just from the deer I saw. Hopefully the rest of the woods were just as full of other animals.

The next day I crossed back into Wisconsin, the home of Harley-Davidson. Being more informed about the ABC rules this year, I realized there was an opportunity to collect ABCs points I'd missed in my previous trip at the Harley-Davidson facilities in Tomahawk, Menomonee Falls and Milwaukee. I dutifully posed in front of each with bike and magazine. The Harley staff were much more used to this sort of activity than the employees at government buildings.

In Milwaukee, I took a quick refresher walk through the Harley-Davidson Museum to see some of the displays and bikes I enjoyed most the previous year. I watched some clips from *Then Came Bronson*, and got an echo of that familiar feeling for adventure that I'd experienced watching that show as a youngster. Little had I known back then.

Funny thing, Bronson's show only lasted one season. So far, I've made it two.

I'd been sensing a growing underlying pressure for some time now, compelling me to keep moving. Sturgis was just about to start and I was still a long way away. After missing the event last year, I wanted to make sure this year wasn't a repeat of that disappointment. Yet, I didn't want to rush along and miss out on the "Here and Now" for a "Maybe" in the future.

Such are the quandaries of everyday life, and of life on the road.

Wisconsin

MD 144.08.09.08:52

August 9, 2017

Pilots are trained to keep an eye out for places to land should their engines quit. I was the same when it started to get dark. But since leaving Milwaukee, I'd found very few options.

My growling stomach urged me to pull over for some supper in Dodgeville. And (speaking of places to land) after topping up my stomach and the Pearl's gas tank, I stopped to look at a Boeing C97 Stratofreighter parked beside the highway.

How it got there I don't know – there were no obvious runways nearby and the wings were too big to have trucked it down the highway. *Could they have landed it there?* Though the years had taken a bit of a toll on the internal insulation fabric, and they'd screwed wire mesh (with gigantic lag screws) over the engine cowlings to keep the birds out, she was still a grand ole bird. Everything had been left intact. You could sit in the pilot's seat and play with the controls all you wanted.

Which I did.

Just as I was touching down at O'Hare International Airport in a gusting crosswind with a load of vintage automobile parts onboard, a young man stuck his head into the cockpit.

"Hi," he said sliding into the co-pilot's seat. "I've made a special trip from Chicago just to see this old girl."

"I used to work at Boeing and was able to see the first 707 ever made," I said while he surveyed the controls. "But this is the first time I've been aboard one of these." Out the side window, I noticed his motorcycle parked beside mine. "Nice bike," I said, as I grudgingly relinquished the pilot's seat so he could take command.

"Thanks. I like to get out on the road when I have time between flights. I fly 737s," he divulged as he flicked through the instruments with knowing movements.

"Really? I hold a private pilot license but it's been years since I've flown."

Turns out, we had much to talk about and I was surprised at the amount of knowledge this lad carried around in his head. I didn't ask, but he couldn't have been more than 30. I guess it makes a difference when you know what you want to do from an early age.

Dodgeville had a state park just outside of town, but when I arrived, I discovered they were charging an exorbitant rate for a tent site. And then an additional charge for the bike!

"Why so expensive?" I asked.

"The state has cut our funding," said one of the four staff members working the gate, which was a one-person job.

"Are you full up for the weekend?" I inquired.

"Hardly anyone here," they answered in unison.

"I think I know why," I said, turning the bike around and riding away.

About ten miles back I'd noticed a new lifestyle development on the edge of town with a "Lots for Sale" sign. I decided it was the place for me. The last of the daylight had all but disappeared by the time I arrived. There were a number of vacant lots, including one atop a knoll at the end of a cul-de-sac, which suited me just fine. The nearest house was mostly screened by a tree windbreak, but its design and size told me my new campsite was going to be a high-class neighborhood.

Just as I threw the sleeping bag inside the tent, the most glorious full moon rose above the corn. I lay there gazing across the valley spread out before me, awash in silver light. Magic!

Next morning, a pickup came over as I was strapping my tent onto the Pearl.

"Thought I'd come by and see who my new neighbor is," said the driver. Pointing towards the windbreak, he said, "That's my house and this development is all my land."

Uh-oh! I swallowed hard, unable to come up with a quick reply.

"Looks like you're on a bit of a trip," he said getting out of his truck. "I used to do a bit of riding myself."

To my relief, we immediately got off to a good start with an in-depth discussion about riding around the country.

"You should stop and see Taliesin East – Frank Lloyd Wright's second design studio. It's only 20 or 30 miles down the road."

I knew of this building, but had no idea it was so close. "Great. Thanks for that."

And, after a cheery goodbye, I was off for another day of discoveries!

On the way to Taliesin, I came across a sign that said, "House on the Rock – Viewing area ahead." After stopping for a gander, it was evident from what I saw that there was sufficient merit to go and take a closer look.

It was astounding! Beyond anything I could ever imagine. A cross between Disneyland, the Smithsonian and Ripley's Believe It or Not, House on the Rock was built by Alex Jordan Jr, beginning in 1945. It was first opened to the public in 1959, around the time his neighbor Frank Lloyd Wright was remodeling his place down the road yet again after three separate fires.

In a supreme act of endurance, Jordan started by carrying bricks up the rock. His organic house grew and grew, and people came to see what all the fuss was about. The attraction was so popular, he began charging admission, and the proceeds were put back into construction.

"Allow about three and a half hours minimum to take the tour," the ticket-taker woman said in a monotone voice.

"I'm on my way to see Taliesin East down the road," I explained, "and I've only got an hour and a half. I'll just whizz through."

The woman looked skeptical.

Four and a half hours later, I emerged back at the carpark. And I had whizzed through!

It was incredible. I could have easily spent the whole day inside. The actual house was a maze of unique spaces, jam-packed with oddball artifacts. It's hard to believe Jordan was six-foot-four though – I had to bend over constantly to protect my head. He must have been influenced by Frank in that regard.

It was the infinity room that I had seen from the highway. The exterior lines tapered to a point, as the white structure cantilevered out some 197 feet (60 m). Viewed from the interior, there was a strong optical illusion of the room going on forever. Walking out towards the end of the room revealed a glass floor where you could look down through a canopy of trees to the forest floor, 154 feet below.

There were multiple living rooms, bedrooms and kitchens, all organically woven together over various levels. Actual tree trunks and branches had been cut and placed in such a fashion that it felt like the building had been built around them. Recesses in the rock at first appeared to be dead-end caves but opened up to reveal other spaces.

Some of the fireplaces were the length of a room, with hearth-mounted hooks supporting a copious collection of cooking pots that could swing out over the flames and back.

Huge adjacent buildings, largely hidden from the outside, held an assorted collection of merry-go-rounds (including the largest one in the world), doll houses, ivory carvings, model ships, cannons, guns, suits of armor, cars, horse-drawn wagons, clocks – and a multitude of other things too obtuse and numerous to mention (such as a black steam-driven hearse.)

Jordan had made a vast array of instruments that played by themselves. Each were artworks in their own right, but he had joined them together into groupings for various pieces of music. There was even a full orchestra, with manikins attached to the self-playing instruments to add a surreal sense of realism.

House on the Rock was one of the biggest highlights of my trip, and until I stumbled across it that day, I'd never even heard of it. Since then, I've only spoken to a handful of people who are aware of its existence. Either there are a lot of people in the dark as much as I was, or indeed it is one of those best kept secrets.

The day was quickly wearing away, so I scooted on down to Taliesin and arrived six minutes before the last tour.

As we were shown around Frank Lloyd Wright's home and parts of the still-functioning Frank Lloyd Wright School of Architecture (now known as The School of Architecture at Taliesin), our guide told numerous remarkable stories about the history of the site, the buildings and the antics of the master himself. It seems that when you're as talented as Frank, acceptance of behavioral peculiarities is easier to obtain. By now, I was able to predict what I would experience when I entered one of his buildings, but it was still a delight to see the intricate details and appreciate the thought that had gone into their making.

Plywood was a new material back then and Wright experimented with it in interesting ways. The floor of the house was constructed from sheets cut into four-inch widths and laid on edge to span the distances between the wide-spaced floor joists. The result was many parallel lines of layered wood, creating a fascinating surface effect. Visually, it wasn't unlike a carpet style that has risen to popularity in the last few years.

The house also included a theater, furnished with a stage curtain made for Wright by his students and covered in an abstract design. They had presented it to him as a Christmas present. He said he liked it, but the upper white area was too white. So he had them spread the curtain on the floor, then proceeded to pour tea on it, staining it to an off-white that was more to his taste.

So to speak.

I was running on stimulus overload for the day. So much to absorb and think about. It was nearly seven o'clock in the evening and I'd only covered 25 miles. Should I go on and leave the "Dairy State," or go back to my knoll in the luxury development for another night?

Go on, of course.

Iowa

MD 144.08.10.12:16
August10, 2017

I headed through Iowa. "Fields of Opportunity" is their state slogan. And those fields are seeded with corn, corn, corn and more corn. It's enough to give an Aztec wet dreams for a month.

Certainly, a very large percentage becomes silage for feed lots, but what surprises me is that we don't have more corn products. Corn bread and cornflakes should be practically free if the laws of supply and demand are working properly. Not to mention corn whiskey!

There are changes, albeit subtle, as you travel through the state. Sometimes, the fields waver between corn and soy beans. Then, later, its soy beans and corn to give the soil a chance to rest. My preference was traveling through the eastern end of the state along the Mississippi River, due to the hillier nature of the topography there.

Via an email newsletter, I would typically send several photos of each state to friends and relatives as I traveled. For Iowa, I took a single photo of a barn surrounded by fields of corn as far as the eye could see. Then I pasted the same photo into the email three times, giving each a different caption: "Eastern Iowa," "Central Iowa" and "Western Iowa. Not really fair.

But not too far off the mark either.

The exorbitant rates I'd turned my back on at the state park campground just outside Dodgeville a few days earlier had left a bad taste in my mouth. Actually, there was a definite pattern arising, the more I thought about it.

My first night in Iowa, I found myself at yet another expensive campsite that wasn't suited to tenting.

"You're pretty staunch sleeping in a tent on a concrete pad," observed a man sitting under the canopy of his large RV camper.

"Not my first choice," I replied trying to find rocks that could act as anchor points for the guy ropes. "The host has closed off the primitive area that's ideal for tents. I have to pay double because these sites are paved and have water and power. And I'm not allowed to pitch the tent on the adjacent grass."

"This is really set up nice for us," he admitted. "We plan to stay here the whole month. The concrete pads are spacious and level. And there's a pump-out facility just over there by the toilets, laundry and showers."

"Yeah, it's definitely set up for RVs. Tell me," I inquired, "do you use the toilet and shower facilities?"

"No. Why would we? We have everything we need in the RV," he said proudly, as I finished unloading my gear into the tent. "What've you got against RVs anyway?"

"Don't get me wrong," I responded. "I've got nothing against RVs. My cousin lives in one and I've met many a great RV adventurer. I just think there should be equal opportunity for all types of campers."

"How so?" he asked offering me a seat in one of his fold-out chairs.

"For instance, nothing is geared for tents or short overnight stays for people who aren't 'glamping'. With the number of people riding bicycles and motorcycles, or even hiking cross-country, I would have expected to see some facilities that made allowance for them," I explained. "Not only the well-to-do."

"So, what sort of campgrounds do you prefer?" he asked handing me a beer.

"Thanks. In order of preference: city or county campgrounds, Army Corps of Engineers, federal or national, private (non-chain), and lastly state campgrounds," I said, ticking them off on my fingers. "I'll concede some of my favoritism does reflect the 50 percent senior discount."

"Why do you list state campgrounds last?"

"Because they're usually the most expensive and don't honor senior passes from other states."

"Well, it costs money to run these places," he justified.

"Since tax payers have already paid for state and federal campgrounds via purchase of land and buildings, it's beyond me how the nightly rates, which should only involve running costs and maintenance, are often more than private campgrounds that are funding everything themselves," I countered.

"I hadn't looked at it that way before," he conceded. "It has gotten darned expensive the last couple of years. If it keeps going up, it will be cheaper to stay in a hotel."

"They also tend to have too many employees working, and often close their front gate offices at 4:00 pm – about the time I assume most campers would be arriving."

"Well, this one has hosts instead of employees to keep an eye on things," he pointed out. "They let you register after hours. And they don't get paid."

"True," I said. "And I think that's a positive thing in general. But hosts don't pay for their own campsites. Usually there are two hosts – so one can take a break during the week – which means, of course, two campsites are lost as a source of revenue. In small camping areas like this one, which has just 20 sites, that's a ten percent loss of capacity right off. So, although hosts aren't being paid, they still come at a cost. And I don't think my cash payment tonight made it to the deposit box."

"You're being awful cynical now," he admonished taking a swig of his beer.

"Yeah probably," I admitted. "But let me tell you of an experience I had recently."

"Alright," he said leaning back and putting his feet up on another chair.

"'In order to serve you better,' as they say, some campgrounds now require you to reserve sites online."

"What's wrong with that?" he interrupted.

"It's a great option if you have access to the internet and have worked out your travel itinerary ahead of time – but as far as spontaneity and flexibility goes, not so much."

"Mmm. I see your point. Carry on."

I told him my story. I had stopped at a campground for the night. I arrived five minutes after the office closed and found the attendant just locking up...

"I'm closed," said the attendant. "You need to go online or call the hotline and register for a campsite."

"There's no cell phone reception here," I said looking at my phone.

"I know. But there is about five miles back," he replied. "You have to go back there, reserve the campsite, then come back here."

"How about I just pitch the tent now and pay you in the morning?"

"No can do. Someone else could reserve the site online and you would be in their spot when they arrived."

"There appears to be a lot of empty sites. I doubt that many more people will show up tonight. Surely they could just take an empty one and we can sort it out in the morning."

"No. They might schedule the one you set up in. I'd be responsible," came the bureaucratic reply.

The RV guy responded to my story with a perplexed look, and another swig of his beer.

"I couldn't believe he was willing to send a paying customer away just in case someone else showed up," I said. "Especially with heaps of empty sites. It would have taken him less time to sign me in than it did to tell me why he couldn't. Only a government employee," I scoffed, recalling Rockefeller's belief no 2.

"It does seem a bit pedantic."

"State and federal campgrounds seem to be set up to fail. By closing off the tent area and forcing tenters to stay in RV areas, they can say, 'No one uses the tent spaces.' By upgrading the RV sites and addressing only top-end RV users, thereby weeding out the average Joe, they can say, 'Use is way down.' And with the high charges, it looks like even the RV users are dropping off.

"The stage is now set," I continued as twilight slowly descended upon us. "Campgrounds have been made luxurious at considerable cost. Facilities that require power, water and maintenance have been erected, all funded by the taxpayer traveler who probably didn't even ask for the extras in the first place. Add to that cleaners, staff and management personnel. Then income-generating spaces have been removed for host occupancy, and fees have been increased to offset all these costs. Average people can no longer afford the fees. And inevitably, occupancy drops making the operation no longer financially viable."

"So, what are you getting at?" he said stepping inside for another couple of beers.

"Eventually the government will end up with two options: either let the under-used campgrounds run at a loss or turn them over for privatization. And the latter will provide a select group of people the opportunity for permanent private campsites with high-end facilities. In other words, their own holiday homes in state and national parks."

"You really think so?" he asked with a slight look of consternation.

"Mark my words."

We sat with our own thoughts and listened to the crickets and owls for a while.

"OK, I feel better now. Thanks for the beer. Maybe all this corn just got to me," I said leaving the confused man and crawling into my tent.

Towards dark-30 the following day, with no campground listed on my app, I pulled into a farmer's yard and asked the owner if I could pitch my tent on the edge of his field.

He looked doubtful.

"I promise not to eat any corn and to be gone first thing in the morning," I reassured him with a big smile and the best innocent look I could muster as he hemmed and hawed. I could see his wife was still a bit nervous so I said, "Hey, no big deal. I'll just keep moving along."

I was walking back to the bike when she offered, "There's a small town ten miles north that has a city park. I don't understand why you wouldn't just stay there?"

"I didn't know it was there," was, of course, my answer. "Great! Thank you so much for that information," I stated, while kicking my leg over the saddle, then rode off into the impending nightfall.

Adjoining the park, I found a lovely, laid-back, no frills campground run by the local Boy Scouts. The price was a reasonable $10 a night for a tent, and the place had one of the highest occupancy rates I'd seen. There was a generous mix of trailers, tents, vans and RVs, and all the people I talked to were great. What a fantastic public service for travelers and an educational experience for the youth of the town.

On that positive note, and with an inkling of hope for the future of camping, I left Iowa early the next morning for South Dakota.

South Dakota

MD 144.08.12.209:33

August 12, 2017

The prairie and badlands lay spread out before me as I thundered across South Dakota. Traveling on the frontage roads was great. There were heaps of cars and bikers on the adjacent Interstate I-90, but most of the time I had the two-lane road to myself. Generally, it paralleled the freeway, occasionally breaking off for several miles to pass through small towns. With higher speed limits, minimal traffic and long stretches of straightaways, I was making excellent time. Since the Sturgis Motorcycle Rally had started a couple of days ago, it was imperative that I keep up my momentum.

Billboards demanding that I stop and visit Wall Drug had been appearing for the last 150 miles (240 k) prior to the actual town itself.

So I did.

Starting off as a little drug store in 1931, Wall Drug had just kept getting bigger, and it had grown even more since I was last there. In fact, I think the entire town of Wall is associated with it in one way or another. True to the advertisements, if you want it, they've got it. Pretty much every knickknack and souvenir for the entire western side of the United States of America can be found as you wander from store to adjoining store. All under one roof. That is, until you come to the end of the block. Then you have to go outside to cross the street and re-enter the next series of Wall Drug stores.

Back on the road, the appearance of bikers was becoming more prevalent. I was now passing several hundred a day on their way back home from Sturgis, and I observed a similar number heading in my direction every time I stopped for gas.

When traveling by Harley, it's common practice to drop the left hand from the handlebars and flick a gentle two fingered V wave to oncoming Harley riders − sort of a silent salute or nod of acknowledgment and recognition from one biker to another. However, I had to give up this practice from Wall Drug onwards. There were just too many bikes and I would have had to ride one handed the whole way to Sturgis.

During the annual motorcycle rally, Sturgis bears a close resemblance to Las Vegas. You can see just about anything – people puking in gutters, naked women covered only in body paint (or not), tattoos, beards, very flash bikes, musicians and lots of gawking people-watchers (like yours truly). But without the glitz, or phony over-the-top architecture. The focus is solely on motorcycles and having a good time. Deus ex machina!

Entire streets were blocked off to cars, allowing only motorcycle circulation and parking, and thousands upon thousands of bikes were parked there, with thousands upon thousands more arriving, parking, leaving and riding around. There are a lot of thousands upon thousands in half a million. And this wasn't even a big year. In 2015, attendance was closer to three quarters of a million. That's a lot of decibels.

With the constant rumbling of motorbikes cruising up and down the streets, the noise was similar to being inside a giant thunderhead at the peak of a storm. Every conceivable space was filled with Harleys.

Awesome in the extreme!

I found the Buffalo Chip Campground just out of town and pitched my tent amongst the great unwashed. Fearful of the heavy rains forecast, I looked for someplace on higher terrain, and settled on a ridge above Bikini Beach that appeared dry enough. Then I set out to explore.

Bikini Beach was the optimistic name given to an area around a small reservoir about the size of a tennis court. People were sitting in deck chairs but I didn't observe much beach action. As far as the name of the campground goes – Buffalo Chip – I suppose I should point out to the uninitiated that a "chip" is a dry cow patty found on the range. Or in this case buffalo poop. Which actually conjures up an appropriate image for this campground.

An undulating sea of tents and RVs, all compressed into 600 acres of grassland, engulfed me as I wandered around to get a feel of the place. The campground was only slightly larger than the Gettysburg battlefield. And while there were a number of Confederate flags on display, I felt glad we were all there to share a good time with beer and music. And not to shoot at each other.

George Thorogood & the Destroyers were playing that night at the main stage, to be followed by Blink 182. Yeah! Once I found out the location of the stage, I gathered my jacket and headed over to get a good seat.

I wasn't prepared for the biker protocol of riding your bike right up to the stage. Rows and rows of bikes radiated outwards, sort of like going to a drive-in movie – only this was a live performance with really big speakers, negating the need for your own. Not only does your bike provide a place to sit, but after each song, in lieu of applause, the audience would start their engines and rev 'em up!

I could only imagine what that must have sounded like for the performers on stage. But no imagination was required for what it sounded like in the audience: LOUD!

With the hum of bikes arriving and departing at all hours of the day and night, sleeping might have proved a challenge for those with good hearing. But I removed my hearing aids and slept like a baby. OK, the substantial number of beers consumed might have helped as well. I don't call it passing out as long as two thirds of the body makes it into the tent.

"Great Faces, Great Places" is South Dakota's motto. The next afternoon, I took a short ride up to Mount Rushmore to see the faces, only to come shooting back down with rain splattering right behind me. I reached the comparative safety of the vendor tents at the Rapid City Harley-Davidson dealership just minutes after the rain caught up. Water flowed across the parking lot and under the tents soaking everything on the ground. So deep it was actually flowing over the toes of my boots for a while.

The deluge carried on for some time. Two people came by on stand-up paddle boards and I caught a lift to the entry of the main store, where vast numbers of wet bikers roamed the aisles waiting for the weather to break. Consider the image and odors associated with being stuck in a two-man tent with two large, wet German Shepherds and a sheep. That should give you a close approximation of the actual experience of being inside the Harley-Davidson dealership that day. But everyone was in a good mood and easy to get along with.

Back in town, Harley-Davidson had put on some freebies for HOG members. Manicures and finger nail painting were offered for the Ladies of

Harley. Haircuts, boot shines and back massages were available for everyone. I decided to take advantage of several.

I'd just finished my haircut, and noticed there was a long queue for the boot shine. No one was in the manicure line and I thought, *What the heck...* The primary attraction being the two cute women standing there (with skimpy bikinis below and nothing but body paint to cover their more-than-ample top halves).

We flirted back and forth, while I showed them photos of the Black Pearl and told them about my travels. In truth, I wasn't really paying much attention to anything other than the wobbly bits right in front of me. You can imagine my surprise to discover that, while I'd been distracted, they had painted my fingernails! The red and black they had chosen matched the Black Pearl perfectly, my thumbnails were decorated with little H-D logos, and the words LIVE and RIDE were painted in glitter on the nails of my right and left hands. They had done a fine job indeed.

If... you like to have your nails painted. I didn't have the heart or courage to say anything negative. "Great. Ah. That looks nice. Er. That matches my bike perfectly," I stammered as the giggles overtook them. Sending tremors down their bodies and causing everything to wobble even more.

Unfortunately, no one was going to get the chance to appreciate their delicate handiwork as I immediately put on my gloves.

One vendor was selling LED accent lights. These are stuck on the bike frame at strategic locations hidden from view during the day. But come night time, they bounce light off the chrome so that the whole engine appears to be emitting its own beautiful glow. Having not really treated myself to anything more extravagant than a manicure and nail-painting – or perhaps because of the manicure and nail-painting – I decided to live a little more recklessly. I splurged and purchased a set. Once I'd made my mind up about either keeping or selling the Black Pearl, I'd install them or take them back to New Zealand.

Three days and two nights was a short visit to Sturgis, but mostly it was just more of the same. Perhaps 15 years ago, when I wore a younger man's clothes, I might have stayed longer.

And probably remembered less.

Montana – Wyoming – Montana

MD 144.08.14.19:13

August 14, 2017

I was still singing George Thorogood's version of "One Scotch, One Bourbon, One Beer" as I crossed the boarder into Montana near Alzada. Then I took a detour north to visit Rita, an old classmate who lived nearby, and for the simple fact that I'd never been to the town of Ekalaka before.

The hills around the wide-open road into Ekalaka featured stunning land formations. Later, I discovered Medicine Rocks State Park is only another ten miles on the other side of town. It is supposed to be an amazing park full of interesting rock formations. But there you go. The penalties of doing things on the fly with no research. Maybe some other time.

On the phone, Rita informed me that the county fair and rodeo was in full swing. I love small town fairs and rodeos. Everyone is so relaxed. So friendly. And so accepting.

Rather than riding a number of miles on the gravel road to Rita's ranch, I arranged to meet her at a relative's house at the city's edge and watch the parade scheduled to travel down main street the next day.

It turned out to be a rather long parade. So long, in fact, that there was a shortage of road length within the city limits. Being a small town, and since nearly everyone within a 100-mile radius was there for the parade already, they decided to close off the highway and use it for the extra staging distance required. In so doing, four carloads of tourists, two motorcycles and a tractor were all delayed for 45 minutes. But everyone on the highway got out of their vehicles and into the spirit of things.

That evening there was a street dance with live music, a big feed at one church and gospel singing at another. All up, the town swelled from the 350 regular inhabitants to two or three thousand spectators.

Naturally, the rodeo was the central attraction, with wild bronc riding, bull riding and calf roping for the cowboys, and barrel racing and goat tying for the cowgirls.

I particularly enjoy calf roping. A calf is released from a chute between two mounted cowboys. Positioned on either side, one is the roper and the other keeps the calf heading in a straight line. Once the first cowboy ropes the calf, his horse stops then backs up, keeping tension on the lariat. Meanwhile, he leaps to the ground with a short rope between his teeth, runs to the calf, picks up the animal, throws it on its side, hog ties three of its legs together with the short rope, then raises his hands to signify he's done, thereby stopping the clock. If the calf remains unable to escape within the next ten seconds, it's a success. And the lowest roping time wins.

Watching this was a real treat for me after being gone from the west for so long. It was a warm and sunny blue-sky day, and I was enjoying myself immensely.

Until I took my gloves off.

Now, I have great admiration for cowboys. It takes tremendous skill, strength and courage to rodeo. Most are friendly and humble. In spite of this, however, many have a low tolerance for slackers, liars and homosexuals. Several took exception to my painted nails.

"Hey! What's this with the painted nails then?" accused a cowboy sitting two seats down to my left.

"Er…" I stammered.

"Yeah, Klingon?" asked another just behind me. "You one of them thar' sissy types?"

Thinking quickly, I realized he had given me an out. I responded, "It's a sign of Klingon achievement." While rising up from my seat, I further explain, "For defeating three or more opponents at once in hand to hand combat. Episode 415." And for good measure, I spat on the ground.

Such a statement from an ominous six-foot-two, 200-pound biker in black leathers, who was possibly a real Klingon, seemed to confuse them somewhat and keep things in check. But fearful that my advantage may not hold, I thought it prudent to head out right after the barrel races. Just in case.

As I was going down the bleachers someone hissed, "There ain't no Episode 415. They're gonna gitcha at the gate. Lying fairy."

Bloody smart-phones.

Sure enough, there were five big brutes in two pickups, one parked either side of the gate at the only exit from the carpark. And cowboys with lariats in the back of each one. They had set up a calf-roping situation with me as the calf!

For the first time ever, I had empathy for the helpless calf. There was only one thing to do, and that was grab the bull by the horns. So to speak.

Shoulders back, head high, I strode purposefully towards the Pearl, while giving them a menacing stare.

They stared right back.

I mounted the bike.

They started their engines.

I spat on the ground.

They revved up their engines.

I put on my helmet.

They began twirling their lariats.

I brought the big V-Twin motor roaring to life. Kicked the bike into gear.

And...

Rode right past them, pretty as you please.

After all, remember the number one rule for motorcycles? You Are Invisible. Sometimes that can work to your advantage.

I high-tailed it back down into Wyoming.

Devil's Tower rises up 1,367 feet (420 m) above the surrounding countryside like a giant corrugated cork. There are several stories on nearby plaques about how this lonely sentinel came into existence.

Native American lore says a group of young squaws were being chased by a giant bear. They climbed on a rock and prayed for the Great Spirit to help them. As they did, the rock rose up in the air. All the while, the frustrated bear clawed at the sides trying to climb up. Thus, creating the vertical striations on the rock's surface.

Scientists, however, would have you believe it's the remnants of an old volcano plug, and that molten igneous rock solidified as it rose up vertically, creating the crystallized rock formation.

And finally, as those of you who watched *Close Encounters of the Third Kind* will remember, it is actually a huge pile of mashed potatoes, scraped by a giant fork, that's hardened over the years.

I guess we'll never know for sure which one is right. But it sure presents a majestic sight as you ride over the hills.

Further along, I passed a coal strip-mining operation. They had removed a good couple hundred feet of earth down to the layer of coal – which is itself another good couple of hundred feet thick. Coal is shoveled onto a conveyor belt, which runs several miles, before passing under the highway to the train tracks and a power plant on the other side. Overall, it's an impressive display of human engineering and determination. I only hope they're putting the topsoil back in place and leaving the countryside pretty much as they found it – albeit a couple of hundred feet lower down.

I couldn't help but sing John Prine's "Paradise" as I motored on westward into Buffalo. "…Mr. Peabody's coal train done hauled it away."

I achieved two more big ticks in Buffalo – not for the ABCs, but of the personal kind.

One was visiting another cousin, Lois, whom I'd not seen for 45 years. She's a writer and plays bass guitar in a band on weeknights, alongside her regular job. She autographed three of her books and I slipped them into my saddle bag for a later read.

It had been really enlightening discovering the hidden talents of my cousins. Without the necessary time to delve down into where the real struggles of our lives were fought, Lois and I settled for skimming over the highlights. There was so much to learn and I hoped I wouldn't have to wait too long before continuing our conversation again.

The other big tick was calling in to see my old classmate Wayne, who (with his lovely wife Shelly) had visited me in New Zealand a few years back. I had taken them sailing and was looking forward to seeing their ranch. The property lay a few miles to the north of Buffalo in a beautiful location at the base of the Big Horn Mountains. They put me up in the bunkhouse – a funky kind of log cabin with dynamic views that had previously been owned by Michael Damson, an actor in *The Young and Restless*.

I was accompanied on my morning walk by several deer and a few flocks of turkeys. It was a grand start to the day and my spirits were high as I loaded my gear, said thanks, waved goodbye and, releasing the clutch, throttled northwards into the heart of Montana.

And then it began to rain.

Montana On Fire

MD 144.08.16.10:24

August 16, 2017

The site of the Little Big Horn battlefield (Custer's last stand) features a splendid memorial with excellent exhibits covering all the details of the conflict from a neutral viewpoint. But having visited a few years previously, and with the rain and all, I elected to give it a miss. As I passed by, I remembered attending several marvelous re-enactments there over the years, and was reminded how often I had crossed paths with Custer on this trip. He had certainly covered a lot of ground to get here.

Hoping to get to Bozeman before dark, I just more or less waved as I passed through Billings. Fragrant smells flowed under my helmet and assaulted my senses as I moved from the open prairie towards the Yellowstone River. Sagebrush and wild onions. Freshly cut alfalfa hay. Rich summer fallow soil. Cedar shrubs. Hot asphalt... then burning pine.

To my great disappointment, forest fire smoke began to overpower the sweet odors. A thick haze filled the air from Billings westward. I was so looking forward to seeing the familiar shapes of the Beartooths, Crazies, Absorakas, Hyalites, Spanish Peaks and Bitterroot Mountains. They're like old friends that really anchor me to the land. But the best I got were slight impressions through the haze.

Bozeman was the town where I'd built a house and lived for a number of years while working for the Milwaukee Railroad. It's also home to Montana State University, where I later received my degrees in architecture. But the changes since I'd left were mind-boggling. Urban sprawl gone wild.

I stayed at my friend Stephen's apartment in what had once been fields of wheat – the whole area now dominated by medium-rise apartments and shopping centers. I can appreciate the need for development, however the whole character of this lovely town seemed to have been lost in the transition. Too much, too fast. I felt the need to find some link to the past, and decided to take a ride up Hyalite Canyon towards the reservoir – at least until the pavement ended.

In the early spring before the road was opened for the season, my good mate Rob and I used to ride our dirt bikes up the narrow canyon to the lake. Snow drifts would block the shady portions of the road, and where there was sunlight, the mud would be ankle deep. Sometimes we would take one bike at a time through the drifts with one of us either side. Using the motor for assistance, I would half drive, half carry my 350 cc bike over the drift and back into the muck.

At least three or four times on the way up, we would stop to prevent overheating. After scrapping off chunks of muck, we'd use a slender stick to dig baked mud out from between the aluminum cooling fins, until the motors resembled themselves again and ran cool enough to proceed further.

We considered all this strenuous effort to be great sport. But our real reward was arriving at the ice-covered lake. There would be open patches at the perimeter where the ice had begun to recede, and usually there was sufficient room to stand on the rocky shoreline with the snow banks directly behind. Perfect for fishing. Cutthroat trout, which had been in starvation mode from the long winter, would strike at anything that moved. The fishing was so good that if we didn't catch anything after two casts, we felt cheated. Sometimes we would snag one which escaped after a brief struggle then catch another before we had finished reeling in the line. If the fish we brought to the shore were sufficient in size, we would unhook them, then stick them in the snow bank behind us to keep them fresh.

All up, in those days it was about a three-and-a-half-hour ride to the lake, allowing for time spent traversing drifts and cleaning the motors. It took about 15 minutes to catch our limit of ten trout apiece, followed by a similar three-and-a-half-hour ride home. Another hour at the car wash to spray down the bikes and ourselves. And finally, 20 minutes to fry up a fantastic fresh trout supper.

Well, that's changed too! The dirt track of our youth is now paved all the way to the top, and proved to be a pleasant, crisp 20-minute morning ride. I guess some changes are beneficial. The smoky atmosphere was less intense in the canyon, and following the stream was magical. The lake level was already way down in anticipation of the following year's winter snow melt. The calm water nearly perfectly mirrored the reflection of the surrounding mountains. However, once I returned to the valley, disappointment descended again with the heavy gray blanket of smoke that still lay over everything.

My next objective was to follow the old Milwaukee Railroad as closely as possible along the route where I used to work, starting from the Three Forks Train Terminal. An old Milwaukee caboose was set up as an information center, and the woman working there knew most of the people in town. Lo and behold, she also had a local phone book! For any younger readers, prior to Facebook, a phone book allowed you to look up a person's phone number and address. The neat thing was, if you knew the person's name, you could find their address. And if you knew the address and last name, you could find the first name and phone number. Using this method, I discovered that some of my old rail pals still lived in the area and I made a few calls.

Following the old railway tracks was a bit of a lark in the smoky haze, as I couldn't really see more than a few miles at any given time – especially once I left the enjoyable Jefferson River canyon and branched out across the valley. The visibility continued to be poor even as I continued up the constricted switchbacks of the normally beautiful mountain road, then over the Continental Divide at Donald Pass.

The enormity of the forest fires was impressed on me when I passed several fields containing large tent cities set up as accommodation for fire fighters.

You've got to hand it to the locals though, they seem to take everything in their stride. In one area near Georgetown Lake, where the smoke was particularly thick, fishermen were hanging their recent catches on clotheslines with clothes pegs. Smoked trout is a real delicacy.

That evening, in Missoula, my classmate Scott and I sat up on the ridge at the edge of town. Drinking Moose Drool Brown Ale, we watched the fire engulfing the forested mountains as it approached the city. Clouds of smoke were illuminated by a subtle pink glow. Suddenly, a wind shift exposed the extent of the fire, showing the entire mountainside aflame. Clusters of trees heavily laden with pine cones were igniting, propelling fireballs hundreds of feet high into the night sky.

It was horrifyingly beautiful.

Overnight, the fire continued to spread, and by sunrise the next morning, this conflagration alone had spread from 28,000 to 39,000 acres.

I was able to lunch with my cousin Sandy and her husband the next day. They were in town because the fire was within a mile of their house at Lolo Pass. The authorities wouldn't let them return to collect valuables, and they were very distressed. I've yet to hear if the house survived.

The ride to Kalispell the following morning took me through more hazy, smoke-filled air, reducing visibility to sketchy outlines of the Mission Mountains and Flathead Lake. At one point I stopped alongside the lake to watch a fire. The flames were visible within a mile up the side of the mountain. Helicopters roared overhead filling monsoon buckets from the lake, then raced back up the slopes to deliver their payloads, before repeating the process again. And again. And again.

I cried.

OK, so the smoke may have had a lot to do with that. But it still broke my heart to see my beautiful home state aflame. By the end of that week, there were over a million acres burning in Montana. While Florida suffered flooding from hurricanes Emily and Irma, Montana would have gladly taken the rain.

The county fair was in full swing at Kalispell when I arrived to stay with Allen and Becky. (The hedge had mostly recovered from the trimming I'd given it on my previous visit.) It was a short walk to the fairgrounds from their house. We passed through a jungle of RVs, trailers, pickups and horse trailers to get to the entry gate. The front half of one trailer was set up for people and the rear half for horses. I still wore my gloves even though most of the nail polish had scraped off by now – just in case. That stuff is tenacious. I've had car paint come off easier.

We took in the livestock, artwork, photography, quilting, flower arrangements and food exhibits. But ultimately, we continued on past the carnival rides along the midway to the Rodeo Arena. This rodeo was larger than Ekalaka's and featured several world-ranking rodeo cowboys, as well as some less seen events, such as bull dogging. Riding pell-mell on your horse alongside a steer would be thrilling enough, but these courageous cowboys lean down from the saddle, grab the horns of the steer, then drop off and wrestle the 2,200 lb (1,000 kg) bovine onto its side. All this requires timing, precision and strength, as well as that courage I mentioned before.

And they do this for sport!

"You're in luck, they're having the Indian relay horse race again this year," Allen advised as we stood in line to buy delicious thick huckleberry milkshakes. "In essence, a single rider from each team rides four laps around the racecourse bareback," he reminded me. "Each lap is on a different horse."

"I remember," I said. "His support crew holds the next mount ready. The rider alights from a still running horse in a mad dash and bounds up onto the fresh critter."

"Right. This year there are four teams in each of the two heats followed by a four-team final," he continued. "Each team represents a Native American tribe from around the area."

At the end of each lap came the exhilarating exchange. With no less than four tired horses, four fresh horses, four riders, and eight handlers on the track, total pandemonium was assured. The horses were exceptionally high-strung or freshly broken, and half the race was realized just by motivating them in the right direction – especially at the start. All this amounted to a very exciting race, from the circulating clustered start, through to the mayhem while exchanging spent horses, and finally, the competitively tight finish crossing the line. Some horses arriving rider-less. Yeehaa!

I'd experienced parching heat, storms, tornadoes and forest fires during the trip. Next came a total eclipse of the sun. Well, it was actually a 94 percent eclipse in this part of the world, but going further south and trying to find a place to stay with all the idiots wasn't really worth that extra six percent. I'd heard enthusiasts tell of several-hundred-dollar fees just to pitch a tent in a field – and prices too fierce to mention for motel rooms.

Donning our special spectacles to keep from burning out our eyeballs, and looking like 1960s 3D movie audiences, Allen, Becky and I watched the rare phenomenon. The temperature dropped markedly when the eclipse reached totality, as the sky turned dark and stars could be seen. Even though I'd observed a full eclipse in Montana in the late 1970s, it was just as much fun to watch it all again.

I'd heard rumors of a scenic mountain road that had been recently paved. It would take me over a mountain pass near the Idaho border, and deposit me on Highway 12 close to my next destination. A wind shift during the night had finally delivered reasonably clear weather for the next leg of my journey. Just what I needed.

With Washington as my target, I was off. Banking the bike over around the tight curves. The high decibel roar of the motor climbing and falling as I ran through the gears. Feeling the exhilaration and freedom that never got old. Laughing, with my hair blowing in the wind, as I cruised down the highway.

Well, all true except the bit about my hair blowing in the wind. I was wearing a helmet. And I don't have much hair on top of my head anymore. But still, you get my drift.

Idaho – Washington

MD 144.08.31.11:40

August 31, 2017

The recently-paved mountain pass turned out to be an excellent shortcut and a brilliant motorcycle route. Just me and the Pearl the whole way, gliding around the turns. About 40 miles in, I passed a bicycle fence. Which is to say, a continuous line of bicycles tied nose to tail to form a fenceline. It always brings a smile to my face to see the creativity, ingenuity and humor of the human spirit.

Back on I-90, I crossed Lookout Pass and kept my eyes peeled for more out-of-the-way roads. This endeavor cost me a bit of time, as two of them ended rather suddenly about ten miles in. But it was sunny and warm, so who cares?

Turns out, in the end it was me who cared. These fruitless detours meant that, as the day wore on into late afternoon then early evening, I'd still not arrived at my sister's house near Spokane. Riding westward meant I was staring directly into the sun. While this may look romantic in the movies, in real life, not so much. I sure could have used those eclipse glasses that I'd been wearing a few days before. With white spots burning into my retinas, I decided to stop for supper and wait for the sun to set.

Unfortunately, I made the mistake of leaving my headlights on when I went into eat. Dead battery. Bummer!

I was rescued by a couple of kindred spirits who patiently stood by while I unloaded everything off the Pearl, then removed the seat so we could reach the battery terminals to jump start her. I kept trying to hurry, until I realized they were enjoying our conversation as much as I was. By the time the bike was running again and all the gear tied back down, there was no longer any issue with the sun. It had well and truly set. I said my thanks and motored back onto the Interstate. The deer were already out and about, playing their nightly game of "Dodge the Cars" as they traversed the highway from the hills to the river.

It's funny how after a while the body and mind need a holiday from a holiday. I discovered I was thoroughly run-down from the physical strain of continuous travel and the mental strain of stimulus overload. I was genuinely in need of some good old R&R, and staying with my sister was the perfect opportunity. Judy let me sleep pretty much straight through for the first two days, then with short breaks to swim in the lake, eat and watch movies for a few days after that.

Judy's grandkids were also staying the week, and with uncertainty surrounding my correct familial title, they began calling me Grunkle Rod – short for Great Uncle Rod. I kinda liked that. It seemed to cover the primary elements of our relationship. We had heaps of fun playing along the shore, burying the kids in sand, and splashing in the lake.

Judy helped me advertise the Black Pearl for sale on Craig's List. After four days, I'd only received five responses. All from scammers. By then I'd pretty much decided to ride to California, and ship the bike home to New Zealand.

Once that decision was made, and I was revitalized, installation of the LED lights I'd purchased at Sturgis became the priority. They came with a terrific double-sided foam tape made by 3M that rivals duct tape for stickiness. An acclamation I do not make lightly. With instructions in hand, I began to adhere the LEDs under the tank and on the frame.

The salesman had said a four-year-old could install them in an hour and a half. Therefore, I felt reasonably satisfied when it only took me two days. And barring the one light that accidentally got stuck to my forehead when I leaned against the gas tank, the whole project came together rather smoothly.

The results were stunning. With light bouncing off gleaming chrome, the Pearl's engine was illuminated with a surreal glow. From an app on my phone, I could change the colors from white to red, blue, green and purple, and there were program options that allowed the LEDs to strobe, pulse, "breathe" and shift through color patterns.

"But you don't usually ride your bike after dark. So who would ever get to see them?" asked my sister.

"Picky. Picky. Picky." But sometimes, when I stopped for the night, I'd wake up at two in the morning, stick my head outside my tent and turn them on for a few minutes. Just because.

Before I put the Pearl on a boat in California, I wanted to make the most of my remaining time in the United States. I set off a few days later, through central Washington with the aim of eventually ending up in Seattle. The sky became hazy again. I'd passed out of the smoke from the Montana fires and into the smoke dispersion area for the fires of western Washington.

Near Othello, I began crying again. It got worse and worse, with tears streaming down my face, until I realized I was following a farm truck hauling onions. There were a lot of onions along the edge of the road that had fallen off other tucks, and many had been run over where the vehicles entered from the fields, sending onion gas into the air. Phew, was I glad once I'd passed on through and could dry my eyes.

Parched and in dire need of a drink, I arrived at Rob and Sandy's house. I'd been looking forward to seeing Rob ever since reminiscing about our dirt bike escapades outside of Bozeman. He handed me a beer as I killed the engine and removed my helmet. Now that's service. "Heard you coming and figured a Klingon might be thirsty," he smiled.

"Ha ha. Mostly it was the Yakima Valley," I explained. "After the peach and apple orchards, there were miles and miles of pungent hops hanging out on cables. Subliminal messages of Washington's famous beers kept passing through my head. If that doesn't awaken a thirst, nothing will."

"I thought it mighta been the fires," he laughed. "We had a close call last week," he said, pointing to the adjacent burned field. "I had the hose out watering down the roof and praying the winds wouldn't turn against us. It got to within a stone's throw of the house."

"Wow, that was close! There were miles of rolling prairie hills burned black and bare between Othello and here."

"Yeah. Those were from last year's fires," he informed me. "Grass fires burned the treeless hills down to the nib and nothing has grown back yet."

Rob and I reminisced over our railroad years and biking experiences. The sun set dark orange. And a blood-red moon rose through the thick smoke haze as we sat on the back deck. Talking and drinking until the beer was gone. Which was pretty late.

The next morning, I was surprised to notice that the Pearl's rear tire was nearly bald. Fortuitously, there was a Harley-Davidson dealer in town who could fit a new one that day.

When Rob took me back to collect the bike, he suggested, "When you set off, you should take the old river road through the Yakima Canyon. It's a pretty ride."

"The smoke is so bad I don't expect I'd see anything," I said.

However, his recommendation turned out to be the perfect route because, once in the canyon, visibility improved markedly. Green shrubbery and sporadic pines lined the river. Steep mountains, bare of any growth except brown grass between rock outcroppings, rose up on either side. Rock slides created ravines and fell right to the river's edge. The valley floor was just wide enough to hold the winding river and the railroad tracks that ran along its banks. Meanwhile, the two-lane highway was carved into the steep hillsides, climbing and descending around curves and over cuts as it sought out the most economical route. An enjoyable ride made even more stunning by the dramatic scenery.

Running parallel to the Rockies, I continued north with the hope of escaping the fires, or more accurately the smoke. This route took me on a brilliant mountain ride to Leavenworth.

The mountainous location and architecture of this little town is designed to make you feel as if you're in the Swiss Alps, and people dress in costumes reminiscent of old Bavaria. There are lots of novelty shops to explore, like the Christmas Store where all they sell is Christmas items all year around.

Leaving Leavenworth after a bratwurst hotdog for lunch, I headed higher up into the mountains. Finally, as I yodeled over the pass, the air cleared. Visibility returned. The sky was blue. Stopping frequently to take photos of the peaks behind me, the ride down through the mountains and into Seattle was spectacular.

In some ways, Seattle was a bit like coming home. I'd lived there aboard *Bontekoe* before venturing out on the high seas, and ending up in New Zealand. The city was also home to numerous relatives, classmates and friends I intended to see, and I set out to visit every one I could find. I took the opportunity to base myself at my cousin Lee's house. It was a perfect location, especially since my cousin Marvin lived with him, and two of my nieces and Lee's son lived within five minutes' drive. In just a few days I had caught up with them all, plus several friends and former classmates to boot.

"Since you've got some time left over," said Lee, "let's drive around town and see what's changed and what hasn't."

Our first stop was the Aurora Bridge. Located underneath the bridge sits a sculpture of a giant troll eating a VW Beetle. "Good thing I had my silver bell to ward off such dangers during my travels," I said to Lee.

A little further down by the Fremont Bridge, is a sculpture called "Waiting for the Interurban," consisting of several people and a dog standing under a bus shelter. It's probably one of the most interactive works of art I've ever seen. People constantly decorate it by adding signs, balloons, dressing the characters in clothing and posing for photos.

"I've always enjoyed this artwork," I said. "Especially the human head on the dog."

"Rumor has it, the face is that of the mayor, who caused some strife in the sculptor's life," said Lee.

"Bad move by the mayor," I laughed.

I had a lot of fond memories as we crossed the draw bridge and drove by the marina on Lake Union, where *Bontekoe* had once been moored. In those days, I'd intended to sail around the world. Ha! New Zealand was a fair distance, but I guess I still have a long way to go.

We made several stops at marine stores around Lake Union to drool over things I can't buy in New Zealand, or at least refuse to buy because they're twice as expensive.

The city's skyline was certainly changing. "Seattle currently has 65 cranes erected for building high rises," commented Lee. "That's a fair bit of construction underway. Especially when you consider the next closest US city only has 35."

About that time, I received a call from a local guy who had seen my Craig's List advertisement and wanted to buy the Pearl. Unfortunately, he wasn't a scammer. Dang! Well, OK, I'd let her go. But there was still the opportunity for another ABC point by going to Canada. So, I agreed to sell him the bike with the proviso that I be allowed to ride it for another week. And, on a handshake, the deal was done.

I left Seattle, headed north and spent the night with my former wife's brother Bob, and his family. It was an entertaining catch-up. They lived near the coast, close to Anacortes, which made it easy to catch the early vehicle ferry to Vancouver Island, Canada, the next morning.

So once again, on a crisp clear morning at 6:30 am, with calm wind and smooth waters, I was going to sea

Canada

MD 144.09.03.14:43

September 3, 2017

The ferry ride from Anacortes to Sidney passes through the San Juan Islands. At one time, I'd had *Bontekoe* moored in Anacortes. From there, it's a 20-minute sail into the islands for a fantastic gunkholing holiday… along with the entire sailing population of Seattle and Vancouver. Hundreds of protected anchorages await the patient yachties who sail these waters where tidal currents are often stronger than the wind.

Several pods of killer whales live in the area. Dungeness crab, salmon and the local rockfish provide a seafood platter that makes your mouth water. The briny smell of the ocean is strong. And the views of Mount Baker, or the Olympics, turning pink in the sunset are stunning. A sailor's paradise. These memories made for a pleasant passage as the ferry plowed along.

While I could have simply ridden over the border into Vancouver to get my ABC point, my friend Larry, a cruising sailor, lived halfway up the east coast of Vancouver Island. And there was no way I could pass up his offer of a place to stay and the chance to spin some sailing yarns.

The rugged and mountainous island granted a fun ride over a pass with breath-taking views of inlets and bays. I'd heard that the ride out to Barkley Sound on the west coast was equally stunning. But time was still a constraint and since I'd seen it from the ocean side in the past, I decided to skip it and headed straight on to Larry's place.

After dinner, we took a leisurely walk along the waterfront. It was dark by the time we returned, so I showed off the new LEDs and Larry was suitably impressed. As we experimented with the controller app, I discovered the lights had been set at only half their potential brightness. *Wow!* I thought. *I must try this during daylight hours.*

After breakfast the next morning, I headed out to catch the Black Ball vehicle ferry from Victoria to Port Angeles on Washington's Olympic

Peninsula. Choosing to make an impressive departure, I turned the LEDs on to high as I waved goodbye and roared out onto the highway.

I found that motorists on the island were very courteous to motorcyclists. Every time I rode up behind a car, the driver would pull over and let me pass. Because of that, I was making incredibly good time and really enjoying the outlooks across the Gulf Islands. But, I'm sorry to say, that came to an abrupt end 15 kilometers short of Victoria.

Turns out, the Royal Canadian Mounties take exception to anyone other than themselves using blue and red strobing LED lights.

It was Labor Day Weekend and there were all sorts of activities going on in Victoria – live music, buskers and art festivals, combined with the normal lively activities of the harbor. Cruise ships, float planes, water taxis and pleasure boats were going to and fro. I secured a ferry ticket, left the bike at the terminal and took off on foot to partake in the festivities until departure time.

After boarding the ferry and strapping the bike down, I headed up on deck to soak in the view. While the Strait of Juan de Fuca can sometimes get a bit bumpy, our passage was pretty typical, with barely a ripple on the sea at the start, and only a very light swell in the middle. Which made it a piece of cake to spot a pod of killer whales.

The male orcas have a dorsal fin that reaches six feet high and looks not unlike a submarine periscope rising up out of the water as they climb up for air. They blast out a plume of mist, then slowly descend again. In still, crisp conditions, the plume hangs for several minutes.

The wind had changed direction during the night and once again the atmosphere was heavy with hazy smoke. Even though there was a blue sky directly overhead, the magnificent view of the snow-capped Olympic peaks revealed only a fraction of their potential beauty – sort of like looking through a screen door at a newspaper lying on the front porch. You might be able to read the headlines but you can't quite make out the stories.

"I guess I'll just have to take a closer look to see what those stories are when I get to shore," I said to the seagulls.

Washington Olympic Peninsula

MD 144.09.07.08:55

September 7, 2017

Highway 101 begins at the top end of the Olympic Peninsula and continues all the way down the west coast to Mexico. A spectacular and famous scenic ride. And while I wasn't going to do it in its entirety, there was no reason I couldn't enjoy the top third as it followed the ocean with occasional jogs inland on this farewell ride aboard the Black Pearl.

The first inward jog was through Olympic National Park where most of the forest is old growth. Access off-road through here is exceptionally difficult due to the density of undergrowth.

I'd read somewhere that when they built this highway, the foliage was so thick that the average lifespan for a pair of Levi's jeans was six weeks. And this was back in the days when the denim of shrink to fit jeans was so thick, it was like putting on a pair of cardboard pants until they had soften after the first couple of washes.

I've ridden down tree-lined roads before. Some had trees bent over from both sides forming a veritable green tunnel. And some formed dense green walls along both sides. But man, I'm telling you, I'd never seen anything quite like this. These trees were huge! It was like riding down 4th Ave in Central Manhattan, with high-rises on either side, leaving only a thin sliver of blue sky above.

After I passed the Crescent Lake area, I noticed a sign saying "A Really Big Cedar Tree". I stopped to see just how big "Really Big" is. Turns out, "Really Big" is REALLY, REALLY BIG! We're talking sequoia-sized here. I just love honesty in advertising,

Following a lovely path that meandered through the forest from the carpark, I saw huge spider webs everywhere alongside the trail. I heard the delightful babbling of a stream off to the left somewhere through the trees. A pungent earthy smell filled the air. The whole place had a primitive mystical feel to it.

The legendary Sasquatch supposedly resides in this area.

Actually, to my mind, several trees along the way qualified as "Really Big" trees. But there was no mistaking the one referred to by the sign. It reminded me of seeing Tāne Mahuta, the huge kauri tree in Northland, New Zealand. Gawking at the immensity and beauty of it, I thought of the poem "Trees" by Joyce Kilmer, which ends with the lines: "Poems are made by fools like me, / But only God can make a tree."

After a couple of photos and a wander around the cedar's base, I noticed an alternate trail leading back towards the carpark. Feeling adventurous, I thought, *Aww, what the heck.*

A thick cushion of long pine needles covered the forest floor making for a springy walk, as I avoided the abundance of spider webs by bobbing and weaving my way along the narrow path.

A bird let out a warbling whistle and, turning my head to try and spot him, I lost my balance and tumbled forward five or six steps. Right into two huge spider webs. Waving my arms frantically while pulling backwards, I succeeded only in entangling myself in three more webs. I let out a long, low growl of anguish.

Due to my arm waving, gyrations, general exertions and forlorn attempts to get free, the webs now pretty much covered my entire body.

Of course, my eyes were covered too, causing me to trip over a root, fall and roll several times down a small incline. When I came to a stop, I found that I was now also covered in long gray-brown pine needles, brown moss and other organic materials found on the forest floor, which had adhered to the spider webs. The whole mess looked somewhat like long brown shaggy hair. I let out another long, low growl of anguish.

Remembering the stream I'd heard earlier, I thought it best to head cross country in that direction to see if I could get cleaned up.

Still vision-impaired and motion-restricted from the attached foliage, I made my way through the forest, with a somewhat cautious, lumbering gait and outstretched arms, towards the stream.

Once there, it took what seemed like hours of painstaking, tedious work to pluck the organic matter from my clothes. And, since I had no towel, I used the solar-drying technique afterwards – basking, if you will, in the tree filtered sunlight.

By the time I got back to the carpark, it was late afternoon and the whole place was abuzz with cars and people. A small crowd had gathered around a highly agitated Asian fellow who was pointing into the forest, waving his hands, pointing at his camera and talking a mile a minute.

Evidently the tourist had seen a Sasquatch not less than 200 yards from the carpark! His wife was nodding enthusiastically and continually jumping in with her version of events. The man rewound the video he had captured, replaying and pausing it at key points as other tourists crowded around and asked a myriad of questions. It was difficult to see over the multitude of people but all I could make out was a fuzzy image of a tall, gray-brown creature, lumbering through the trees with outstretched arms.

Just my luck. The first sighting of a Sasquatch in some time and even though I was in right in the same area, I'd apparently missed it. Bugger!

On the short ride to the campground, I kept a vigilant eye out just in case he came close to the road and made another appearance. But no such luck.

The next day, the road jogged out to the North Pacific again and I got to thinking about taking a swim. That way, I would be able to say, "In the last two years I've swum in the Yellow Sea, the Tasman Sea, the South Pacific Ocean, the Caribbean, the North Atlantic, the Great Lakes and the North Pacific."

The weather being foggy, overcast and not a little chilly, the venture took some serious self-persuasion. But finally, common sense gave way to ambition. I stripped bare and waded out about thigh deep into the icy water, then realized I'd actually already swum in the North Pacific – the previous year at Santa Monica!

What was I thinking? Just as I turned to go back to shore, I lost my balance on the rocky bottom and had to sit down suddenly to keep from falling. The intake of air that accompanied my surprised gasp was audible over the entire beach. Which was lucky because, almost immediately, the next wave rolled in over the top of me, completing my immersion.

Since my lungs were already filled to capacity, I was unable to inhale any water with the shock of it all, which probably saved me from drowning.

Now I can say, "I swam in the North Pacific and the further North Pacific." As if any of that really matters.

A sign reading "World's Largest Spruce Tree" tried to tempt me a few miles later. I'm not sure if it was bigger than the cedar or not, but I was just too stiff and cold to make the hike. Looking back, I wish I'd stopped. I might have had another chance to see the elusive Sasquatch.

Eventually the Columbia River arrived on the route south, and I'd scarcely warmed up enough from the swim to feel my toes again when the impressive sight of the 4.067-mile-long (6.7 k) Astoria-Megler Bridge came into view shortly afterwards.

Oregon – Washington – California

The last leg of the Astoria-Megler Bridge over the Columbia River descended and curved for a dramatic entry into Astoria, Oregon. This was a memorable arrival as it completed another milestone for the Black Pearl and me.

While I'd personally been to all 50 of the US states, over the last two years the Black Pearl and I had now been in all 48 of the continental states, plus Mexico and Canada. I'd formed a pretty strong bond with the bike and I was feeling some remorse about selling her. Perhaps I should have kept her, and gone through with my idea of riding on down Highway 101 to California, then shipping her home to New Zealand. Shoulda, woulda, coulda. *What would I do with two bikes anyway?*

The cool sea breezes were a welcome change to the blazing heat I'd encountered down south and out east earlier in the year. And I'd been riding dry since Sturgis. The upshot of all this was that the salt-water blisters on my backside had finally begun to reduce in number and some had even healed outright.

Seaside, Oregon was where I'd decided to leave the coast and head eastwards again. It is also where Lewis and Clark had finally found the Pacific Ocean after leaving St Louis. It's a good thing too. Pretty much everywhere you go in the Northwest you see signs of their wanderings. Who knows how many more Lewis and Clark trails we would have had to mark if they hadn't finally found the edge of the continent?

It seems to me 90% of everything explored and named between Australia and the Mississippi River can be attributed to Lewis and Clark or Captain Cook, The epitome of adventurous explorers.

So they built a nice sculpture to mark the occasion where the city joined the beach. To celebrate their achievement, I took a short barefoot jaunt along the sandy beach that ran for miles in either direction.

Rising up over the pass between Clatsop and Tillamook State Parks, two things happened simultaneously. The temperature rose dramatically and visibility dropped in inverse proportion, due to the smoke from still raging forest fires. At one point, I saw a "Scenic Viewpoint Turn Left" sign, but whatever the view, it wasn't there when I looked. In fact, I couldn't see anything beyond the end of the carpark.

My cousin Don – of early motorbike riding legend – lived with his wife Sharon in McMinnville, and this was to be my furthest southern destination in Oregon before heading back towards Seattle. Given that, in some ways, my recent excursions had been the fulfillment of the adventures he and I had had riding together in the late 1960s, I was eager to see him and relive some of our earlier escapades.

"So, what are your plans now?" asked Don as we all settled onto his couch after our initial greetings.

"Well, I managed to meet up with Karen and her husband Terry earlier today," I responded. "We watched a baseball game together." Karen was the sister of my former wife.

"That just leaves time with you and our classmate Janice."

"I didn't know she lived here," came the surprised response.

"Funny that. You two living in the same town for the last 20 years and each not knowing about the other till I show up. Anyway, we're going to join her and her husband tonight for dinner," I informed him.

After dinner, we shared laugh after laugh as Don and I reminisced about our motorcycle trip and days in High School. Sharon sat gobsmacked as I recounted the tale of our encounter with the truck. Don kept turning to her and saying, "See. I told you. I told you it all happened."

Turning again to talk of my future plans, Sharon asked, "Are you going to take in the Evergreen Flight Museum before you leave town tomorrow?"

"You know, I love flying, but I've been to so many flight museums this trip, I think I'll pass."

"But this is a really top-notch museum," Don pointed out. "You really should go."

I hesitated.

"It's right on your way out of town," Sharon prompted.

I vacillated. Then they dropped the trump card. "Home to the Spruce Goose," they announced in unison.

I capitulated.

And good thing I heeded their advice too. It's an amazing museum. The Goose is the primary drawcard but the variety of other aircraft was equally enthralling.

I was staring at a WWII German Messerschmitt jet fighter, when a volunteer guide snuck up behind me. "Good thing the Germans weren't further along in the development of this technology, or there could have been some drastic changes during the war," he said.

"It's beautiful," I replied. "First time I've ever seen one of these. I just love the lines. So elegant and sleek."

"Yeah. I appreciate machinery when design, power and efficiency all come together." Pointing to my vest patch he said, "I see you do too with your Heritage motorcycle." Then, chest swelling slightly, he added, "I ride an 08 Deluxe. They call me Spud."

"Always nice to meet a fellow biker," I said as we shook hands.

"The tour of the Spruce Goose is almost over and the next one isn't for 15 minutes. I can give you a short private tour now if you'd like." As if he had to ask.

As we climbed the boarding stairs into the vast aircraft I said, "I believe this bird still lays claim to being one of the ten largest wingspans of any airplane in the world?"

"Yup. With WWII in full swing, there were restrictions on using aluminum. Therefore, its skin is made entirely out of plywood, and the surface, devoid of rivets, is incredibly smooth."

"Spruce?" I asked.

"Actually, birch was the primary wood used, but once the newspapers got hold of the idea of spruce and made it rhyme, the name stuck. Flying her originally required a pilot, co-pilot, radio operator, and two engineers – one either side to monitor the four engines on each wing."

"I can't believe this cockpit is so spacious. It's like being in the living room of a house."

"Here," Spud said, handing me a Howard Hughes hat. "Put that on, sit in the pilot's seat and I'll take your photo."

Several hours later, with prints of the photos in hand and too much left unseen, I finally pulled myself away for the ride north, back to cousin Lee's house in Seattle.

The heat was back, along with my salt-water blisters. The smoky haze was still so thick, it was impossible to see Mount Saint Helens or Mount Rainier. Or little else off to the sides of the road for that matter.

All that, plus the impending separation of me and my machine, cast a pall over the remainder of the ride. I'd gotten a second wind and once again began entertaining daydreams of riding on down the West coast.

Then maybe continuing on through the desert for winter...

And then east again next spring...

Oregon's state slogan is "We Love Dreamers," and it seemed I'd caught the bug.

I brought myself back to reality. I'd made an agreement to sell the bike. More importantly, there had been a handshake.

It was well after dark when I arrived back in Seattle, so I took advantage by cranking my LEDs on high and running them through the entire color spectrum for the final portion of my trip – bringing a smile back to my face.

The next day I handed the Black Pearl over to her new owner. After completing the paperwork, I dismounted, gave her a goodbye pat on the gas tank and turned my head as they rode away.

There was no smoke in the air, but my eyes burned just the same.

Two days later I flew to Los Angeles where I was able to meet up with my cousin Scot for a short visit. It took only a few minutes to reacquaint after 50 years, and soon he was telling me stories of our fathers that I had never heard before. Once again, I was reminded of my good fortune at having such a unique and wonderful collection of relatives. It was a perfect ending to the trip.

And just like that, four months had passed. I'd begun this adventure thinking that riding, countryside and relatives would be the order of importance. In the end it turned out to be relatives, countryside and riding. Of the 19 relatives I'd hoped to see, I'd been able to meet up with all but three. Not to mention numerous classmates and friends. If this had been some kind of ABC competition, I'd surely be right up in the lead.

Now that the four-month journey was over, it suddenly seemed all too short.

But what can you do?

I gave thanks to the Lord for keeping me safe and all I was able to see and do. Then moved up the chute and boarded the plane with the rest of the herd.

Book 6

Australia 2017

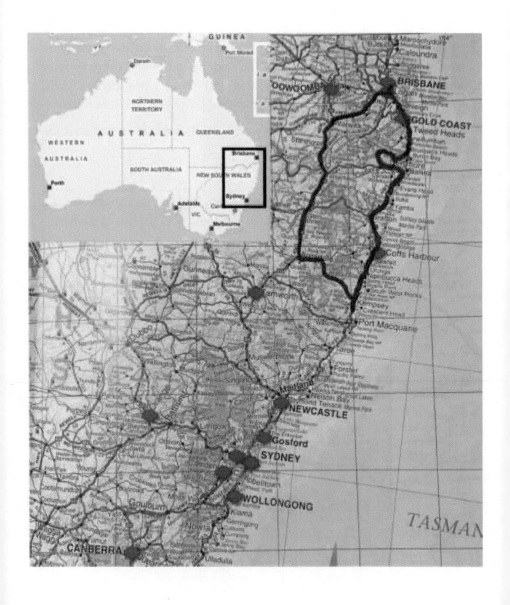

Queensland – New South Whales

MD 144.10.27.09:29
October 27, 2017

Just when you, the reader, thought the adventure was at an end, that all those months in the saddle must surely have satisfied my yearning for travel and it would be safe to get up, stretch your legs, grab a beer and start reading a different book ...

There I was, sitting on my mate Rafe's yacht in Auckland, regaling him about my amazing trip to the United States and the fun I'd had collecting points for the ABCs.

"But unfortunately," I lamented, "I'm not positive I have enough points to win. And the only way to get more would be to go to Australia."

"So, what are you going to do?" he asked.

"Well, I've given it some thought. A short trip of, say, four or five days would allow me to collect ten 'big things,' two states, plus a country point for being in Australia. If I fly to Brisbane, hire a bike, then ride to Port Macquarie and back, I should be able to achieve all that."

"I have some friends I met sailing in the islands who live near Port Macquarie. You could stay with them," he offered.

I was caught up in my own thoughts. "I really want to get first place and the $1,000 prize."

"So, you're saying that, in addition to the several thousand you spent in the States, if you spend another $2,000 for airline tickets, bike hire, and room and board, you *might* win $1,000?"

"It's the principle of the thing, Rafe." At least that's what I kept telling myself as I began to gain a level of insight about how gamblers get in so deep that they cannot quit.

Then Rafe, being an instigating kind of guy, said, "OK, let's do it."

Now, a lot of people have said that to me over the years. The trip with Paula and her luggage immediately sprang to mind. However, Rafe seemed to be quite serious. "Wow! Really? OK then," I stammered. "I suggest we leave next Tuesday and come back Saturday. That will get us the best airline prices."

"But I have a meeting on Thursday," came Rafe's response. "Can you do another time?"

OK, here come the excuses, I thought.

"Sure," I said, feeling pretty certain I'd end up reserving a ticket for one as usual. "Pick a time you like and just let me know in the next day or so."

Next morning, I answered the phone to hear Rafe say, "OK, tickets departing on Saturday night, returning Thursday before my meeting, are booked and paid for."

Yikes! We had a plan. And only a week until departure.

Due to space limitations, some luggage adjustments were required to accommodate two people on one motorcycle. The first casualties were the tent and sleeping bag.

"No worries," said Rafe. "We'll stay in backpackers' accommodation." It would be more expensive than camping, but should prove more comfortable – and we weren't going for long.

The second casualty was the rear storage bag, as the rental wouldn't have a luggage rack. That meant my rain gear and quick access items would have to be stowed in a saddle bag.

Which brings us to our third challenge: we'd only have one saddle bag each. I'd felt pretty good about myself for traveling around for the last couple of years with only three changes of clothes and the absolute necessities. Now I would have to reduce that by a further two thirds.

I packed one change of underwear, a t-shirt, a pair of socks, thermals, a jumper and toiletries. I'd be wearing my leathers most of the time and I'd heard it hardly ever rains in Australia. *Oh well,* I reminded myself again, *we aren't going for long.*

All challenges aside, I was really looking forward to traveling with Rafe. He spoke fluent Aussie, and with his upbeat, can-do attitude, he was a fun guy to be around.

Rafe had purchased discount tickets that only allowed one carry-on bag each, limited to 7 kg (15 pounds). I felt rather conspicuous standing in the queue wearing all my leathers, carrying a bulging waterproof bag under one arm, and my motorcycle helmet stuffed full of gloves and face scarf in the other, as we proceeded up the ramp to the plane.

"I'm sorry sir, you're only allowed one carry-on," said the stewardess at the gate.

"I only have one bag," I responded.

"And the helmet," she noted raising her eyebrows with a smirk.

"Clothing attire," I said with a straight face. Ha! I had her there.

Unfortunately, that meant wearing the bloody helmet for the whole flight. Acoustically, it made for a quiet trip across the Tasman Sea, but proved a bit of a challenge when the meal arrived.

It was a balmy evening as we touched down in Brisbane. Unbeknownst to us, the All Blacks were in town to play a rugby match against the Wallabies (New Zealand versus Australia), which had sucked up almost all available accommodation. Fortunately, Rafe was able to sweet-talk the receptionist out of two of the last three beds at the YHA.

Next day, still functioning on New Zealand time, we arose at 4:35 a.m. – which meant we'd actually slept in a bit. We filled in an hour or two walking about, then found the bus station, traveled down to the motorcycle rental shop and hired ourselves a black and cream 2016 Harley-Davidson Heritage Softail. It may have been a few years newer and boasted a bigger engine than the Black Pearl, but it was not nearly as classy a ride.

Riding on the left side of the road, the same as in New Zealand, made adjusting to our new surroundings a piece of cake. Rafe and I had done a practice run back home aboard my Super Glide and worked out the kinks of riding two-up. I'd hired the Heritage because I was familiar with the way it would handle, and the elevated back seat would give the pillion a good view over my head. Rafe and I were loaded and fully adjusted in less than 20 minutes.

Our first ABC stop was a mere 200 meters (650 ft) from the rental shop! Yeah, this was going to be easy. In fact, according to "The Plan," we would have half the big things we needed by the end of the day. Then we could sit back, cruise along and just enjoy the sights.

"The Plan" began to unravel when we arrived at Surfers Paradise about an hour later. Turns out, a lot of the big things listed on the internet had been relocated, demolished, or destroyed by storms. As a result, we spent hours riding around looking for things that had ceased to exist five or ten years ago.

Lifting my visor at a stop light, I raised my voice above the big engine's exhaust pipe noise, "At least we're seeing a lot of things most tourists miss."

"And with good reason," Rafe shouted back.

After our fifth trip down the seaside esplanade, and with no giant boomerang to be found, I was feeling stressed, so we pulled over to talk to the locals. Several people confirmed that the boomerang had, in fact, been washed out to sea several years previously. And hadn't come back.

Since we'd already stopped, we decided to go down and wiggle our toes in the sand. It was there, on the beach, in the warm sun, that the realization re-emerged. *There's more to life than collecting points.* I began to relax, unwind and slow down, deciding to enjoy the trip for what it had to offer.

Which turned out to be a lot.

Leaving the Gold Coast skyscrapers behind, we followed the coastal back-roads southwards, across the state line from Queensland into New South Wales, through Tweed Heads and the like, until I accidentally turned off at the wrong place, putting us in a loop de loop, over the hills and through the valleys. I was actually quite enjoying myself, when Rafe tapped on my helmet.

"This is the wrong way. We're heading west," he shouted above the rumble.

"Yeah, but it's accidents like these that make a trip fun."

"We don't have time for extraneous exploration," he said, pointing to his watch.

Looking inland, I could see some really interesting looking dome-topped mountains in the distance. *They would be fun to ride through.* We saw sugar cane, apple orchards and huge fields of blueberries. Once I found the coast again, we could see whales close in as they migrated southwards. And jacarandas. There seemed to be one or two of these vibrant purple trees every

356

half a kilometer. In fact, further on in the town of Grafton, there was actually a Jacaranda Festival underway.

Live music was playing and there were hundreds of young university people on holiday in Byron Bay, walking down the streets, on the beach and in the park. Because of this, the town's backpackers' accommodation was fully booked. We decided to sit for a while and soak in the ambiance anyway. And we may have glanced at the young ladies in bikinis.

It was going on late twilight when we got to Ballina, and there were no backpacker beds to be found there either. Our next best bet was Yamba, another an hour and a half further south. I didn't hear Rafe say, "I told you so." Which was gracious of him, as we carried on into the darkness.

Riding in kangaroo country after dark is not recommended. I slowed down to 60 kilometers an hour with my eyes wide open, constantly checking the borrow pits either side of the road, expecting one of those giant-rabbit-like creatures to come bounding out in front of me at any moment.

Then it began to rain.

That turn of events caused us to break all three of the most important rules of motorcycling. Sometimes you just gotta trust that things will work out. Over the previous two years, while sleeping in tents, riding motorcycles and sailing, I hadn't had a single sick day. However, I'd had the beginnings of a cold when we boarded the plane and now it took full advantage of my wet, chilled state to escalate into full-blown man flu. I'm telling you right now, coughing and sneezing in a full-face helmet is an experience you really don't want to know about.

We were winding down the coast the next day when I saw a "Scenic Lookout" sign pointing inland.

Ordinarily, such a sign implies that said lookout is nearby – perhaps half a kilometer away. A full 14 kilometers later, we arrived at the top of a mountain in the Orara East State Forest. There we walked onto a suspended platform out over the tree-tops and surveyed the splendid view. We could see over the forest, down to the coastal beaches where we had been, where we were going and across the Tasman Sea. But it might take more than a clear day to catch a glimpse of New Zealand.

On the way up we had passed several banana plantations, a couple of koala bear crossings, one kangaroo crossing, and a roadside stand offering frozen chocolate-covered bananas. Which, of course, we stopped to try on the way back.

This delicacy consisted of a peeled banana, with stick stuck into it, dipped in chocolate and dropped in a freezer. Simple, yes, but deliciously effective. Rafe pointed out the sign above the honesty payment box: "OLL STeLING WILL Be DispLAeD ON FACEBooK." There must be some real lowlifes out there to take advantage of something that only costs $2.50.

It was late afternoon by the time we rumbled up to the home of Rafe's sailing friends in Port Macquarie. Patrick and Kate welcomed us with open arms and treated us like royalty. To which I responded, "Nice to meet you. Can I go to bed now?" and sneezed on them for emphasis.

Several hours later they came to wake me for supper, which was scrumptious. All the talk was of sailing, and I felt incredibly annoyed and embarrassed that I was too tired and sick to enjoy the wonderful opportunity of sharing stories with these generous people.

The next day I was feeling marginally better. First thing in the morning, Patrick told us to leave the bike parked, loaded us into their Land Rover, then drove us around to see the sights. We were treated to three sandy beaches (each with a different look and character); a drive through a regional park on a narrow, rutted road that rivaled any cross-country mountain travel I've ever done (with the exception of a trip to the volcano on Tanna Island in Vanuatu in 2015); kangaroos running wild; a jail built by prisoners in the late 1800s; and an outlook that gave us views of a dozen or more whales and their calves near the shore. All this was capped off with a climb up a steep walkway to a lighthouse. Eventually we headed back to the house and joined Kate for a late breakfast on the veranda. What a lovely experience.

Fully briefed on the best things to see on our return ride to Brisbane, and with full bellies, Rafe and I headed inland on the appropriately named Waterfall Highway. We stopped to look at the spectacular Ebor Falls, and I once again marveled at the way water carves valleys and canyons through solid rock, revealing layers of geological history.

There were little towns every 50 kilometers (30 miles) or so along the highway, and I began to get slack about monitoring our fuel levels. Big mistake. Suddenly, the towns disappeared, and places like Wongwibinda weren't much more than a wide spot in the road. Eventually, I began to panic.

"Why are you coasting down the hills?" asked Rafe over the idling engine.

"I don't know how far it is to the next town, but I figure we've only got about ten kilometers of fuel left."

"Eight kilometers," said Rafe, pointing at the sign just coming into view.

We made it with four tablespoons of petrol to spare.

The countryside turned greener and the trees thinned out as we continued inland. In fact, it began to look a lot like New Zealand. Proper farms began to sprout up and the fields boasted a wide variety of crops by the time we reached Glen Innes in the Northern Tablelands of NSW.

Gaelic cultural heritage was evident everywhere in this charming little town. In addition to the traditional patterning of brickwork, painted images and the like, they had also erected an impressive Stonehenge type monument called Standing Stones, just outside of town. The stones had been positioned to signify summer and winter solstice, as you might expect, but the layout also included the four points of the compass, and the 12 hours of the day for a sundial.

Checking the sundial against my watch, I noticed it was 42 seconds fast. But not too bad considering it's just a bunch of stones sticking up out of the ground.

Rafe bagged us an economically-priced room in an old hotel, right in the heart of town. Although the hour was late, the manager and owner were both bikers and they held the kitchen open for us, whilst offering a safe place to leave the bike for the night. I could hardly keep my eyes open as I chowed down the last of my veggies, then crawled upstairs to bed. Dang this being sick.

The electric blanket was a godsend as I cranked it on high and tried to sweat out my cold. Next morning the bed was soaked, but I finally felt human again after sleeping in until checkout time. Luckily Rafe had brought along a book and was so thoroughly engrossed in the story, he didn't seem to mind.

The last full day of riding started off with me cleaning the phlegm off the inside of my helmet visor. Sneezing had caused so much build up over the last couple of days, visibility was severely reduced. And everything had acquired a yellow-greenish tinge.

There were only two big things, an apple and a dinosaur, left to photograph and we found both before stopping for lunch, accomplishing the primary objective of the trip and alleviating any remaining pressure I felt about achieving my goals. That meant we could now focus on the secondary objective of the trip: enjoying the countryside aboard our iron horse as we lived out our own movie.

Back in Queensland, we skirted along the edge of Girraween National Park and I began to think how nice it would be to take some of those park roads and explore a bit more. Traffic was non-existent. The speed limit was 110 kph (68 mph). The weather was nice.

Ahhhh. Oh well, next time.

The countryside had turned back to brown bushlands again. I was interested to discover that fires were intentionally set to clear out the underbrush. Montana was aflame and, meanwhile, here in Aussie these guys were setting light to the place on purpose! The ground was black and bare, and the trees were burned black several meters up off the ground. This gave the them an ugly appearance, but they seemed to be able to survive the burning, with green leaves growing just above the scorched area and continuing on to the tops.

We passed several kangaroo crossing signs. The big marsupials seem to keep a low profile during the heat of the day, but we kept a wary eye out anyway. We had spooked a kangaroo alongside the narrow track when we'd been riding in the Land Rover with Patrick. He had raced within inches of us before bounding off into the brush again. I didn't want a similar experience while on the bike.

Like the deer in Montana, we noticed quite a number of kangaroos alongside the road that had been struck by cars or trucks. Unlike Montana, these carcasses had not been dragged off and devoured by turkey buzzards, coyotes or other scavengers. Instead, they were lying there in various states of decay. Some were fresh and bloated. Some were just a pile of bones with hide and hair around them. I'm not sure if there were just a lack of scavengers or if kangaroo tastes so bad nothing will eat it.

It was about this time that I made the critical blunder of asking Rafe if he wanted to swap seats for a short spell. Riding pillion is not nearly as comfortable as sitting in the main seat. And the view is not as nice. Although, you can look at things for longer than five seconds without having to keep your eyes on the road.

After about 50 kilometers (30 miles), my knees began to hurt from being bent and I suggested we swap back. But Rafe wasn't having a bar of that. Having realized what he'd been missing out on, he was enjoying himself to the max. However, at the next petrol stop, I seized my opportunity by jumping into the forward position, and latching tightly to the handlebars before he returned from the restroom.

Turning back towards the coast and Brisbane, we passed through Spicers Gap State Forest and Main Range National Park. These were the same mountains I had seen in the distance from the coast on our first day out. I had speculated correctly: they were indeed a nice place to visit and provided a great ride. Unfortunately, with few pullouts for photography, we had to contend ourselves with simply absorbing the beauty on the run.

Once we arrived at Ipswich, we were pretty much back in the city mode of riding. Of course, I expertly timed our arrival to align with the peak of rush hour traffic all the way to Brisbane. Rafe was not impressed with my uncanny ability and quite verbal about it too. I still managed to drop him off in time for a pre-arranged meeting at a restaurant with a friend, and went to get us a room at the YHA. It was a much cheaper stay now that there were no rugby matches on.

The next morning, we were packed and on the bike early enough to do a quick tiki tour of the city center and along the river. Then, moving against traffic as the commuters began arriving for their daily grind, we managed to arrive at the motorcycle rental shop just as they opened. And thanks to Rafe's masterful use of the internet, caught an Uber cab to the airport five minutes later.

I love it when a plan comes together!

At the airport I realized this two year adventure was coming to an end. And while reflecting back over the highlights, I concluded that even if it might not win an Emmy, it had still been a mighty fine movie.

As we boarded the plane, I noticed a couple of guys with long hair and beards that looked a bit like bikers. One guy had black painted fingernails. A smirk spread across my face as I thought, *Yeah buddy, I bet I know how that happened!* We found our seats – a row of four with Rafe and I stuck in the middle two. Painted fingernails dropped down beside me and the other dude with long hair and a beard sat beside Rafe.

Turns out, they were musicians performing in the support band touring with Alice Cooper. They had completed the Australian leg of the tour and would be performing in Auckland next. Painted fingernails and I had a great conversation during the flight and I grabbed a quick selfie with him when we got off.

Later I noticed him talking to a familiar-looking face as we waited for the shuttle outside. Alice Cooper himself!

"Mr. Cooper, would you honor me with a selfie?" I asked walking up to them.

"Sure," he said. "But you might want to remove your helmet first."

After handing my helmet to Rafe, I stood beside the rock legend, held my camera at arm's length, snapped the photo and gratefully said, "Perfect. Thank you so much."

"Hey, would you send me a copy of that photo?" asked Alice Cooper.

"Sure," I said beaming.

"I've never actually had a photo of me with a Klingon before."

I really must buy a new helmet.

Epilogue

After arriving back in Auckland from my adventures, I noticed that the same questions came up again and again. Hopefully, what follows has captured the essence of those questions.

All up, during the two years, the majority of nights were spent sleeping on the ground in a tent, and I seldom spent more than one night in the same location. Occasionally I would pay for a roof over my head at a motel or Airbnb. My next most common accommodation was either staying with rellies, visiting friends' houses– usually for less than a week. When I was home in Auckland, I was often house-sitting, but mostly lived on my yachts, *Bontekoe* or *Vela Dare* and was seldom in a marina for more than a month at a time. The longest stretch I remained in any one location was a three-month stint staying with my daughter Tristin, prior to and in preparation for her wedding.

I suppose that defines a nomadic life.

I was surprised to discover how enjoyable it felt being in the tent. My body seemed to benefit – if not thrive – from sleeping on the ground. I became more in tune with the world around me. Rain, wind, sun. Each morning offered something new when I poked my head out. A new vista. A new environment. Different people.

Yet there were constants. My motorcycle was always there and ready to go. Coffee from my camp stove started the day. My choices for clothing were always the same, and I knew exactly what gear I had with me.

Yes, I got lonely sometimes. And tired sometimes. And experienced a longing to quit once or twice. All were short-lived. And none of these emotions were any different to those I've had while living in one place and working at one job for any length of time. When I thought of quitting, I envisioned the reward of finishing. When I got tired, I took a break, read a book or changed my pace. When I got lonely, I made an effort to meet and talk to other people.

The same strategies, in other words, that I've used when I'm not traveling.

Would I have preferred to travel with someone? Sure, that would have been nice, but the comfort of consistent friendship would have been at the expense of my individual freedom to choose when, where and what I wanted to do. I managed to achieve the best of both worlds on my short trip with Rafe (an experience which could only have been improved if we'd each had our own bike), but that balance is hard to find most of the time.

Here are some further answers to the most common questions I'm asked...

What's the total distance you traveled?

Motorcycles –

2016:	NZ – Black Beauty	10,500 miles	(17,000 km)
	USA – The Black Pearl	12,000 miles	(19,300 km)
2017:	NZ – Black Beauty	3,700 miles	(6,000 km)
	USA – The Black Pearl	18,000 miles	(29,000 km)
	AUS – Heritage	870 miles	(1,400 km)
Total distance traveled over the two years		45,600 miles	(73,400 km)

Between 2009 and the end of this trip, I have accumulated over 100,000 miles (161,000 km) on Harley-Davidson Motorcycles.

My return flights from Auckland (New Zealand), to Taipei (Taiwan), Spokane (USA) (twice) and Brisbane (Australia) clocked up a further air travel of Total of 44,000 miles (70,600 km).

What have you learned?

A great deal actually. Remembering it, however, is the real challenge!

I learned a lot about different types of people:

In Taiwan, people seemed to feel safe. They left their phones or handbags on restaurant tables to reserve their seats if they went to the toilet. They were also very helpful. But generally, they kept to themselves. It's every man for himself when queuing, and if you dally, you'll find yourself waiting for the next train.

In the US, people seemed happy, interested and helpful. But they also seemed willing to open up and talk about themselves. And almost anything else.

In New Zealand, about half the people I met while riding were actually from overseas. But most Kiwis are honestly interested in what you have to say, where you've been or where you're going. And if you listen back, you discover most have some pretty amazing stories of their own to share.

It's very hard to beat a Miles City girl when it comes to looks, personality, intellect, motivation or positive outlook. They're just great to be around. (I'm sure this statement will cause me a lot of grief so I'll expand it to say all Montana women have these qualities.)

Generally, people are kind, helpful and friendly. People often opened up to me and shared their lives in ways that were wonderful. In fact, I only had two negative experiences during the entire two years. One was when someone ran into my bike when I wasn't there. They left a dent in the top of the front fender, possibly from a trailer hitch. They could have left a note! The other was a federal parks employee. He really took the shine off an otherwise lovely day for no real reason.

My relatives rock.

I found that Route 66 was an intimate experience. I'm glad I traveled east to west. That was the way the country expanded and the way most people originally traveled – which gave me a sense of being part of something bigger. I wonder, though, how many different things I would have seen going the other way. Or how many things I would have seen differently.

In all my adventures, I learned for sure that life is lived along the back roads and not on the freeways.

What were the outcomes of the ABC competitions?

In 2016, the winning number of points was 134. I tied third-equal at 101. My prize was a $500 gift certificate, a third place plaque, a hat, a scarf, a beer insulator and a patch. And a mention in the HOG magazine.

In 2017, I took first place with 136 points. Second place came in at 126. My prize was a $1000 gift certificate, a first place plaque, a hat, a scarf, a beer insulator and a patch. And a mention in the HOG magazine.

Both years, I was the only Kiwi to enter. Since the cost to obtain the points had far exceeded the prize money, you would be entitled to ask "Why?" Same reason people climb mountains or sail oceans. Because it represents a challenge. An adventure. It was a goal I believed was achievable and I set out to prove it to myself and others. The rewards of the experience far exceeded the cost.

To what extent are the events described actually true?

Oh, come on! I will say that actually everything I wrote about happened and that this book should be read as a true account. However, being a sailor, I was once advised not to let the truth get in the way of a good yarn. Storytelling is an art I would like to master. As such, there were a few times I may have interjected a level of "flair."

For example, yes, it did snow two to four inches plus on the Beartooth Highway in 2016. But the part about the debate with the Yeti (or Abominable Snowman) over the merits of Hillary or Trump as president, didn't actually happen. We only discussed concerns regarding climate change.

What were the best things you saw?

However obscure they might seem to some people, there were several things that made a particular impact on me.

The first was the gold sway ball in the Taipei 101 building in Taiwan. Often skyscrapers hide these anti-sway elements as functional necessities that don't need to be seen by the general public. Here, they'd turned engineering into art and painted the ball gold, put it on display, and included it as part of the tour. Good stuff.

In North Dakota I saw billboards that read "Be nice," "Be polite" and "Be kind." They had no other markings on them, and therefore no one taking credit or trying to sell something. What a breath of fresh air! I get so tired of being told I'm not going to be happy unless I do this or buy that. After I saw each billboard, I thought about its message for miles afterwards and tried to put it into practice every chance I got. Imagine my surprise to discover that the people in that area were nice, polite and kind.

The House on the Rock, Dodgeville, Wisconsin, contained such an improbable collection of unusual artifacts and unique artworks. I hadn't expected to discover the place, and it provided a surprise and joy at every turn.

The "This is not a Briggs & Stratton" motor in the Hammer Hardware store in Invercargill, New Zealand, was utterly unique. Even though I've seen it run, there's no way I could explain how it does. It's an imaginative and delightful piece of machinery.

What were your favorite places?

Well, that's a hard one. I really enjoyed every place I went.

Changing weather affects the look of the countryside, and taking a photo at the same time in the same location two days apart would result in a totally different outcome. These shifts and nuances make a difference. As does our perception of places and people, depending on our experiences, personal interactions and our mood at the time.

In Taiwan, I think my favorite place was the Taroko Gorge. Along with the awesome beauty of the natural environment, people had taken the time and significant effort to build temples way up in the middle of nowhere. As you travel around a bend in the road, the sudden appearance of one of these lovely structures adds a particular delight to the scenery.

On Route 66, visiting Winslow, Arizona, with all its references to the Eagles, was wonderful. It was just a perfect day. In terms of the natural environment, Bryce Canyon was like visiting a geological Disneyland. Beautiful, stunning and yet, improbable. The Park Lane Highway through the Appalachian Mountains in Tennessee and Kentucky was awe-inspiring. And the experience of riding through the snow tunnels on the Beartooth Highway was unmatched.

In the South Island of New Zealand, the most impressive ride was the road into Milford Sound and Mount Aspiring National Park, and in the North Island, the Castle Point lighthouse was spectacular.

The beauty of Byron Bay and the ocean expanses of the ride down the New South Wales coast made for a quintessential Australian journey.

Overall, I was constantly amazed at the geology and geography of the places I visited. In the USA, covering such vast distances in such a short span of time really put the landscape into perspective. It was so educational to see the different strata, laid down eons ago, appear at cuts in the earth, change into sloped hills, and morph into vertical mountains, then back to plains. My knowledge is still limited in the technical aspects of geology, but I feel a sense of completeness in seeing how it all unfolds and relates.

The amount of forested land east of the Mississippi River was so far beyond my expectations it's unreal. Previously, I believed there was nothing but big cities and suburbs, both containing masses of people. While there certainly are large masses of people, there's also substantial countryside. I certainly hope the inhabitants of the future will maintain that ratio of separation.

The Appalachian Mountains were far prettier and more expansive than I had previously appreciated. Traveling through them was a real joy.

New Zealand has such a wide variety of landscapes and seascapes, it can be like going to several countries on one ride. Rock formations can change dramatically from coarse lava origins to rounded igneous, layered sandstone, or jagged granite peaks, in less than 100 kilometers travel. Similarly, there are rain forests and deserts a half day drive from each other.

The Southern Alps are very similar to the Rocky Mountains in height and appearance. But without the wild animals.

I've only just scratched the surface of Australia. But I find the big expanses of countryside, sparse growth and arid nature of its bushlands intriguing and to my liking. Definitely more there to see.

Viewing the geography and landscape was a constant reminder of where it all came from. I've always said, "You cannot spend a lot of time on the ocean and not believe in God. Everything is just too perfect."

Well, I would have to say the same for my trips on land. Everything is just too perfect, when you actually take the time to look. Even as the mountains crumble from erosion, they're being pushed higher by the forces of the tectonic plates. Every day, everything is the same, and yet it's different.

While cruising along, deep in thought in 2016, I realized I had never been baptized as an adult. The more I rode, the more I felt it was important to rectify this shortcoming. Upon my return to New Zealand, I took the full immersion plunge and arose reborn.

Was travel in 2017 different because of that? Yes and No. No, I still had to deal with breakdowns, injuries, bad weather and so on. There is no preferential treatment for making that commitment. Yes, everything is the same, and yet it's different. My Christian beliefs were already well established and continued on as before. But I have a greater desire to delve down, learn and understand. There's so much yet to discover. And that sense of discovery and the peace I obtained while riding haven't left.

Riding has been a constant reminder that I am in *the Movie*. Life is happening all around me and it's taking place right now. And, if I want to retain my *star* status, I need to engage and live life as God has asked us to do.

How do you feel?

Pretty darn good actually! The most interesting thing is, I've not really read a newspaper, watched TV or listened to the radio since May 2015. Because of this, I feel a soft underlying sense of happiness and contentedness. Without all the bombardment of media and advertising telling me I'm not happy because I don't have this, or wear that, or drink this, or drive that, and without the news telling me I need to worry about crime or invasions or war or illness or weather, I find I'm automatically happy and less stressed out. Removing those stimuli has left time for inner peace. I seem to do OK just buying what I need instead of what I want, or think I want.

Focusing on what is going on around me instead of things that are out of my control in places hundreds or thousands of miles away, allows me to become more in tune with, and responsive to, the land and people where I am. I also believe I have more empathy for my fellow man, am easier to get along with and less judgmental.

Hours of sitting still while riding the bike, not talking or hearing anything other than the engine's heartbeat, seemed to put me into a meditative state. With distractions removed, I was able to simply be. I could observe and absorb everything around me for what it was. Distinguish between those things that were man-made and those that were not. Contemplate them both and my relationship with them.

Humankind has made some mighty achievements and fantastic creations. Yet they are not perfect and, in fact, consistently fall short, even though people are continually trying to improve them. Spending too much time in cities and away from nature eventually wears on the soul.

Seeing so many everyday miracles unfolding before me as I traveled, and ultimately, fully recognizing and appreciating them as the results of the Hand of God, was enlightening. While it might be enjoyable *most* times amongst man's creations, my soul *always* feels fulfilled after spending time amongst God's creations.

While thus focused, it was easier to hear and therefore, listen, to an inner voice. This is sometimes difficult to hear when I'm back amongst the distractions, and often I have inadvertently ignored or failed to act upon it. But that voice has never steered me wrong. So, I shall keep seeking it.

A nice place to be.

So, what's next?

Well, that too is a hard one. As of this writing in 2019, the plan is as follows;

Immediately- I plan on moving back aboard my sailboat *Vela Dare* and finish her restoration. Also planning on going sailing for short one-week trips to gain familiarity and become confident on her once she is sea worthy. These will be as often as time allows around the islands of the Hauraki Gulf in New Zealand.

And of course, more short trips on Black Beauty around New Zealand. The tent and sleeping bag are always ready.

Turns out, 85 percent of my left shoulder rotator cuff was torn as a result of my fall in Montana. That explained a lot about why it wasn't healing properly. Nearly one year on, I am in recovery mode from the surgery. Hopefully I'll be able to ride again shortly. With luck, I'll be back to 100% in time to head off shore again in 2019.

The upside is, I had sufficient down time to collate the emails and travel logs and put this book together.

Next year and long term. Long term plan is to sail back to the states. That would be by heading west from New Zealand to complete the circumnavigation trip I started back in 1991. It may include a long bike ride in Australia.

Whatever happens, I'm sure it will be an adventure!

Acknowledgements

I would like to acknowledge:

My editors

Andrew Killick who did a marvelous job massaging my cumbersome verbiage and allowing the book to flow, while remaining true to the adventure's story line. Since Andrew and I had not met before the end of the book, there was a steep learning curve as he suffered through the conflict of my Americanisms and proper English prose. Hopefully this book reads with a creditable blend that readers from both hemispheres feel included and represented.

Jill Bodley who kept sending me back to the computer saying "You can do better." Forcing me to really think about what it was the book should be trying to accomplish. And viewing it from the eyes of the reader.

Katie Rickson, who dropped everything to edit the initial draft and provided insightful comments in a remarkably short time period.

All the people who assisted me on my trips. Without them, things might have had an entirely different outcome. Many are mentioned by name in this book.

The other riders I've had the pleasure of riding with and the things I've learned from each.

The Harley-Davidson Motorcycle Company, for designing and building motorcycles that provide safe transportation and allow millions of riders to be in their own movies every day. But most importantly, creating a machine that sets the human spirit free.

Cindy in Taiwan, who did a tremendous job of hosting, planning and organizing my visit, making all of our activities flow effortless. I had a marvelous time experiencing the country and culture.

Rafe, who was a wonderful traveling companion and remains a good friend. Always upbeat and positive.

Everyone who patiently read the news emails I sent out during my trip and encouraged me to compile them into a book.

My beta readers – especially author Vicki Tapia for her support and encouragement. And author John Burgess who dropped everything for the final read.

And finally, my daughter Tristin, who offered support during my travels by collecting my mail, checking on the yachts, sorting out issues in my absence, encouraging me onwards and tolerating my crazy antics. In addition, for being a beta reader and assisting with the cover design. I couldn't ask for a more perfect child.

Maps were downloaded from the internet and no copyright infringement is intended.

Any errors that still remain in this document are mine alone.

To each of you, a big heartfelt THANK YOU

Glossary

Cowboy boots = SKs

Tiki tour = Traveling around to see things in no specific order

Mince = Hamburger meat

Squiz = take a look

Cuzzie bros or cuzbros = Close friends (literally cousin brothers)

Rellies = Relatives

Torch = Flashlight

Jumper = Pullover

Togs = Swimsuit

Rug up = Dress for warmth

Bonnet = Car hood

Boot = Car trunk

Windscreen = Windshield

Metal = Gravel

Choc-a-block = Filled to capacity

My shout = I'm buying

Ute = Pickup

Mate = Friend, buddy or Pal

Conversions

    10 feet = 3.5 meters

    10 miles = 16.1 kilometers

    1 gallon = 3.78 liters

    32 deg Fahrenheit = 0 deg Celsius

    100 deg Fahrenheit = 38 deg Celsius

Appendix A – Luggage and Contents

On My Person

Leathers – Jacket, pants, HOG vest, chaps, gloves, cowboy boots

2 Buff face coverings

Pocketknife

Wristwatch

Money belt for cash, credit card and debit card

Helmet

Rear Seat of Bike

Waterproof bags –Two small bags, one inside each saddle bag, plus one large bag which held the sleeping bag

Two-man tent (Kathmandu 80), motorcycle cover rolled up inside tent bag

Sleeping bag (Holyfill)

8 bungee cords

Cigarette lighter/AC plug (for USB connections)

Phone holder bracket

Apple iPhone 5SE (most photographs were taken on this phone due to ease of access)

Rear Leather Bag

Cooking pot, spoon, cup, gas canister, cigarette lighter, sugar, instant coffee satchels

Sunglasses

Hat

LED flashlight

Rain Gators

Rain Pants

Rubber gloves with one set cotton liners and one set polypropylene liners

1 tool kit – screw driver, 3/8" ratchet, 1 extension, 4 sockets, star wrenches, 2 spare spark plugs, pliers, air pressure gauge, spark plug gapper, Leatherman tool

Drink bottle (2 cups, 500 ml)

Cable bicycle lock

Large envelope for paperwork (receipts, insurance, title etc.)

1 to 2 paperback books

Plastic poncho

1 iPad

HOG Atlas (2016 and 2017 for ABC Points)

*Various state maps

*Hydro vest

*Bear pepper spray

**Rain jacket

Right Saddle Bag

Tennis shoes

3 pairs of two-dollar store variety reading glasses

Toiletries bag – toothbrush, toothpaste, deodorant, calogne, tweezers, fingernail clippers, Aspirin, Panadol, Voltaran (anti-inflammatory), assorted Band-Aids (plasters), moleskin, soap, nail clippers

Polypropylene jumper

Swimsuit

Air mattress (¾ in, 20 mm thick, three-quarter length)

Digital waterproof camera (Leica)

**Nylon web tie downs with ratchets

Left Saddle Bag

1-Levi's 501 button down jeans

3 t-shirts,

3 pair underwear

3 pair socks

3 handkerchiefs

Singlet undershirt

Long-sleeved heavy cotton pullover

Long underwear bottoms

Polypropylene thermal top

1/8" Nylon line (20 ft, 6 m long)

Space blanket

Sunblock (SPF50)

*USA Only **NZ Only

Total weight of Luggage

USA: Suitcase 50 lbs (23 kg), carry-on 16 lbs (7 kg). This included all the gear listed above.

NZ: Approximately the same.

Australia: 15 lb (7 kg) carry-on and helmet only.

Appendix B - Costs in 2016-2017

Exchange Rates

1 NZD = 0.71USD = 0.89AUD = 21TND

1 USD = 1.41NZD = 1.12 AUD = 32TND

Motorcycles

2009 Super Glide (Black Beauty). Purchased new in New Zealand and still own it, so the only costs have been depreciation, maintenance and repairs – about NZD6,000 over the two years. Big costs were the transmission and the wheel bearings. Tires last about 18,000 km and cost about NZD400 installed. Otherwise, I did most of my own servicing.

2005 Heritage Softail (The Black Pearl). Purchased secondhand in the USA. Difference between purchase and selling price was about USD500. Maintenance and repairs were about USD3,500 over the two years. Big costs were the upgrade of the hydraulic cam tensioners, services and tires. Tires cost about USD300 installed and I went through five.

As part of my original negotiations, the Pearl was taken back to Post Falls at the end of my 2016 ride and stored in the shop of the previous owner. He said he had seller's remorse and missed her terribly. He generously agreed to keep a battery tender on the bike and start her up monthly to circulate the oil. And, I think, to make himself feel good. He did a wonderful job looking after the bike. But starting her up and then not being able to take her for a spin, changed his perspective. By the time I returned, he had come to grips with the Pearl not being his bike any longer.

I still have seller's remorse after letting the Black Pearl go at the end of the 2017 ride. But all good things must come to an end, I suppose.

Heritage Softail. Hired from Eagle Rider in Brisbane, Australia. AUD900.

Petrol

NZ – Average price per liter:	between NZD1.90 and 2.25
USA – Average price per gallon:	between USD1.85 and 2.35
AUS – Average price per liter:	between AUD1.50 and 1.60
Average fuel consumption:	43 m/g in USA, 19 km/l in NZ

Food

Generally, I ate an average of two and a half meals a day. In the desert I never ate more than two. I set a rough budget of USD5 per meal in the USA, and NZD10 in NZ. Local diners, Subway and Taco Bell were usually my source of lunch and dinner, and I often ate McDonald's pancakes for breakfast. When I camped for free, I would treat myself to a proper sit-down meal at a nicer diner or restaurant.

Other than bananas and apples, I seldom bought food from grocery stores as there was no way to carry, keep or prepare it with the space I had on the bike. (By the way, bananas don't travel well on a motorcycle. The heat and vibration turns them to a mush in about ten minutes and then they squeeze out of their skins like toothpaste – with about the same texture and consistency.)

I did have a small gas camping stove for my morning coffee, and sometimes I used this to heat up soup. But generally, it was easier, cheaper and more fun to eat at diners or fast food outlets.

The big cost, of course, was coffee. As I observed earlier in this book, it's amazing how a cup of coffee can cost more than a gallon of gas! And it is even more amazing that we are willing to pay that much!

Meanwhile, a single bottle of beer in New Zealand costs about the same as a six pack in the US.

Through the desert and hot areas, I always carried a two-liter bottle of Gatorade, and three bottles of water (containing two liters, three liters and 300 mm respectively). Generally, I refilled these as required at each gas stop. I ditched two bottles once I was back in cooler climates.

Camping

In the USA, camp sites varied from free to USD44 per night. With my senior pass, I was able to stay at all national, Army Core of Engineers and some state campgrounds for half price.

My pass also allowed me into all national parks and national monuments free of charge. A very good deal.

There was a website that listed free campsites, however most of these were based on you traveling in a mobile home or campervan. For instance, they sent me to places like carparks of truck stops, casinos and shopping malls.

Tent sites generally catered for a tent, two people and a vehicle, with no reduction for motorcycles or single persons. I had no offers from any "second persons" so I always paid full rate. Most campsites charged the same for tents as RVs. If I had to pick an average, I'd say the cost was about USD12 to USD15 per night.

New Zealand campsites varied from free to NZD30 per night – probably about NZD18 to NZD25 per night on average.

I used an app called CamperMate, which includes all campgrounds in New Zealand and groups them as free, low price and expensive. Prices and reservations for individual campgrounds are available upon selection.

Motels and Airbnb

The costs of motel and Airbnb accommodation was as follows:

New Zealand Iron Run 2016: one night in backpacker accommodation costing NZD45. Remaining nights with friends or camping out.

USA 2016: Five nights in motels. Cheapest was USD32 (Kingsman, Arizona) and most expensive was USD85 (Pasadena, California) per night. On Route 66, I think there were quite a number you could stay at for about USD45 to USD55.

New Zealand Iron Run 2017: Five nights in backpacker accommodation, at an average of NZD40 per night.

USA 2017: Airbnbs and motels for a total of nine nights. Prices ranged from USD60 to USD75 per night.

Australia 2017: Four nights at an average of AUD32 for backpacker accommodation (AUD45 peak rates due to the rugby game). One night at a friend's house.

Other lodging

In the USA, I shamelessly took advantage of the generosity of friends and relatives when they offered me a place to stay. Other than a week each time at my sister's house, where I started and ended my trips, I spent a total of 12 nights not in my sleeping bag. I would have been happy to pitch my tent in people's back yards, but generally they were embarrassed enough seeing me in my leathers and having the bike parked out the front of their houses. They didn't want to worry about their neighbors seeing me crawl out of the tent naked in the morning and urinate in the bushes as well – so they let me stay inside!

Rental and Hireage

In the USA, I had to rent a car for two days until I found and bought the Black Pearl in 2016. I also hired a pickup to haul my things from the family farm to Miles City, where my brother generously offered the use of his van for transportation to Spokane, where I arranged onward shipping to New Zealand. OK, so I threatened to haul my stuff to his place and leave it there if he didn't let me use the van.

In New Zealand, I hired a car for five days in the South Island to attend the rally, when Black Beauty's transmission failed in 2017.

About the Author

Rod Slater is a native of Miles City, Montana, and now resides in Auckland, New Zealand. He has one daughter and son-in-law, who live nearby.

He holds a Bachelor's Degree in Art and Architecture and a Master's Degree in Architecture from Montana State University. He is currently Director of Rod Slater Art and Architecture, Ltd. His artwork primarily encapsulates two of his great passions: sailing and motorcycling, expressed in the mediums of watercolor, oil, acrylic and sculpture.

He lives aboard his yacht *Vela Dare* and is an avid cruising sailor with over 50,000 blue water miles experience – half of which were solo sailing.

Trialing a variety of professions throughout his life, combined with a variety of experiences and extensive traveling, has enabled Rod to see the world around him in a different light and with more depth and clarity than might have been possible had he stayed focused on a single occupation and location.

Imagination, humor and a thirst for adventure helps him maintain a sense of balance in life. He acknowledges it is by the good grace of God that he is able to continue traveling and learning about this wonderful creation we call earth and the people who populate it.

This is his first book.

www.rodslateraaa.com